THOMAS, LORD AUDLEY OF WALDEN, 1488–1544

Lord Henry Dudley = MARGARET = THOMAS HOWARD, 4TH DUKE OF NORFOLK, 1536–72

William
ancestor of the Carlisle and Corby branches

Margaret = Robert Sackville,
2nd Earl of Dorset

John | Edward, Lord Howard of Escrick | Elizabeth = (1) William Knollys, Earl of Banbury (2) Edward, Lord Vaux | Frances = (1) Robert Devereux, 3rd Earl of Essex (2) Robert Carr, 1st Earl of Somerset | Catherine = Wm. Cecil, 2nd Earl of Salisbury (7 sons and 5 daughters) | three others

HENRY, 5TH EARL OF SUFFOLK, = (1) Mary Stuart
1627–1709,
to whom the house was returned
by the Crown

Catherine = (1) Lord Aubigny
(2) Earl of Newburgh

Elizabeth
= 10th Earl of
Northumberland

three others

HENRY, 6TH EARL = (1) Penelope, dau. of
OF SUFFOLK,   Henry, Earl
1670–1718   of Thomond

EDWARD, 8TH EARL OF SUFFOLK,
1671–1731, *d.* without issue
Disputed the settlement made by the 7th
Earl, but agreed to accept an annuity of
£1,200 in lieu of the estate

CHARLES, 9TH
EARL OF SUFFOLK,
1675–1733

Diana
= Henrietta,
dau. of Sir
Henry Hobart

HENRY, 10TH EARL OF SUFFOLK,
1706–45, *d.* without issue

CHARLES WILLIAM, 7TH EARL OF SUFFOLK,
1693–1722, *d.* without issue
Suffered a recovery and settled the estate on
himself and his uncle Charles, with remainder
to the Effingham branch of the Howard family

James,
d. without
issue

Thomas,
d. without
issue

Arthur,
d. without
issue

Sarah

Elizabeth = Thomas Felton

Elizabeth = John Hervey,
1st Earl of Bristo

John, Lord Hervey = Mary Lepell

Frederick, 2nd Earl of Bristo
Heir to the Lady Elizabeth, younger dau. o
James, 3rd Earl of Suffolk; ancestor of all the
Lords Howard de Walden after the 4th, who
was the last to hold both the title and the estate

AUDLEY END

Audley End

AUDLEY END

BY WILLIAM ADDISON

WITH A FOREWORD BY
LORD BRAYBROOKE

ILLUSTRATED WITH
A COLOURED FRONTISPIECE AND
SIXTEEN PAGES OF PHOTOGRAPHS

LONDON
J. M. DENT & SONS LTD

FOREWORD

AUDLEY END was acquired by the Crown for use as a royal palace in the latter part of the seventeenth century, and was requisitioned for military purposes during the Second World War; but its acquisition by the State in 1948 marked a permanent change of ownership. It is a strange and tragic irony that this great loss to my family is directly traceable to the fact that my two cousins were killed in defending their country. The inexorable pressure of death duties, which, contrary to popular belief, are levied at full rate in such circumstances, coming so soon after the heavy duties incurred on my uncle's death, gave me no option but to part with the house.

Many a time since then I have hoped that further chapters might be added to my great-grandfather's book, *The History of Audley End*, published in 1836. So it was with the greatest pleasure that I first heard of Mr. Addison's plans for this book, which proved to be for something very different from a supplement to the former work. My great-grandfather, the third Lord Braybrooke, who is chiefly remembered as the first editor of Pepys's *Diary*, had written with intimate knowledge and affection of his family home. The change in ownership called for a work of wider interest and scope, and it was felt that this ought to be written while personal associations were still fresh. Abundant material for such a work had accumulated in the muniment room at Audley End, and I have been impressed by the skill and enthusiasm with which Mr. Addison has tackled these tens of thousands of documents, now in the Essex Record Office at Chelmsford, no less than with his keenness to have his data carefully checked.

I hope, therefore, that a great many others will share the pleasure that this book gives to me and my family.

BRAYBROOKE

v

PREFACE

AUDLEY END, in the north-west corner of Essex, for more than three hundred years the home of Howards, Griffins, and Nevilles —of the Earls of Suffolk and the Lords Braybrooke—was acquired for the nation in 1948 as a building too important to be lost, yet too costly for its owner, the ninth Lord Braybrooke, to keep. It was already a monument in that it belonged to the past far more than it could to the present. The first house, built by Lord Treasurer Howard, first Earl of Suffolk, was reduced to about one-third its original size in the eighteenth century, when even Sir John Vanbrugh thought it too large for private use. Between 1762 and 1792 Sir John Griffin Griffin, fourth Lord Howard de Walden and first Lord Braybrooke, spent £100,000 in restoring house and estate, and his, rather than the Earl of Suffolk's, is the Audley End we see now. Its future is assured. But however carefully a building may be preserved, something—and that, perhaps, the greater part—is lost when the family moves out. If, as here, furniture, portraits, and personal belongings of various kinds are allowed to remain, the house may be more than a museum; it is no longer a home.

But the loss at Audley End was less than it might have been. After disposing of the mansion Lord Braybrooke deposited at the Essex Record Office the remarkable collection of estate and family papers accumulated by successive owners, of which the catalogue alone contains nearly two hundred pages. Documents from the collection material to national history were sent to the Public Record Office, papers relating to the Berkshire estates of the Aldworth and Neville families to the Berkshire Record Office at Reading, and others to their appropriate centres; but the Essex Record Office catalogue, referred to as E.R.O. D/DBy in footnotes throughout the present book, remains the key to the entire collection.

The Braybrooke records, particularly with reference to the estate, are unusually full and will be studied by experts. Here they have been used to help the general reader, and in particular the more inquiring among the thousands of visitors who will pass through the Great Hall year by year, to appreciate something of what Audley End and its families have represented in English life during the last four hundred years. That the house

should become a museum is one danger; that its owners—
officers of state, soldiers, scholars, farmers, and men of affairs
—should become portraits in oils, names in pedigrees, and little
more, is another.   Audley End may have been a white elephant;
it has never been an ivory tower.   In the seventeenth century
it was one of the wonders of the kingdom.   For thirty-two
years it was a royal palace.   Then it fell into decay with the
declining fortunes of the Earls of Suffolk until an exciting law-
suit brought it to Sir John Griffin Griffin, later fourth Lord
Howard de Walden and finally first Lord Braybrooke, who
transformed it into one of the great Whig mansions of his day.
In the nineteenth century it was primarily the centre of a large
estate, with a farm at the heart of it, and in order to bring out
the working, practical aspect of aristocratic life in Victorian
times the Lords Braybrooke have been studied, not as isolated
grandees, but in relation to the everyday life of the neighbourhood.

The first half of the book, then, deals with a family and palace
of national consequence; the second with a great house and a
landed family—one of the oldest in the kingdom—both of which,
while less eminent than they had been, continued to be typical.

The preliminary examination of the Braybrooke collection by
the staff of the Essex Record Office first made the work possible,
and it is with pleasure that I acknowledge my indebtedness to
my friends, Mr. F. G. Emmison, F.S.A., the county archivist,
and his senior assistants, Mr. F. W. Steer, F.S.A., and Miss
H. E. P. Grieve, B.E.M., B.A.   I am indebted also to Dorothy
Lady Braybrooke, for so graciously placing at my disposal her
unique knowledge of the house that was so long her home,
to the Rt. Hon. H. U. Willink, P.C., M.C., Q.C., M.A., Master
of Magdalene College, for much valuable advice, to Mr.
Kitteridge, the housekeeper, and the Ministry of Works for
their advice and courtesy.   But my greatest indebtedness is to
Lord Braybrooke, both for giving me full access to all relevant
documents and for his unfailing kindness in discussing them
with me.   'Words are the only things that last for ever,' said
Hazlitt immodestly.   But it must be agreed that the maintenance
of the fabric as a national monument would have fallen short
of its main purpose if the estate and family records had not also
been given means of survival.   W. A.

Loughton,
    Easter, 1953

CHRONOLOGICAL TABLE

THOMAS AUDLEY, BARON AUDLEY OF WALDEN, 1488–1544.

1538   The Benedictine Abbey at Walden granted to Lord Chancellor Audley, 27th March.
1538   Raised to the peerage as Baron Audley of Walden.
1544   Death of Lord Audley, 30th April.

THOMAS HOWARD, FOURTH DUKE OF NORFOLK, 1536–72.

1557   Married as his second wife, Margaret, only surviving daughter of Lord Audley, after the death of her first husband, Lord Henry Dudley.
1564   Death of Margaret, Duchess of Norfolk, 10th January.
1569   Imprisoned for conspiring to marry Mary Queen of Scots and place her on the English throne.
1571   Queen Elizabeth visited Audley End and on 1st September sent Sir Thomas Smith to examine Higford, the duke's secretary.
1572   Executed for treason, 2nd June.
1572   Henry Howard, Earl of Northampton, retired to Audley End to take charge of his beheaded brother's children.
1578   Queen Elizabeth entertained at Audley End on her progress through East Anglia.

THOMAS HOWARD, FIRST EARL OF SUFFOLK AND FIRST BARON HOWARD DE WALDEN, 1561–1626.

1597   Thomas Howard, eldest son of the fourth Duke of Norfolk and Margaret Audley, summoned to Parliament as Lord Howard de Walden.
1603   Created Earl of Suffolk, 21st July.
1603   Began to build Audley End.
1603   Lord Chamberlain of the Household, 21st July.
1604   Joint Earl Marshal.
1606   The King's Players at Saffron Walden.
1610   James I visited Audley End.
1612   Theophilus, second Lord Howard de Walden and subsequently second Earl of Suffolk, married Elizabeth, daughter of the Earl of Dunbar.
1613   Sir Thomas Overbury murdered. The Suffolks involved.
1614   James I visited Audley End. The Earl became Lord Treasurer.
1614   Chancellor of Cambridge University.
1616   The original Audley End completed. The Earl and Countess in retirement at Audley End following the arraignment of their daughter, the Countess of Essex, for the murder of Sir Thomas Overbury.

1618　The Earl removed from the office of Lord Treasurer after being charged with embezzlement.

1619　Heavily fined and imprisoned.

1619　Birth of James, afterwards third Earl of Suffolk, named after the king, who sent the Duke of Lennox to represent him at the baptism in the chapel at Audley End.

1626　Death of the first Earl, 28th May.

THEOPHILUS HOWARD, SECOND EARL OF SUFFOLK AND SECOND BARON HOWARD DE WALDEN, 1584–1640.

1626　Lord Lieutenant of Cambridgeshire, Suffolk, and Dorset.

1628　Lord Warden of the Cinque Ports.

1640　Death of the second Earl, September.

JAMES HOWARD, THIRD EARL OF SUFFOLK AND THIRD BARON HOWARD DE WALDEN, 1620–88.

1642　Sold the Howards' Charing Cross house to the Earl of Northumberland, who gave it his name.

1646　Joint-commissioner of Parliament to Charles I.

1647　Suspected of Royalist sympathies and imprisoned.

1654　Description of Audley End by John Evelyn.

1660　Pepys at Audley End.

1661　The Earl served as Earl Marshal for the Coronation.

1665　Gentleman of the Bedchamber.

THE CROWN.

1666　Audley End sold to the Crown for use as a royal palace (conveyance dated 1669).

1667　The Earl appointed Keeper of the King's House at Audley End.

1667　Pepys again at Audley End.

1669　Audley End described by Cosmo III, Grand Duke of Tuscany.

1670　Queen Catherine of Braganza at Walden Fair.

1670　The Prince of Orange, afterwards William III, slept at Audley End after receiving an honorary degree at Cambridge.

1673　The Earl commissioner for the office of Earl Marshal.

1681　Audley End described by Ralph Thoresby.

1687　Settlement made by the Earl on which the Countess of Portsmouth and Lord Hervey based their claim to the estate in 1746.

1688　Death of the third Earl, December.

1689　William III at Audley End.

1691　Death of the fourth Earl (b. 1626), April.

HENRY HOWARD, FIFTH EARL OF SUFFOLK, 1627–1709.

1697　Audley End described by Celia Fiennes.

1701　Audley End returned to the fifth Earl of Suffolk by William III on the Earl's promise to relinquish his claim to the £20,000 of the purchase price still unpaid.

1706　Henry Howard, afterwards sixth Earl, created Baron Chesterford and

Earl of Bindon, the Howard de Walden title having been in abeyance since the death of the third Earl without male issue.

1706   Appointed Deputy Earl Marshal, to act in the stead of the hereditary holder of that office, who was a Roman Catholic.

1709   Death of the fifth Earl, December.

HENRY HOWARD, SIXTH EARL OF SUFFOLK, *c.* 1670–1718.

1714   Appointed Lord Lieutenant of Essex.

1714   The Hon. Charles Howard, afterwards ninth Earl, returned with his wife to England from Hanover after making the acquaintance of the Elector, afterwards George I, from whom they received court appointments.

1717   The Earl became first Commissioner of Trade and Plantations (President of the Board of Trade).

1718   Death of the sixth Earl, September.

CHARLES WILLIAM HOWARD, SEVENTH EARL OF SUFFOLK, 1693–1722.

1720 (*c.*)   Mrs. Charles Howard became the mistress of the Prince of Wales, afterwards George II.

1720   Death of Anne, widow of James, third Earl of Suffolk.

1721   The buildings round the main court at Audley End pulled down on the advice of Sir John Vanbrugh. Stone screen by Vanbrugh set up at the south end of the Great Hall.

1722   Death of the seventh Earl without issue, 9th February.

EDWARD HOWARD, EIGHTH EARL OF SUFFOLK, 1671–1731.

1724   The eighth Earl, probably of weak intellect, in trouble with the House of Lords for improperly selling written protections from arrest.

1725   The eighth Earl illegally agreed to his brother, afterwards the ninth Earl, enjoying full possession of Audley End in return for an annuity to himself of £1,200 a year.

1731   Death of the eighth Earl, June.

CHARLES HOWARD, NINTH EARL OF SUFFOLK, 1675–1733.

1733   Empowered by Act of Parliament to raise money by sale or mortgage for the payment of debts accumulated by the late earls of Suffolk.

1733   Death of the ninth Earl, September.

HENRY HOWARD, TENTH EARL OF SUFFOLK, 1706–45.

1735   Married Sarah Inwen, daughter of a wealthy brewer.

1740   Loggia overlooking the Mount Garden enclosed.

1745   Death of the tenth Earl, intestate and without issue, upon which the title passed to the fourth Earl of Berkshire, by descent from the second son of the first Earl; the estate, by a settlement made by the seventh Earl, passed to Thomas, second Earl of Effingham, from whom it was claimed by the three descendants of James, third Earl of Suffolk, namely, Elizabeth, Countess of Portsmouth, Anne Whitwell, and Lord Hervey, afterwards second Earl of Bristol.

ELIZABETH, COUNTESS OF PORTSMOUTH, *d.* 1762.

1747   Decree in Chancery in favour of the Countess of Portsmouth and others. The house and park, however, were excluded on the ground that they had been the property of the Crown when the 1687 settlement was made. The Countess bought the house and park from the Earl of Effingham.

1749   John Griffin Whitwell, whom the Countess made her heir, took the name of Griffin by Act of Parliament and married Anne Mary, daughter of Col. John Schutz.

1749   The east side of the inner court demolished.

1753   Deed of Partition of the Estate between the Earl of Bristol and the Countess of Portsmouth.

1762   Death of the Countess of Portsmouth.

SIR JOHN GRIFFIN GRIFFIN, FOURTH LORD HOWARD DE WALDEN, FIRST BARON BRAYBROOKE, 1719–97.

1763   Grecian Temple erected on hill-top west of Audley End to commemorate the end of the Seven Years War.

1763–5   Extensive rebuilding and restoration of the house; the grounds laid out by Capability Brown.

1764   Death of the first Lady Griffin, 18th August.

1765   Sir John married as his second wife, Katherine, daughter of William Clayton of Harleyford, Bucks, 11th June.

1767   Death of Henrietta Howard, the ninth Earl's countess and George II's mistress.

1771   The three-arch bridge over the Cam built by Robert Adam.

1774   Obelisk erected north of the house in memory of the Countess of Portsmouth.

1783   Palladian bridge and tea-house built.

1784   Sir John summoned to the House of Lords as fourth Lord Howard de Walden.

1785   Lord Howard appointed Lord Lieutenant and *Custos Rotulorum* of Essex.

1786   Entrance gateway with the Howard lion restored.

1788   Lord Howard created Baron Braybrooke of Braybrooke, with special remainder to Richard Aldworth Neville, his heir.

1792   Temple of Concord built east of the house to commemorate George III's recovery from illness.

1796   Lord Howard promoted to the rank of Field Marshal.

1797   Death of Lord Howard de Walden, first Baron Braybrooke, May.

RICHARD ALDWORTH NEVILLE (GRIFFIN), SECOND BARON BRAYBROOKE, 1750–1825.

1798   Lord Lieutenant, *Custos Rotulorum*, and Vice-Admiral in succession to Lord Howard.

1799   Howard de Walden barony claimed by the Bishop Earl of Bristol, at
        whose death it passed to his grandson, Charles Augustus Ellis,
        and was thus separated from the earldom of Bristol. It remains
        in the Ellis (Scott-Ellis) family.
1799–1800   High prices and much hardship on the estate as the result of
        an exceptionally severe winter.
1802   The second Lord Braybrooke first enjoyed the revenue of the estate
        following the death at the age of eighty-eight of Dr. Parker,
        widower of Lord Howard's sister.
1803   About 3,500 acres in Great and Little Chesterford enclosed by Act
        of Parliament. Rents increased between ten per cent and twenty
        per cent.
1803   New garden walls built.
1809   Diary of Henry Neville, Captain of Dragoons, who died of excessive
        fatigue after the Battle of Talavera.
1811   Jersey herd of cattle established at Audley End.
1814   Final settlement with Lord Bristol on the purchase of the Littlebury
        part of the estate. Lord Braybrooke to pay £20,000.
1819   Richard Neville, afterwards third Lord Braybrooke, married Lady
        Jane Cornwallis, eldest daughter and co-heir of the second
        Marquess Cornwallis.
1823   The Cornwallis collection of pictures and heirlooms came to Audley
        End on the death of the second Marquess.
1823   Agreement to publish the *Diary of Samuel Pepys*, edited by the third
        Lord Braybrooke.
1825   Death of second Lord Braybrooke at Billingbear, the Berkshire seat
        of the family, 28th February.

RICHARD NEVILLE (GRIFFIN), THIRD BARON BRAYBROOKE, 1783–1858.

1826–31   New suite of rooms on first floor.
1827   Ice House Lodge built on hill at southern extremity of park.
1833   540 trees blown down on the estate during exceptional gale.
1834   Lodge at main entrance built to design by Thomas Rickman.
1836   *Audley End* by Lord Braybrooke published.
1842   *The Private Correspondence of Jane Lady Cornwallis* (1581–1659) pub-
        lished.
1842   Cambridge New Lodge built. Cricket pitch laid on front lawn.
1844   Alexander Pope's chair came to Audley End.
1845–7   Excavations by the Hon. R. C. Neville, afterwards fourth Lord Bray-
        brooke, of the Roman station at Great Chesterford.
1849   Central heating system installed.
1852   R. C. Neville, afterwards fourth Lord Braybrooke, married Lady
        Charlotte Toler, daughter of the Earl of Norbury.
1853   The Hon. Latimer Neville, afterwards sixth Lord Braybrooke,
        succeeded his uncle, Dean Neville-Grenville, as Master of Magda-
        lene College.
1854   Two sons of the third Lord Braybrooke fell in action while leading
        their men at Inkerman.
1858   Death of the third Lord Braybrooke, March.

RICHARD CORNWALLIS NEVILLE, FOURTH BARON BRAYBROOKE, 1820–61.

1858   On succeeding to the title, the fourth lord renounced the name of
        Griffin, which by the terms of the Countess of Portsmouth's will
        he was required to take, and retained the name of Neville.
1859–60   The Hon. Latimer Neville vice-chancellor of Cambridge
        University.
1861   Death of the fourth Lord Braybrooke, February.

CHARLES CORNWALLIS NEVILLE, FIFTH BARON BRAYBROOKE, 1823–1902.

1865   The Arcade behind the Great Hall enclosed.
1880   Cornwallis family papers deposited at the Public Record Office by
        the fifth lord.
1902   Death of the fifth Lord Braybrooke, June.

LATIMER NEVILLE, SIXTH BARON BRAYBROOKE, 1827–1904.

1903   Celebrated his golden jubilee as Master of Magdalene College.
1904   Death of the sixth Lord Braybrooke, January.

HENRY NEVILLE, SEVENTH BARON BRAYBROOKE, 1855–1941.

1916   Gale blew down large cedar south-east of the house. A section of
        it was made into the table now in the temple on the Ring.

1941–6   House in occupation of army.

CONTENTS

ACKNOWLEDGMENTS

The coloured frontispiece is reproduced by courtesy of the Essex County Records Committee, and the black and white photographs by permission of the Controller of Her Majesty's Stationery Office.

ILLUSTRATIONS

I

AUDLEY END

WHILE A MANSION no less than a cottage derives most of its charm from those who live in it, houses and their families have a curiously varying relationship. With Hatfield, if we think of the House and not of the Palace, the Cecils mean everything. With Knole, family and dwelling are more evenly balanced in that the Sackvilles mean practically as much to Knole as Knole to the Sackvilles. Perhaps we see the personal and impersonal contrasted most clearly in Hardwick and Chatsworth, the two Derbyshire homes of the dukes of Devonshire. The latter may be associated with the family in general; the former is haunted —at least metaphorically—by the shade of its builder, Elizabeth, Countess of Shrewsbury, the proud, irrepressible Bess of Hardwick.

Audley End is in a different group. The Howards and Nevilles are families too large to have a single focal point. Their shades as well as their monuments are dispersed. So while they are at Audley End and Saffron Walden they are less obtrusively there than the Cecils at Hatfield, the Sackvilles at Knole, or the Cavendishes at Chatsworth. In short, Audley End has a life of its own in a way that so many great houses have not— an elusive, challenging life. The Audley End of history has made and unmade its owners, and unmade far more than it has made. In fact, of the long line, with its ten earls of Suffolk, Charles II, James II, William III, the Griffins, and the Nevilles, not one was able to master it until it came into the hands of a woman comparable in spirit with Bess of Hardwick—Elizabeth, Countess of Portsmouth, of whom Cole the antiquary said: 'She was as stately and proud as Lucifer; no German princess could exceed her.' From her imperious fingers it passed into the strong and manly grip of her nephew, Sir John Griffin Griffin, afterwards fourth Lord Howard de Walden and first Lord Braybrooke.

Seen from the London to Newmarket road, with the Cam

flowing through the park before it, as though to symbolize its hereditary link with Cambridge, the Audley End of to-day may suggest repose and serenity rather than pride. It is no longer the palace built between 1603 and 1616 by Thomas Howard, first Earl of Suffolk, and designed to be the largest private house in the kingdom; for even his lowlier-born fellow East Anglian, Wolsey, was not more ambitious with Hampton Court than Howard was with Audley End. The foundations of the original buildings can still be traced from the air in dry weather, the lines corresponding with those in the drawings of Henry Winstanley of Littlebury, Clerk of Works in James II's reign. To compare the present house, the Audley End of the Braybrookes, with the original house, the Audley End of the Suffolks, we must identify the existing ranges in Winstanley's careful drawing, facing page 2. They run along the south, west, and north sides of what he describes as the innermost, or smaller, court. The front seen from the Newmarket road is the west range, and though most of its ashlar was renewed by the fourth Lord Howard de Walden in the eighteenth century, in appearance— apart from the rooms above the hall—it is still substantially as it was when the first earl entertained his sovereign here in 1610 and 1614. It was on the second of these two visits, when the building would be nearing completion—externally, at all events —that James remarked: 'By my troth, mon, it is too much for a king, but may do for a Lord High Treasurer,' the office to which Suffolk had lately been advanced. There was more point to the remark than may now be apparent. Several of the great houses either built or rebuilt by Tudor and Stuart favourites may be traced to lord treasurers. The office, says Fuller, 'was ever beheld as a place of great charge and profit,' adding:

One well skilled in the perquisites thereof, being demanded what he conceived the yearly value of the place was worth, made this return, 'That it might be worth some thousands of pounds to him who, after death, would go instantly to heaven; twice as much to him who would go to Purgatory; and a *nemo scit*—nobody knows what—to him who would adventure to go to a worse place.'

Thomas Howard, first Earl of Suffolk, as we shall see presently, belonged to the third class!

From the west front we have a prospect of lawn and river, with a low hill rising beyond the road to a circular Grecian temple built by the fourth Lord Howard de Walden, after a

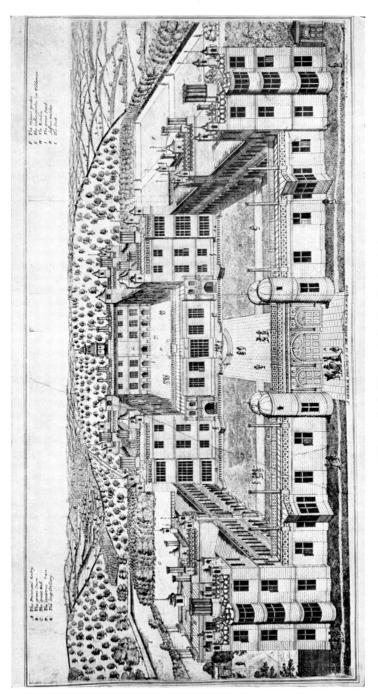

Winstanley's View of Audley End, 1676

design by Robert Adam, to commemorate the British victory of 1763. This displaced an ancient hunting tower described in Stukeley's *Itinerarium* as 'placed in a great Roman camp [1] called Ring Hill,' where a golden coin of Claudius was found along with other Roman money, and at another time 'a silver cup, of verie ancient making . . . eared up by a plough, but of such massie greatness, as it weighed more than twenty ounces.' [2] This flowing landscape is the work of 'Capability Brown,' who transformed the grounds as effectively as Lord Howard de Walden transformed the house. Brown's is not the art that conceals art so much as the nature that conceals nature; but at Audley End he had both to conceal. The formal gardens of the old palace, though a wilderness of decay and neglect when Brown was called in to advise in 1763, extended to the road, and these, as well as the distant landscape, had to be cleared to make way for his lawns and plantations. But he would see at a glance that all the essentials were here. The serpentine line, which since William Kent's pronouncement that 'Nature abhors a straight line' had been accepted as the true line of beauty, required just such an undulating landscape as north-west Essex provided. Brown required a stream in the middle distance, and here it was. Perhaps there was less timber in 1763 than he could have wished. The impoverished Suffolks had sold what they could. But the park at Audley End as we see it now, with its hardwood trees, including the cedars that Brown always required at focal points, is typical of its age and a perfect setting for the reconstructed house, which, noble as it is, owes much to the river flowing through its grounds, to the bridge that spans it, to the walks and parterres. And east of the house we find that other feature so typical of Brown, the ha-ha, practically the only unnatural barrier he allowed himself, and one he had doubts about.

These gardeners of the landscape school are often criticized for having sacrificed the charm of the earlier gardens for the sweep of their rolling parkland and colourless plantations. But at Audley End a formal 'Elysian Garden' was laid out to the north of the house, with flower-beds and walled enclosures. The mill-race of the monks was converted into a cascade, and a Palladian tea-house was set up on a bridge at the northern tip. The cascade and tea-house are still there, but the flower garden, designed with such care for the fourth Lord Howard de Walden

---

[1] Prehistoric, actually.　　[2] Holinshed's *Chronicles*, vol. i; Braybrooke, p. 136.

and his lady, has gone. The soil on this side of the house proved to be too cold and damp for anything but evergreens, and the flower-beds were transferred to the east and south.

When we turn to the house itself we find little except the west range to remind us of the Suffolks. The east front is entirely late eighteenth-century. Part of the south front is original, but much altered. Only from the west do we have a true, if partial, impression of the house as it was when Thomas Howard built it. Whether it is better or worse for this must be a matter of taste. Experts have had curiously divergent views about both the origin of its style and the value of its architecture. The traditional story is that it was built to a model brought from Italy, for which the earl paid £500. But if this is true, the model cannot have been followed at all faithfully, for there is much about its form and decoration that could hardly be Italian. Evelyn, to whom Audley End was a 'goodly palace,' found it 'a mixt fabrick, twixt antique and modern,' and so it is, with survivals of the native style embellished with detail not readily identified—in short, an admirable example of the hybrid style sometimes called 'King Jamie's Gothic.'

The first quarter of the seventeenth century was not a good time for the building of large houses. Inigo Jones had not yet introduced the classical in pure form, and Sir Henry Wootton's *Elements of Architecture* did not appear until 1624. Meanwhile, the stubborn English temperament, while willing to allow foreign embellishments, clung to its native tradition, which was not at that time capable of producing palaces.

The two-storeyed porches, with round-headed openings enriched with arabesques, have coupled columns at the angles. These, following a common adaptation of the classic, are Ionic below and Corinthian above. But whether predominantly Italian or Germanic these porches are particularly interesting in that they are so distinctively Jacobean, as also are the enriched strapwork of the balustradings, the chimney-shafts, and the copper-capped turrets at the angles of the corner blocks. Whatever purists may say of the detail, the proportions of the building are noble and impressive, and the arrangement of windows and doors instructive from the point of view of architectural development. The medieval plan is retained to the extent of having a door at one end opening into a screened passage. But at the same time the growing desire for classical symmetry required from the builder the emphasis of a central feature. He was not bold enough to use the door for this purpose. That arrangement was not usual until the beginning of the eighteenth century. But the eighteenth-century arrangement of a central door with windows on either side was anticipated in reverse. That is to say, here we have a central window with doors on either side, thus requiring two doors where one would have served. The hall, however, is still entered at one end, in the manner of the Middle Ages.

The two doors, pleasing in themselves, have carved tympana above, with Peace depicted in one and War in the other. But it is to the great window that we look with particular satisfaction —not least, perhaps, because it is a feature so rich in associations. Were not such oriels described by Bacon as 'pretty retiring-places for conference'? The great window at Audley End must often have served this purpose, as it must also have served almost daily the gentler ends of intimate family conversation. And as we reflect on these things we may remember those earlier windows—oriels in 'full perfection, glazed with right roiall glasse, fulfylled with ymagery.'

This part of the house, and this part only, retains its original character internally as well as externally. The Great Hall still belongs in spirit to the Howards, with its massive oak screen at one end—one of the finest in England, and comparable with similarly flamboyant screens at Knole and Hatfield. According to a tradition that may well be founded on fact, it came from Italy. It is clearly of early seventeenth-century date, and it has been doubted whether England had wood-carvers at the time capable of rendering the human face so skilfully. But the design is hardly Italian of the high renaissance, and surely London sculptors had already achieved considerable skill by 1610. The possibility of the Audley End screen being carved by one of them can hardly be ruled out entirely. There was a highly skilled wood-carver in St. Bartholomew's Close who might have done it. He appears in official records in 1608 as 'Master Sculptor in all the King's Palaces,' and in 1609 as the 'Carver in Wood and Stone of all His Majesty's Works.' This man was the son of a Huguenot refugee who took the name of Colt. Others may have settled in England at the same time and have taken English names. Whether the work of London craftsmen or not, the Audley End screen is one of the most typical examples of early seventeenth-century craftsmanship remaining. It is in three richly ornamented bays, with the middle one exceptionally wide to add dignity to the entrance. Between the bays are massive double caryatides, supporting an enriched entablature with projecting cornice. Round-headed arches filled with pierced arabesques occupy the upper panels of the side bays between the figures, and again form the centre-piece of the gallery front above the doorway.

About 1740 the entire screen, and with it the oak chimney-piece, was painted white. Such are the vagaries of taste. Oak panelling had then gone out of fashion, and where it was retained, as here, painting was by no means uncommon. The paint was removed by the third Lord Braybrooke a hundred years later, at the time when he did so much to improve the appearance of the Great Hall generally. Incidentally, the plaster figures on the mantelpiece were brought from the mantelpiece of the old library, and are later than the woodwork. The arms are those of the seventh Earl of Suffolk and his wife, Arabella, daughter of Sir Samuel Astry. It was he, as we shall see later, who employed Sir John Vanbrugh at Audley End, though practically the only constructive thing Sir John did here was to set up the screen at the south end of the hall about 1721, and this was a purely utilitarian device. It was built to support the roof when a double staircase was introduced by Vanbrugh to replace the original stairs.

The ceiling, with its moulded tie-beams and hammer-beam brackets, has forty plastered panels charged with the arms of the Howard family, whose arms also emblazon so many of the silken banners, along with the arms of holders of the estate from Geoffrey de Mandeville to the Braybrookes.

The Great Hall, though less noble than we might expect, and considerably smaller than the Great Hall at Hatfield, is the core of the house both architecturally and historically. And here, as nowhere else in the house, we are gripped, not by the dead but by the living hand of the past—a strong hand like that of a friend we have not met for a generation, whose welcome bursts the flood-gates of memory. It is natural that we should feel thus at Audley End, because here, more than in most great houses, the shadow is more than the substance, and it is in the Great Hall that the shadow falls, though the logs no longer blaze evocatively as they did for centuries, inspiring so many with affection for the house, from Evelyn or Pepys to the Quaker banker, Francis Gibson of Walden, who, when he called with the mayor on Lord Braybrooke in the January of 1836, to lay before his lordship a scheme for so mundane a matter as a site for the new gas works, forgot to record in his diary the outcome of his business and wrote instead: 'The park looking beautiful in the hoar frost, and the blazing log fire in the Hall finely contrasting.'

In the main, both outside and inside, Audley End is Whig and Hanoverian in its solid—almost stolid—magnificence. It is true that the Howard lion surmounts the entrance gateway, which, though restored in 1786, may date from 1616, and that of the six old rain-water heads one has the initials and date 'I.R. 1686' for James II, another 'W.M. 1689' for William and Mary, as reminders that for thirty-two years Audley End was a royal palace; but apart from such minor features as these there is little to conjure up the shades of the Suffolk Howards who disported themselves in the Lord Treasurer's courts, to say nothing of earlier shades—Lord Chancellor Audley, his daughter Margaret, or her second husband, Thomas Howard, fourth Duke of Norfolk, who was beheaded on Tower Hill in June 1572 for his part in the plot to place Mary Queen of Scots on the English throne. Yet to know what Audley End has represented in English life these and earlier shades must be invoked.

First comes Geoffrey de Mandeville, Constable of the Tower of London and first Earl of Essex, grandson of the Geoffrey de Mandeville to whom a hundred and eighteen lordships were granted—thirty-nine of them in Essex—for his services to William of Normandy. The first Geoffrey de Mandeville built the castle at Walden, intending to make it the principal seat of his family; the third, about 1140,[1] founded a priory near Audley End, where Chestnut Avenue joins the London–Cambridge valley, and endowed it with nineteen churches 'in free, pure, and perpetual alms, with all the appurtenances of the same churches, in tithes and offerings, in lands and rents, in men and their services, in meadows and pastures, in wood and plain, waters and ponds, in fishponds and fisheries, in ways and paths, in all liberties and free customs.' In addition to these he granted to the priory one hundred and twenty acres of arable land 'in my clearing of Walden,' with one hundred acres of wood, a meadow, and 'the land set aside for a vineyard,' a mill at Walden, another at Enfield, a hermitage at Hadley in Middlesex, with pasturage for sheep and pannage for pigs. The consecration

[1] The date is in dispute. See *Essex Review*, vols. xlv, xlvi, xlvii, and *Victoria County History*, vol. ii, p. 3.

ceremony was performed in the presence of the bishops of
London, Ely, and Norwich, of the earl's wife, Rohesia, daughter
of Alberic de Vere, Earl of Oxford, and of all the military
commanders in Geoffrey's honour.

To those present on this solemn occasion the priory must
have seemed a most promising foundation. But before the
monks had time to establish themselves Geoffrey, who had
plotted against Stephen in the interests of the Empress Matilda,
was declared a traitor and deprived of all his possessions,
including his castles at Pleshey and Walden.   He thereupon fled
to the Isle of Ely, where he maintained himself as a robber
chieftain, attended by the wildest ruffians he could collect, and
from his lair in the fens attacked every town and manor within
reach, pillaging and burning them, and leaving a trail of ruin
behind him.   Though himself the founder of churches, he
showed no respect, let alone reverence, to any of God's houses,
and such was his name among the folk he terrorized that they
were wont to say that Christ and His saints must sleep that such
a man should live.   Finally, after a dastardly attack on Ramsey
Abbey, he was cornered at Burwell, and just when the world
might be thought well rid of him he made a gambler's last throw
for the salvation of his soul, with dramatic consequences.   As
he lay dying, certain Templars stood by, of their charity tending
him in his last hours.   When Geoffrey saw what they were he
confessed his sins with such a show of repentance that they
were moved to pity, and when he died they wrapped his body
in the garb of their order and bore it to London, where it was
placed in a leaden coffin.   But for all that he died unshriven
and excommunicate.   So prayers were said for his soul night
and day until, nineteen years later, William, first prior of Walden,
a simple God-fearing man, obtained absolution for the founder
of his house from Pope Alexander III, and though he had little
cause to honour the memory of such a man, he went up to
London to claim the body for burial.   But the Templars, having
heard of his intention, had buried it secretly.

It was under the second prior, Reginald, a man of noble birth
who ruled for thirty-six years, that the foundation was raised
to a place of respect among the religious houses of eastern
England.   In 1190 it became a Benedictine abbey with Reginald
as first abbot.   Its later history need not concern us here; but
the choice of site is important.   Geoffrey is said to have founded
the house at this point because it was at the intersection of four

main roads and in the angle of two streams.[1]   The monks would
thus be able to offer alms to wayfarers travelling between
London and Cambridge, or from Hertfordshire into East Anglia.
The priory, therefore, was principally to be marked as a place
where travellers might sleep the night and sing their matins
before departing next morning.   This being so, it is interesting
that the only part of the old abbey buildings remaining to-day,
apart from traces of the foundations, a brick water gate on the
north of the house, and other mere fragments, is the building of
mellow Tudor brick between the river and the road, which is
now called the Stables, but may have been the monastic pilgrims'
hospice.   Much of it is of sixteenth-century date and could not
have been built much before the dissolution of the abbey in 1537.
The third Lord Braybrooke attributed it to that period.[2]   But
the Royal Commission on Historical Monuments dated it later
in the century.[3]   On the whole, it seems probable that a building
stood here before the dissolution, but that it was much altered,
or partly rebuilt, by Audley or the Duke of Norfolk.   The old
abbey had been in decline for some time, so it is unlikely that
much building had been done in the last few decades.   At the
dissolution only seven monks remained, and all were old.   The
abbot, Robert Barrington, had been removed several months
before the confiscation was completed in the October of 1537.
He was reported to be 'a man of good learning' but secretly
married, who declared openly that 'there was no sanctity in
monkery.'   He and his monks were ejected and William More,
rector of Burnham-on-Crouch and suffragan Bishop of Colchester, acted as the king's agent until, on 27th March 1538,
the abbey and all its endowments was granted to Lord Chancellor Audley, from whom the present house, built by his
grandson, takes its name,[4] a name he did not have the joy of
seeing continued in his own descendants.

[1] It was later moved to a site on higher ground to the east.
[2] *Braybrooke*, pp. 132-3.
[3] *Roy. Com. Hist. Mon.* (N.W. Essex).
[4] The name first appears in a book of accounts belonging to the almshouse,
under date 1547. Braybrooke, p. 1. For branches of the Audley family see
A. L. Reade, *Audley Pedigrees*, 1929.

II

LORD CHANCELLOR AUDLEY
AND THE DUKE OF NORFOLK

LORD CHANCELLOR AUDLEY was a man of commanding presence and uncommon sagacity, who had a way of displacing his betters and outwitting his rivals by methods that were neither honourable nor particularly subtle. He simply anticipated the Stuart doctrine of the Divine Right of Kings in favour of his own king, Henry VIII, and made it effective by using his position, first as speaker and afterwards as lord chancellor, to set the seal of legal authority on whatever the king wished. Henry, indeed, placed him in those offices for that very purpose. On Wolsey's fall in 1529 he was made Chancellor of the Duchy of Lancaster, and in the same year appointed Speaker of the House of Commons expressly to preside over the Parliament that authorized the break with Rome. He was neither more nor less than the king's mouthpiece in preparing the way for the Act of Supremacy, and in May 1532, on succeeding Sir Thomas More as lord keeper of the great seal, he received a knighthood for that service. The following January he became lord chancellor, and soon afterwards stooped to what must be accounted the basest act of his career when, in 1535, he passed judgment on More and Fisher, after presiding over a trial that showed little or no respect for justice.

Audley confessed that he had 'no devotion to any sects of religion,' so having sanctioned the divorce from Catherine of Aragon and the marriage with Anne Boleyn he would hardly be perturbed in removing the most influential critics of the king's political and domestic policy, nor, for that matter, in removing Anne herself the following year. In fact he both presided at her trial and was present at her execution, and when, after the marriage with Anne of Cleves, Parliament met to disinherit the Princess Elizabeth, he addressed the two Houses in these terms:

Lord Chancellor Audley (1488–1544)

What man of middle condition would not this deter from marrying a second time, when he remembers that the first marriage was a vast expense and a great trouble of mind to him; and the second ran him into great and imminent dangers, which hung over him during the whole time of it?   Yet this our most excellent prince, on the humble petition of the nobility, and not out of any carnal lust or affection, again condescends to contract matrimony; and hath at this time taken himself another wife, whose age and fine form denotes her most fit and likely to bring forth children.

Henry had married his third queen within twenty-four hours of the death of the second.   Anne of Cleves, his fourth, was the most fortunate of his six wives; but in spite of her fine form Audley was soon asked to remove her, as he was later asked to remove her successor, Catherine Howard.

Such, then, was Thomas Audley, yet Lloyd [1] could write of him:

His soul ennobled his body, and his body graced his soul, the one quick, solid, apprehensive, and judicious; the other tall and majestic. King Henry loved a man; here was one whose austerity was allayed by debonairness, whose gravity was sweetened with pleasantness, whose knowledge was as large as his authority, whose wit was equal to his wisdom, whose memory was strong and judgment solid.

We may be sure that so useful a lord chancellor would not go unrewarded.   The king had learnt his worth.   He would also learn his price.   When the abbey lands were for disposal—and no one had done more than Audley to bring them and their revenues into the king's possession—Sir Thomas pleaded that 'never had Chancellor so little to live by.'   His eight hundred a year, he said, would 'scarce suffice for his housekeeping.'   But on receiving a grant of Church property, and that a not inconsiderable one, he acknowledged that he had more than housekeeping in mind.   'In the busy world,' he confessed to the Bishop of Colchester,[2] 'I susteyned damage and infamy, and this shal restore me to honeste and comodyte.'   The lord chancellor knew that he had sullied his honour in the king's cause, and he made it clear that he expected his reward in this life, fearing, no doubt, that he could expect little in the next.

The priory of Christ Church, Aldgate, which Fuller refers to as 'the first cut in the feast of abbey lands, and I assure you a

[1] *State Worthies*, 1766 (1st ed., 1665).
[2] MS. Cotton Cleopatra, E. iv, fol. 197.

dainty morsel,' was given to Audley. Then in 1536 came
St. Botolph's Priory, Colchester, with all its revenues. Walden
fell into his lap in 1538, and it was in that same year that he was
created Baron Audley of Walden, thus making it clear that, like
Geoffrey de Mandeville five hundred years earlier, he intended
to make this the principal seat of his family.

But so far the lord chancellor had no family, and his wife, a
Barnardiston from Suffolk, must have trembled to see what the
king and her husband would do in their determination to
provide an heir to the throne, fearing that what happened to
queens of England might happen to herself. As far as we know,
her death in 1537 or 1538 was from natural causes, but we cannot
help feeling that in spite of his speech about remarriage it would
be highly convenient to her husband. Certainly he lost little
time in marrying a lady of higher degree, namely, Elizabeth,
sister of Henry, second Marquess of Dorset and afterwards
Duke of Suffolk, the father of Lady Jane Grey. This lady, we
are told, he married at the king's behest and was pleased to say
that he repented 'never a whytt' of it, but, on the contrary, had
'gret cause to thank the kyng's Majeste for enduying' him to it,
for the lady was much to his liking. So he wrote to Thomas
Cromwell,[1] while confined to his house by an attack of gout,
or, as he put it, 'syttyng in my chayr with a sore foote.'

By Elizabeth, his second wife, Audley had two daughters, of
whom one only survived. But although he had no son to
inherit his estates, he would have been a proud man if he could
have known how many illustrious families would be descended
from his daughter Margaret, Duchess of Norfolk, how noble a
mansion would perpetuate his memory, and that the possessors
of that mansion would so long remain, as he had ordained they
should be, Visitors—with the privilege of appointing the Master
—of the Cambridge college he re-established and re-endowed
in 1542.[2] Audley died at his Aldgate house on 30th April 1544,
after resigning the Great Seal on the 21st. He was buried in
Saffron Walden church, and of his tomb we may echo Fuller
and say that its marble is not blacker than the soul, nor harder
than the heart, of him whose bones were laid beneath it.

Although Lord Chancellor Audley held the Walden estate for
six years, and presumably lived at the abbey, we have no docu-
mentary evidence of his having altered the buildings to make

---

[1] MS. Cotton Cleopatra, E. iv, fol. 193.
[2] Magdalene College, formerly Buckingham College.

them more suitable for domestic use. Undoubtedly he would do so; but none of his surviving letters refers to work of this kind, and, in fact, not one of them is addressed from Audley End, or Walden Abbey, though several were written from other Essex houses, such as Leez Priory, Easton, and his old home at Earls Colne. Some, however, lack superscription, and these may have been written from Walden. His will certainly makes it clear that the abbey was 'his chiefe and capital mansion house' at the time of his death. He bequeathed it to his widow, 'with the parke adjoining, and all houses, barnes, etc., within the precinct thereof.' Evidence of her residence there is found in the Corporation Book of Walden, where an entry under date 1559 records 'VI Capons given to my Lady Audley, 15s.'

It is not surprising that soon after Audley's death his widow, young and rich as she was, should have married again. Her second husband, Sir George Norton, was high sheriff of Essex in 1550, the year after the marriage, and we may assume that they lived at Audley End until Lady Norton's death, which occurred about 1557. With them would live Margaret, the lord chancellor's daughter, who was born in 1540, and would be four years old when her father died. At fourteen she married Lord Henry Dudley, fourth son of the Earl of Northumberland; but there was no issue of the marriage and Dudley was killed at St. Quentin in August 1557, shortly before his wife came into possession of her father's estates, which were vested in her mother for life. It is thus her second husband, Thomas Howard, fourth Duke of Norfolk, whom she married within a few months of her first husband's death, who comes into the Audley End story, and the more so because Margaret's own life was so brief. She died on 10th January 1564 and was buried at Framlingham, Suffolk, where her effigy may be seen on one of the splendid Howard tombs, her head resting on a tiger, a wyvern at her feet. The Audley End portrait by Hans Eworth[1] was painted in 1562, when she was twenty-two years old. But if short, the marriage was fruitful. Margaret left five children—three sons, from whom are descended the Earls of Suffolk, Berkshire, Carlisle, and Bristol, as well as the Lords Howard de Walden and Howard of Escrick; and two daughters, from one of whom, also named Margaret, the Sackvilles of Knole are descended.[2] It is of her that we read in the *Memoirs of the Countess of Arundel*,

[1] Formerly attributed in error to Lucas de Heere.
[2] She married Robert Sackville, second Earl of Dorset.

and in Miss Sackville West's *Knole and the Sackvilles* how much she was loved by her husband's family.

'By courtesy of England'—that is to say, by permission of the queen—the Duke of Norfolk was allowed to hold his second wife's estates for life,[1] and by adding these to his other lands he became—at least by repute—the wealthiest subject in the kingdom, living in princely style at his castles of Kenninghall and Framlingham, with occasional visits, no doubt, to the abbey at Walden, by this time generally known as Audley End, where the duchess's fifth and last child was born shortly before her death. There is evidence of the duke's continued interest in his Essex estates, which he held for nine years more.

Among the many illustrious owners of this noble house none has lived more boldly or more recklessly than the duke. He is our gay Elizabethan, our most spectacular figure. The queen delighted to honour him. In 1559 she created him Knight of the Garter, styling him her cousin in recognition of the relationship of the Howards with the Boleyns. His position was always unique, both as duke and earl marshal. Ever since succeeding his grandfather in 1554 he had been the only duke in England. The Somerset title had been lost in 1551; those of Northumberland and Suffolk in 1553. And in consequence of this unique status the Duke of Norfolk held the lord lieutenancy of practically every county in southern England, apparently with an overriding commission in others. But his ambition was unbridled. In 1567 he married a third rich heiress in Elizabeth, daughter of Sir Francis Leybourne of Gunswick Hall, Cambridge, the widow of Thomas, Lord Dacre of Gilsland, who brought with her a family of one son and three daughters. In order to secure the Dacre wealth to his own offspring the duke married his eldest son by the first marriage, the Earl of Surrey, to Ann Dacre in 1571; his first-born of the second marriage, Thomas, to Mary Dacre, who died, alas, at the age of fourteen; and Elizabeth, the youngest of the Dacre girls, to his third son, William. His plan to marry his daughter Margaret to the infant Lord Dacre was frustrated by the prospective bridegroom's death at the age of eight, after which he aimed higher and schemed to marry her to the young King of Scotland, afterwards James I.

The third duchess died the year after her marriage, and in

---

[1] His first wife was Mary, daughter and heiress of Henry Fitzalan, twelfth Earl of Arundel.

Margaret Audley, Second Wife of Thomas, Fourth Duke of Norfolk,
by Hans Eworth

casting his net for a fourth the duke overreached himself. He aspired to marry Mary Queen of Scots, and place her on the English throne.

The facts of the story are familiar. What lay behind them can be neither fully understood nor rationally explained, except in terms of the twin madnesses of passion and ambition. When Mary sought refuge in England after the battle of Langside in 1568 Elizabeth, to whom she had appealed for protection, set up a commission to inquire into the charges laid against their queen by the Scots, and invited Norfolk—handsome, gallant, bold, and well established in her confidence at the time—to preside over its deliberations. It was a most unhappy choice. Mary was an old hand at using her charms to bring men to her feet; the duke was susceptible. He was also experienced in using women to further his ambition, and he may even have seen in her smiles the promise of a greater honour than any he had yet dreamed of. However that may be, when all the evidence had been heard he professed himself convinced of her innocence. But whatever he said in public, in private he soon began to see himself as Mary's consort. And the duke's ambition was matched by the queen's passion. Before long letters were passing between them that professed the most ardent affection. How much was genuine it would be difficult to know. Both were old hands at the game. But whoever was deceived, either about them or by them, Elizabeth herself had no illusions. In the August of 1569, while the duke was dining with her, she teased him as she had teased so many, without allowing him to see how much she knew until, as the duke bowed himself out of her presence, in accents that betrayed at last the woman as well as the queen in her, she bade him beware on what pillow he lay his head.

But this was no private affair. Europe as well as Britain was concerned and in every court on the Continent the political implications of such an alliance were being canvassed. The French ambassador approved. The pope gave twelve thousand crowns to Robert di Ridolfi, who with Norfolk's support was plotting to invade England in Mary's cause. Philip II was marshalling the Catholic forces, and it seemed likely that the clash would come quickly. Meanwhile, however, Cecil's spies were active on Elizabeth's behalf, and when the hour was about to strike the duke was summoned to Windsor. He feigned illness and retired to Kenninghall. The Queen of Scots was

c

then moved to Tutbury and placed under stricter control. Her papers were seized and were found to contain all that Cecil needed to justify him in committing Norfolk to the Tower. But Elizabeth was reluctant to charge him with treason. He had, she hoped, learnt his lesson, and on his promises of loyalty to herself she released him. Cecil, however, had no faith in the duke's word. His watch continued, and was fully warranted, for letters again passed between the duke and the Queen of Scots, and again he was arrested and committed to the Tower.

The irony of this second committal is that Elizabeth was actually entertained at Audley End while the duke was held prisoner at the Charterhouse, his London residence, to which he had been moved from the Tower because the plague was prevalent there and his case was still untried; and it was 'from our Court at Audeley' that on 1st September she issued a commission to Sir Thomas Smith, himself a Saffron Walden man, 'to examine the Duke of Norfolk touching the money he had sent to Scotland, and other matters.' The Walden accounts show that Lords Burghley and Leicester were present, because on this occasion of the visit of 'our moste gratious and Soverayne Ladye Elyzabeth,' the recorder of Walden delivered an oration and presented 'a cupp of silver doble gilt, with a cover, weying 46 ounzes,' to the queen, 'a podd of oysters' to Thomas Berenger, and sugar loaves to Burghley, Leicester, and Sir Thomas Smith.

The duties thus laid upon Sir Thomas in his native town must have been the most painful in his long and honourable life. His great work, *De Republica Anglorum*, shows him to have been one of the most enlightened men of his age. In it he had written that torture, of which he had seen so much in Mary's reign, was against the laws of England and should have no place among a free people. This belief he still held, yet he was ordered by Cecil on 15th September, in a letter signed by the queen, to put the duke's servant, Barber, and his lawyer, Lawrence Bannister, to the rack if necessary in order to make them talk. Sir Thomas received this letter as master of requests. He acknowledged it on the 16th, but boldly made plain to Burghley his disgust at being employed in such a service, craving a revocation and adding: 'I assure you, I would not wish to be one of Homer's Gods, if I thought I should be Minos, Aeacus, or Rhadamanthus; I had rather be one of the least shades in the Elysian fields.' Nor was this the only attempt to weaken Burghley's resolve. His own son-in-law,

Edward de Vere, seventeenth Earl of Oxford, an intimate friend of the duke, pleaded with him 'for the preserving him [the duke] from destruction, but not prevailing grew so highly incensed against Burghley, knowing it was in his power to save him, that he said he would do all he could to ruin his daughter.'[1] But Burghley remained unmoved.   Incriminating evidence was taken from the duke's lawyer on the 17th, and after four months in prison, cut off from access to any books that might help him in preparing his defence, and from all communication with his friends—denied even a copy of his indictment—Norfolk was brought before twenty-seven carefully selected peers, with Shrewsbury as lord high steward.   When he asked for counsel to be assigned to him, Catlin replied brusquely: 'You must have none.'

'That's very severe,' the duke protested.   'I have had very short warning, not more than fourteen hours, night and all.   I am no lawyer.   I could not have books to inform myself . . . but must fight without weapons.'

Then a message was brought into court from Elizabeth, stating that she had received confirmation of the duke's guilt from a foreign ambassador.   This message was communicated to the twenty-seven peers, but not to the duke himself.   He had, therefore, no opportunity of answering it.   There could be only one verdict.   Shrewsbury asked the peers one by one whether they found the duke guilty or not guilty, and all replied 'Guilty.' When this finding was announced to the duke he drew himself up and said solemnly: 'The great God and my own innocence be judge between me and my false accusers.'

'Thus fell,' says the account,[2] 'that illustrious Prince, whose greatness in Estate and title was his only crime, for being of an antient and splendid family, the blood Royal of England and France not being out of his veins.   Having an estate to support that greatness of £100,000 a year, besides fortunes he obtained in marriages.'

But the queen was still reluctant to exact from him the due penalty for his treachery.   She signed several warrants for his execution, and revoked them before they could be put into effect until, in the early summer of 1572, she was at last convinced that if her throne were to be safe the duke must die.   Accordingly he was beheaded on Tower Hill on 2nd June 1572.

[1] Dugdale's *Baronage*, vol. i, p. 199.
[2] *The Arraignment of Thos. Howard, Duke of Norfolk*, 1685.

William Camden, the antiquary, who witnessed the scene, relates how he

was brought upon the scaffold at eight o'clock in the morning, when Alexander Nowell, Dean of St. Paul's, who was there as his ghostly comforter, desired the multitude that stood round, to keep silence, after which the duke spoke as follows:

'It is no new thing for men to suffer death in this place, though since the beginning of our most gracious Queen's reign I am the first, and God grant I may be the last. I acknowledge my Peers have justly sentenced me worthy of death; nor have I any design to excuse myself. I freely confess that I treated with the Queen of Scots in things of great moment, without my Sovereign's knowledge, which I ought not to have done; whereupon I was cast into the Tower. But I was afterwards set at liberty, having made an humble submission, and promised upon honour to have nothing more to do with her; yet, I confess, I acted contrary; and this, in truth, disturbs my conscience. But I neither promised nor sware it at the Lord's Table, as is commonly reported.'

He went on to confess that he had conferred with Ridolfi, though not, he swore, to the queen's prejudice. He alleged that he had not approved of either the Catholic rising in the north or the pope's intervention, declaring himself a Protestant who had always been 'averse to the popish doctrine.' And he may well have been telling the truth. His tutor had been John Foxe, the martyrologist, for whom he had retained so great a respect that he desired to see him again in the last hours of his life. The Roman Catholic tradition in the Howard family after the Reformation begins with the duke's sons, Philip and William, whose tutor was a gentleman named Martin, afterwards a priest of the Roman Church.

The scene at the scaffold moved the people deeply. 'It is incredible,' says Camden,

how dearly the people loved him, whose goodwill he had gained by a munificence, and extraordinary affability, suitable to so great a Prince. The wiser sort of men were variously affected; some were terrified at the greatness of the danger, which during his life seemed to threaten the State from him and his faction. Others were moved with pity towards him as one very nobly descended, of an extraordinary good-nature, comely personage, and manly presence, who might have been a support and ornament to his country, had not the crafty wiles of the envious, and his own false hopes, led on with a show of doing the public service, diverted him from his first course of life. They called likewise to mind the untimely death of his father, the Earl of

Surrey, a man of extraordinary learning, and famous in war, who was beheaded in the same place five-and-twenty years before.

Whatever his faults—and they were grave—there was, as Camden noted, something in the duke's personality that endeared him to the people not less than to the queen herself. As he prepared himself for execution he wrote to his children a letter, which has a passage showing that Audley End and his tenants there were not forgotten in his last hours. It refers to St. Aylott's, a grand old farmhouse two miles east of Walden, and is addressed to the son who was to inherit the estate. 'Tom,' runs the letter,

I had forgotten to request one thing at your hands, which I hope you will hereafter, when the time cometh, perform. It is this: I promised Bowles a lease of a farm of yours in your hands called St. Aylott's, which if I had lived I would have performed; and now I hope you will, if God send you to come to years, perform as much as I would have done. He hath been as honest and true a servant to your father as any that he hath had, and therefore I hope at this my request, he shall have the lease at your hand.

After the duke's death his brother, afterwards Earl of Northampton, lived at Audley End, attending to the education of the children, whose lives he influenced even to the second generation, and not always—if indeed ever—for good. Northampton may, perhaps, be regarded as the evil genius of the family. Bannister, the duke's lawyer, had said in the evidence extorted from him on the rack that it was Henry Howard, not Thomas, who had first been put forward as a suitable consort for the Queen of Scots by those who plotted in the Catholic interest. It is true that the circumstances in which the evidence was given detracts from its value; but it was commonly believed that Henry had been pulling the strings throughout, and was largely responsible for his brother's downfall.[1] As with so many of the Howards, his character presents a wellnigh insoluble problem. Horace Walpole in *Noble Authors* reminds us that he was said by Bishop Godwin to be 'the learnedest among the nobility, and the most noble among the learned,' which is probably true. Bacon recorded some of his witty remarks in *Apophthegms*.[2] He had all the high-flown ambition of his house, and much of its moral instability. When we come to discuss

---

[1] Birch, *Memoirs*, vol. i, p. 227, and *D.N.B.*
[2] *Works*. Edited by Spedding, vol. vii, pp. 154, 164, 171.

the ladies of the Howard family we shall see how discreditable a
part he played in the shocking affair of the Earl of Somerset
and the Countess of Essex, daughter of the first Earl of Suffolk.
Plotting was in his blood, and even after his brother's death for
scheming in her cause his own relations with the Queen of
Scots were open to suspicion. In 1574 he was said to be
exchanging tokens with her, and though he contrived to give
an explanation of his conduct that was apparently accepted at
the time as satisfactory, Elizabeth continued to doubt his
integrity, and with good reason. His own story was that the
purport of his advice to Mary was to 'abate the sails of her
royal pride.' Elizabeth he certainly flattered grossly, and we
can hardly doubt that he played on Mary's vanity in the same
way. After all, Mary had a son. The future was in her blood,
not in Elizabeth's. At the end of Elizabeth's life Henry
Howard, as Scott reminds us in a note to *The Fortunes of Nigel*,
conducted 'with great pedantry, but much intrigue, the correspondence between the Scottish king and the younger Cecil.'
The pedantry being, as Cecil well knew, the best bait for that
particular fish.

Of the duke's children Philip, the eldest, who was fifteen at
the time of his father's death, was a favourite with Elizabeth,
even though he bore the name of her sister Mary's consort.
He had been baptized in the chapel at Whitehall in the presence
of the queen and her court, with Philip as one of his godfathers.
As a youth he spent two years at Cambridge, and was doubtless
in attendance at Audley End when Elizabeth, in 1578, paid her
second visit. He was then a tall and handsome man of twenty-
one, somewhat swarthy of skin, with a manner that was both
dignified and debonair.

There were no sinister shadows in the background at Audley
End in 1578. The vice-chancellor of Cambridge and the heads
of the colleges came out into Essex to offer Her Majesty their
presents, which included a Greek Testament bound in red velvet
and lettered in gold, and a pair of perfumed and embroidered
gloves. They were received most graciously by the queen, who
promised that she would always be mindful of the university.
Her courtiers, among whom were Burghley, the earls of Leicester
and Oxford, Sir Christopher Hatton—recently appointed vice-
chamberlain of the household—and Sir Philip Sidney, also
received gloves, with verses 'annext to them.' It was on this
visit that 'the Nobilitie and Schollers of the Universitie went

into a gallerie, and there called for beare and wine to welcome
the Schollers; and from thence into the chambre of my Lord of
Leicester, where was handled a Disputation of Philosophy.'
As there were not enough beds either at Audley End or in
Walden for them, the scholars were obliged to return to the
university the same night.

We do not know how many members of the Howard family
were present at Audley End on this occasion. It would be
interesting to know if Philip's wife, Anne, was there. The
married life of this particular couple began badly. For one
reason, the queen 'could not endure the lady,' and Philip was
as desirous as his ancestors had been for the sweets of royal
favour. Later in life, Philip and Anne were reconciled through
their devotion to the Roman Church, to which Philip, by
this time Earl of Arundel, publicly avowed his allegiance in
1583. Like so many of his family he suffered for his faith. In
1585 he was imprisoned in the Tower for having, as a Catholic,
attempted to leave England without the queen's licence. While
still in custody he was attainted, in 1589, and fined £10,000
for having procured a certain Father William Bennett to say
mass for the success of the Spanish Armada.[1] According to
Camden [2] he died as the result of his religious austerities. Philip
Howard never enjoyed the Norfolk dukedom; but it was restored
to the family in the person of his son in 1644.

But whatever the piety of his later years, Philip, who as a
young man bore the title of Earl of Surrey by courtesy, was
one of the most profligate of the queen's favourites. Perhaps
he was an illustration of Fuller's saying: 'They that marry where
they do not love, will love where they do not marry.' At all
events, his fancy was inclined to roam, and this roving fancy of
his caused some disturbance in the quiet life of Saffron Walden,
as we read in *A Noble Mans Sute to a Cuntrie Maide*,[3] the maid
being Mercy, daughter of a Saffron Walden rope-maker and
sister of the illustrious Gabriel Harvey, one of the Cambridge
scholars who disputed before Elizabeth at Audley End in
1578.

If the fourth Duke of Norfolk had served England's queen
instead of Scotland's, or if Philip had made amends for his

---

[1] It is only fair to point out that this accusation has no better foundation than a
confession extorted from Father Bennett on the rack.
[2] Camden's *Elizabeth* in *History of England*, 1706, p. 587.
[3] *The Letter Book of Gabriel Harvey*, Camden Society, 1884.

father's treachery and folly, we might have had a Tudor mansion instead of a Jacobean at Audley End. When Philip's name was mentioned during the trial of the Queen of Scots at Fotheringhay in 1586, Mary burst into tears and said: 'Alas, what has the House of Howard suffered for my sake.' That suffering was remembered by Mary's son. When he came to the English throne he made what restitution he could, and the eldest son of the Duke of Norfolk and Margaret Audley was among the first to receive honours. It was this son who built Audley End.

III

'TOO MUCH FOR A KING'

IN THE FAREWELL letter to his children already mentioned, the duke entreated his sons, especially Philip, 'to beware of the Court, except it be to do his Prince service, for that place hath no certainty, and either throweth a man down headlong, or he liveth there unsatisfied.' He added: 'You may, by the grace of God, be a great deal richer and quieter in your low degree, wherein I wish you to continue.' His own father, the poet Earl of Surrey, whose life also ended on the scaffold, had counselled humility no less movingly; but both father and son bequeathed to their children a blood more potent than any counsel. The Howards of Tudor and Stuart England were not made to be content with low degree. Nor had they cause. Philip was dead when James became king, so the two we are now concerned with are Henry, the late duke's brother, and Thomas, eldest son of the Audley marriage—Henry as family guardian, Thomas as builder of the palace that was hardly in keeping with the father's pious injunction. Both were in the select company that assembled with Cecil at Theobalds in May 1603 to pledge their allegiance to the new king before he went up to London to be crowned, and both were appointed to the Privy Council there and then. Shortly afterwards they continued in step, as it were, in that both were made earls— Thomas of Suffolk, Henry of Northampton. Such was their ascendancy in the new reign that they were rapidly established as two of its most influential figures, both at court and in the nation's counsels.

Long before this, however, Suffolk, still known to the people as Lord Thomas Howard—the Lord Thomas Howard of Tennyson's poem *The Revenge*—had captured the popular imagination by several daring feats of seamanship. Lloyd, in his *Statesmen*, says he was 'as plain as his brother [by which he must surely mean his uncle] Henry, was subtle, as obliging as he was insinuating, as knowing as he was cunning, the one conversing with books, the other with men. . . . He was a man never endued with much patience, and one that much retarded the progress of his fortune by often speaking publicly with too much liberty.'

Between the fourth duke's death and the new king's accession the political complexity of the Howards had not diminished. While Philip had attended mass for the success of the Armada, Thomas had commanded the *Golden Lion*, a vessel of 500 tons, with 38 guns and a crew of 250, under his kinsman, Lord Howard of Effingham, in the fleet that destroyed it. For his gallantry in this encounter he had been knighted at sea by the lord high admiral. Three years later, sailing himself in the *Elizabeth Jonas*, a ship of 900 tons with a crew of 500, and in command of a squadron of ships sent to attack the Spanish plate fleet, he had come into conflict with a vastly superior force from Spain, and, after cruising for six months off the Azores somewhat provocatively, had so distinguished himself that Camden, in his life of Elizabeth,[1] writes in high praise of his conduct. He had held commands in the 1595 and 1597 expeditions, in the latter—when Cadiz was taken—leading the third squadron, with the admiral himself leading the first, Essex the second, and Raleigh the fourth. It was shortly after this last exploit that he was summoned to Parliament as Lord Howard de Walden.[2] So when Elizabeth died in 1603, two months after he had entertained her at the Charterhouse, Lord Thomas was a national hero, and his advancement to an earldom by James served the dual purpose of settling the family debt and at the same time gratifying the people. His direction of the search that brought Gunpowder Plot to light still further enhanced his reputation.

But honoured and acclaimed as he was, Suffolk soon realized that if he was to take the place he intended to have in the new court he must be worthily housed. As a Howard he was not to be satisfied with the old house at Walden, which had not been his father's capital residence, and which his grandfather had doubtless intended to rebuild. The Earl of Northampton would support him in this ambition. He may even have inspired it. Shifty as he was, Northampton was a man of culture, whose house at Charing Cross, afterwards Northumberland House, was evidence of his taste in architecture, and equally of his flair for magnificence. His skill was shown again in the enlargement of Greenwich Palace. So in view of Northampton's acknowledged interest in architecture, and of his tutelage of the family,

[1] Camden's *Elizabeth* in *History of England*, vol. ii, p. 565.
[2] *Journal of Parl.* 39 *Elizabeth*.

it is odd that several writers, in referring to the building of Audley End, should question statements in the *Dictionary of National Biography* article giving him credit for a hand in the work. With all the circumstances of their lives in mind it is surely inconceivable that the uncle should not have been interested in what the nephew was doing, or that the nephew should not have consulted him. With a fabric so mixed in style there is, perhaps, no point in pursuing the argument; but it ought to be said here that the authority for Northampton's interest is a passage in *Aulicus Coquinaire*, 1650, where it is stated of the Earl of Northampton that:

He assisted his nephew, the E. of Suffolk, by his designing & large contribution to that excellent fabrick, Audley End. He built the noble structure at Charing Crosse, from the ground, Northampton House, & presented it, a New Year's gift to the Lord Walden, Suffolk's eldest sonne, & now called Suffolk House: and yet left his other nephew, the E. of Arundel, the rest of his estate, so to appear to the World his equal distribution to such even kindred.

The writer of this, in dealing with Sir Anthony Weldon's insinuations about Northampton being peeved at not receiving the lord treasurership, says:

He died in Anno 1613, full of years and honorable fame, though our pamphleteer [1] will not know so much, & yet no doubt must needs be intimate with his person, for he tells us his thoughts, that he had assuredly promised himself the Treasurer's staff although we can produce this lord's letter, & other testimonies, employing all his own & his friends interest for that preferment upon his nephew Suffolk, & excusing himself of the burden and weight of that office by his known infirmity of stone, of the which he died.

Weldon had said that Northampton altered his will on his death-bed because he was so annoyed at his nephew's rival candidature for the treasurership. The author of the *Aulicus Coquinaire* disposes of that error; but it is doubtful whether he is himself correct about Northampton's provision for the Suffolk family. He says nothing about Henry, Northampton's namesake, to whom he left much of his property, knowing that Theophilus—to whom he may or may not have given Northampton House as a new year's gift—would be provided for as Suffolk's heir, and that Thomas was to have the Wiltshire estates of his mother's family. There is no need to enter fully into

---

[1] Sir Anthony Weldon.

these finer points of inheritance. We are chiefly concerned with Suffolk himself, and towards him the will expresses affection in terms that are plain enough. He is referred to as 'my most dear and entirely beloved nephew, Thomas Earl of Suffolk,' and to him Northampton left his

> jewel of the three stones, one of them being that rubie which his excellent Majesty sent me out of Scotland as his first token, which jewel I cannot better repose with any, than with him that is so faithful and trusty to his Majesty. And I give him also a cross of diamonds given me by my Lady my Mother.[1]

What until recently was the other great problem about the designing of Audley End, namely, the part of John Thorpe in it, disappears as a result of John Summerson's important contribution to the *Architectural Review*, November 1949, 'John Thorpe and the Thorpes of Kingscliffe,' in which he shows conclusively that Thorpe, if an architect at all, was one of no consequence. He was, says Mr. Summerson, one of the most eminent land surveyors of his day, and the famous volume in the Sir John Soane Museum, which has deceived so many, is Thorpe's record book, and not a book of original designs. 'John Thorpe's fame,' is thus, as Mr. Summerson puts it, 'a freak of history.'

No accounts survive to show the actual cost of the original Audley End; but the Earl of Pembroke recorded that he heard the lord treasurer tell King James that first and last, inside and outside, with the furniture, it cost him £200,000.[2] The present main block was always the core of the building, and from this, with Winstanley's help, we can reconstruct the whole. When it was completed in 1616 the range containing the Great Hall overlooked the greater court, with the main entrance in the range facing it. Arched cloisters ran along the north and south ranges of the greater court, their columns supporting upper storeys with mullioned windows and turrets, so that the whole resembled, shall we say, the galleried and cloistered courts, or quadrangles, of our larger medieval colleges. The stone parapet was pierced to form what Evelyn called 'a bordure of capital letters,' bearing the legend *Prudentis est in consilio fortunam semper habere* on one side, and on the other the motto of the Garter. As the roofs were flat and leaded, the sky formed a backcloth against which both were clearly legible.

[1] Braybrooke, p. 78.   [2] Braybrooke, p. 82.

Looking eastward from the greater court, beyond the single-storeyed Great Hall—as it then was—could be seen the Clock Tower, surmounting the east range of Winstanley's innermost court, below which, in this now demolished east range, was the Long Gallery, 226 feet long, 32 feet wide, and 24 feet high, with its panelled walls and oak chimney-piece carved with a representation of the labours of Hercules. Its ceiling, decorated to portray the loves of the gods, was much admired by visitors, and indeed the entire gallery was so fine that Evelyn described it as 'the most cheerful, and I think one of the best in England.'

From this east range, which completed the enclosure of the innermost court, two wings projected eastward again, the one containing the Chapel, the other one of the kitchens, while the Great Kitchen projected northward from the north range of the greater court.

Westward from the greater court, the main entrance gave access to the outer court, walled but without service buildings, through which a double avenue of limes led from the main road to the house. Bowling greens, cherry gardens, ponds, and stable yards are shown by Winstanley to have filled up the ground, the extent of which can be appreciated by noting that the river flows through the middle of the outer court.

A feature of Suffolk's Audley End was its extensive cloisters. The outer court, as we have seen, had arcades along both the north and south ranges. There was another along the west side of the east range, under the Long Gallery, and yet another, now converted into rooms, along the outside of the south range, overlooking the Mount Garden, with its mound of earth encircled with a spiral walk, 'writhen about with degrees, like the turnings of cockil shelles, to come to the top without payne.' A high wall screened these gardens from the envious poor who passed by them, but from the Mount, perhaps, the family might themselves gaze no less enviously at the country folk gathered on the green outside for a village fair.

The Mount Garden on the south was balanced on the north by another feature of the age, the Wilderness, which, as its name implies, afforded relief from the dominant formality of the plan as a whole. Of the completed palace, Evelyn says that it 'shews without like a diadem, by the decorations of the cupolas and other ornaments on the pavilions.' Many travellers have described this dazzling fabric. Perhaps the most interesting— though again, like Evelyn's, it belongs to a later reign—is that

of Cosmo de Medici, afterwards Grand Duke of Tuscany, who
travelled through England in 1669. In order to get as clear a
picture as possible of the original house at this point, it is,
perhaps, better to take it now than leave it for a later chapter.
The original manuscript, in the hand of the Grand Duke's
private secretary, Magalotti, with its three large drawings of
Audley End, is in the Laurentian Library at Florence.

'Descending into the valley below,' writes Magalotti,

> by an easy acclivity, we came to a spacious avenue, planted with
> elms [1] of considerable height, which terminated at the mansion. The
> entrance is into a quadrangle Court, whose sides are surrounded by
> porticoes of stone, which, extending with perfect regularity to the
> distance of several bowshots, inclose a large meadow. The balustrade,
> which runs round the court, is formed on one side, of the letters which
> compose the following words: *Sapientis* [2] *est in Consilio fortunam semper
> habere*; and on the other, with those of the motto belonging to the
> arms of the Order of the Garter, *Honi soit qui mal y pense*. The interior
> of the house consists of many apartments, well proportioned and
> judicially disposed; and of a well-lighted Gallery, ninety paces or more
> in length, having the ceiling of stucco, adorned with arabesques, and
> walls lined with wainscot, which is the custom in all the houses of the
> English Nobility, as a protection against the cold. The Architecture
> of the Palace, although it was built only sixty years ago, is nevertheless
> not regular, but inclines to the Gothic, mixed with a little of the
> Doric and Ionic. . . . Upon the roof [3] is a Gallery, in the midst of
> which rises a small Cupola, containing a clock, the sound of which
> proclaims to a great distance the magnificence of this vast fabric.

Cosmo was a friend of Henry Neville of Warfield, one of the
Nevilles of Billingbear, and it is interesting to note that some
curtains of crimson Florentine damask, with the saltire, the
first quartering of the Nevilles, worked into the pattern, given
to Henry Neville by Cosmo, were brought to Audley End when
a descendant succeeded as second Lord Braybrooke. They
hung in the South Library.

In such a palace as this the earl and his countess must have
looked forward to living as nobly as the dukes of Norfolk had
lived in other generations in their East Anglian castles. And
at the time of its completion the earl was still a popular figure.
When he was appointed lord treasurer on 11th July 1614,
according to the Birch MS. No. 4173, there was public rejoicing:

[1] Evelyn says they were limes.
[2] Actually *Prudentis est in consilio*, as given above.
[3] The gallery was on the first floor, above the arcade.

'Yesterday being the last day of Term,' runs the account, 'the Lord Treasurer went to Westminster Hall, accompanied with the greatest number of nobility and gentlemen of fashion that hath been seen on the like occasion.' The same account tells us that the appointment was made not for his 'learning in Greek and Latin, or that he could make epigrams and orations, but for his approved fidelity and integrity.'

Though this early confidence was to prove misplaced, the earl would continue to have his following. He had the Howard flair for doing things in the grand manner, which always wins the plaudits of the crowd. He was as popular at Cambridge as chancellor as he was at court as lord treasurer, and for the same reason. When James came down in March 1615, the earl entertained him so lavishly at St. John's that the cost of the table is said to have been at the rate of a thousand pounds a day. And while the earl entertained at St. John's, the countess and her retinue were at Magdalene, the college refounded by Audley, the earl's grandfather.

But the Earl of Suffolk, like his father before him, was living beyond his means, large as these were, with the result that after scheming to live like a prince he found himself reduced to comparative poverty. The cost of building the place had been greater than he had bargained for. So although, according to Morant, he sold estates in the North of England to meet it,[1] his debts continued to mount until he and the countess were reduced to resorting to various forms of political corruption, in a vain effort to ward off, or delay, the inevitable result of their extravagance. The countess, the earl's second wife and the mother of his fourteen children, was the daughter of Sir Henry Knyvett of Wiltshire. She was a famous beauty in her day and none the better for it. 'Lady Suffolk,' says Anne Clifford in her Diary for 1619, 'had the small-pox at Northampton House, which spoiled that good face of hers, which had brought to others much misery, and to herself greatness, which ended in much unhappiness.' When disaster befell the Suffolks in 1618 the countess was thought largely to blame. Weldon, in his *Court and Character of James I*, says:[2]

The Constable of Castile so plied his master's business (in which he spared no cost) that he procured a peace so advantageous for Spain, and so disadvantageous for England, that it, and all Christendom,

[1] The third Lord Braybrooke doubted this. See Braybrooke, p. 83.
[2] Page 27.

have since both seen and felt the lamentable effect thereof. There was not one courtier of note that tasted not of Spain's bounty, either in gold or jewels; and, among them, not any in so large a proportion as the Countess of Suffolk, who shared in her Lord's interest, being then a potent man; and in that interest which she had in being mistress to that little-great secretary [1] (little in body and stature, but great in wit and policy), the sole manager of state affairs; so it may be said she was a double sharer; and in truth, Audley End, that famous and great structure, had its foundation in Spanish gold.

In the early summer of 1618, two years after the completion of the house, it became known that the earl was suspected of having embezzled money received from the Dutch for the Cautionary Towns, and on 19th July he was relieved of office, but was allowed to retire to Audley End until the following March, when he was summoned to London for examination. It was not until August 1619, however, that a full inquiry was held, and he was not publicly charged in the Star Chamber until 20th October.   On 30th November, according to a manuscript in the University Library at Cambridge,[2]

The Informacion ag[st] the Earle of Suffolke and his Lady and their Serv S[r] John Bingley came to Censure.

S[r] Edw. Coke began the censure to this effect. 'My Lords in this Informacion exhibited in this Court against the Earle of Suffolke the La: his wife and S[r] Jo: Bingly, for divers misdemean[rs] in the office of high Treasurer of England. In misimploying of treasure, falshoode of distribucion of paym[ts] of the matter of Allom, translating of debts, and issuing of money by false records, extorcion, and bribery.'

After S[r] Edward's speech come those of S[r] Fulke Grevill, Hobert Chief Justice, the Master of the Rolls, the L[d] Chief Justice of the King's Bench, Secretary Calvert,[3] Secretary Nanton, Lord Digby, Marquis Hamilton, the Bishop of London, the Lord Pembroke, the Duke of Lenox, the Lord Archbishop, the Lord Chancellor.

Both the earl and the countess were committed to the Tower; but were released after nine days on promising to pay a fine of £30,000. As for this, the *Calendar of State Papers*, August 1620, informs us that 'All the Earl of Suffolk's fine is remitted, except £7,000, which is to pay Lord Haddington's debts. The King was entertained by Sir Thomas Howard at Charlton during his progress.'

It seems to be generally agreed that the countess, who in age was as much detested for her rapacity as in youth she had been

---

[1] Cecil.   [2] Add. MS. 27.   [3] Afterwards Lord Baltimore of Maryland.

The North Porch

courted for her beauty, was the more guilty of the two. Nevertheless, the Howard record being what it was, it seems a little
unfair to lay the husband's faults as completely as some have
done to his wife's charge. They were probably a well-matched
couple. The earl was kept busy gaining power and influence
for himself and his family; the countess, usually through her
creature Sir John Bingley, was fully employed in turning her
husband's position to profitable account by selling offices at
court. What is abundantly clear is that all the money the pair
of them could raise was poured into the building of this fabulous
mansion they were destined never to enjoy.

It was a tragic end to so proud a story; but nevertheless the
earl continued to hope that Fortune's wheel would even yet,
revolve in his favour, particularly when the king had been so
gracious as to receive him again as early as the January of 1620,
and had so substantially reduced his fine. But the king's mind
was never easily read, and perhaps the cruellest thrust of all the
earl was to suffer was a letter from James asking for the resignation of Suffolk's two sons, still in the royal service. It was to
this request that the earl replied in the most pathetic of his
surviving letters: [1]

Most gratious Soverayn,
Your pryncely favour in delevering me and my wyfe out of the
Tower, must and shall ever be acknowledged by us with all humble
thanks; and now be pleased to geve me leave to be an humble sutor
to your Ma^ty, that out of the tender compassion of your pryncely
hart, you wyl be pleased to cast your eye upon the meserable estate of
your dystressed, afflycted, and owld servant, now brought into feare
of recovery of your Ma^te's favour; and, so wretched my case ys as
the little hope that remayned in me to lyve in your memory was my
two sonn's servyse to your gratious self, and the Prynce. Yt is now
requyred of me to impose upon them the resygnation of their places,
which, wyth all humylytie, I beseech you to geve me leave to say, I
wolde sooner use my power over them to wyll them to bury themselves quycke, than by any other way than inforcement to geve up
their places of servyse.

He points out that both are married and have children of
their own and humbly begs to be spared the ruin of these two
young men. At the same time he wrote a letter to the Duke of
Buckingham, the king's favourite, for whom he can have had
no love, imploring him to plead his cause with the king. But

[1] Quoted in *Portraits of Illustrious Persons*, Edmund Lodge, F.S.A., 1825.
D

James was not to be moved. He insisted on being obeyed, and the two young men were compelled to resign. Then, having given himself the pleasure of abasing his victims, he forthwith restored them to the very offices he had required them to quit.

But it is easy to exaggerate the earl's distress. This was not a commercial age, and it was usual for a nobleman to live recklessly. Nor was the Earl of Suffolk exceptional in his passion for building. There was hardly a nobleman of the day who did not indulge it to a greater or lesser degree, and several others came near to ruining themselves while the fever was on them. Sir Francis Willoughby comes to mind. And having built their great houses, they entertained so prodigally that if the building had left gold in their coffers their tables would have consumed it. To us, the building of Audley End may appear to be madness, the earl's fall the tragic end of a course of wickedness and folly; but the earl and his contemporaries may not have seen it so. In fact, for a man who lived at such a rate the extent of his debts at the time of his committal to the Tower—£40,000, according to his own statement [1]—would not seem ruinous. He had sold the Charterhouse for £13,000, but he still held Lulworth and Framlingham castles, as well as Charlton in Wiltshire, the seat of the present earls of Suffolk. His large family had been well settled. His daughters had married into powerful houses; his sons had either married rich heiresses or been appointed to lucrative offices under the Crown, and, after the one frightening episode, they might now be thought safe in them. Moreover, however great the cost, the palace on which he had staked so much was completed. Bleak as his last years were, there would be some satisfaction in that. Audley End would stand, and his descendants, he must have hoped, might even yet find in its courts the life that he had missed, but nearly, so very nearly, achieved. Such would probably be his thoughts in the last six years of his life, which closed on 28th May 1626.

The countess outlived her husband by several years. For her there can have been little consolation in the great house she could not occupy. A Mr. Garrard,[2] writing in 1633 to the Lord Deputy of Ireland, says:

The Countess of Suffolk is run away, or hid herself that she cannot be found, because she refuses to pay £1,400 arrear, and £200 pension to Mrs. Clare, now Harding, decreed now a second time upon review

---

[1] Braybrooke, p. 83.   [2] *Strafford Correspondence*, vol. i, p. 165.

by the Lord Keeper, the King rejecting once, twice, thrice, petitions that have been offered from her, and telling others that interceded for her, that it was just for her to pay it, and she should pay it. She pretends poverty; and I believe she is so, for she has dissolved her husband's hospital at Audley End,[1] not being able to maintain it any longer. Sergeants-at-arms seek her daily, but she cannot be found. Her eldest son is so far from taking care of her, though it be his own case, that he thinks not of freeing her, no, nor of paying his own debts, which will eat out his inheritance.

It is also worth noting that Mr. Garrard tells us that Theophilus, the second earl, was disinclined to relieve his mother's distress. It is true, as we have seen, that these great houses, built in the fullness of the English Renaissance, belong to an age with little concern for cost; but it is also true that the extravagance of one generation was bitterly resented by the next. The second earl was not alone among the noblemen of his day in lacking appreciation of what his parents had done. The ninth Earl of Northumberland, the 'Wizard Earl,' said when his father, the eighth earl, died: 'I was . . . so well left for movables as I was not worth a fire-shovel or a pair of tongs; what was left me was wainscots, or things riveted with nails; for wives are commonly great scratchers after their husband's death, if things be loose.' Theophilus could have said the same with feeling. The first countess would certainly have been a great scratcher if there had been anything left to scratch for!

Theophilus, the second earl, who, while still a minor, was summoned to the House of Lords as second Lord Howard de Walden when his father became an earl, married Elizabeth, daughter of George Home, Earl of Dunbar, Lord Treasurer of Scotland. Lord Walden was twenty-eight at the time, which was old for a man of his rank to marry. But the bride was only eleven. In the first earl's eyes she was evidently a prize worth waiting for. In November 1606, when Elizabeth was a child of six, the two fathers put their heads together and concluded an agreement, 'with the full assent and good-liking of Theophilus Lord Walden, and also with the assent and good-liking of Lady Elizabeth Home,' that the wedding should be solemnized within three months after the Lady Elizabeth's twelfth birthday. If Lord Walden did not wait for her, but married another, the Earl of Suffolk should pay to the Earl of Dunbar £6,000 lawful

[1] Now the College of St. Mark, a place of retirement for elderly clergy of the Chelmsford diocese.

money of Great Britain.   The marriage, which anticipated the
bride's twelfth birthday, may have been hastened by the Earl
of Dunbar's anxiety to attend it.   If so, he was frustrated, for
he died in January 1612 while making magnificent preparations
for the long-awaited nuptials at Candlemas.   The marriage may
remind us of a passage in Weldon's *Court and Character of
James I* (p. 58): 'They that lived at court,' he says,

and were curious observers of every man's actions, could have thus
affirmed, that Salisbury,[1] Suffolk, and Northampton, and their friends,
did get more than the whole nation of Scotland (Dunbar excepted);
for whatever others got, they spent here; only Dunbar laid a foundation
of a great family, which did all revert into England again, with his
daughter's marriage with the house of Suffolk; so in truth all the
water ran to their mills.

The second earl was a delicate man, and must have been
hard pressed at times to maintain his family of nine children, to
say nothing of having his mother pestering him for several years.
Fortunately he was given appointments that would help.   He
was granted the governorship of Jersey for life in 1610.   He was
Captain of the Band of Gentlemen Pensioners, and in 1628 he
became Lord Warden of the Cinque Ports.   Theophilus was as
proud and gallant a courtier as his father and grandfather had
been, and he enjoyed his share of royal favour—particularly
through his friendship with Prince Henry, who shared his love
of jousting.   He figures in the records of several tournaments
devised for the prince's entertainment, the most illustrious of
them being the one at Whitehall in honour of the creation of
Henry as Prince of Wales, at which Lord Walden, as he was then,
carried off the honours.   That was in 1610.   In the same year
he quarrelled, while serving as a volunteer at the siege of Juliers
in Flanders, with Sir Edward Herbert, afterwards Lord Herbert
of Cherbury, who gives an account of the incident in his *Life*.
It appears that Theophilus had been drinking with some of his
cronies in Sir Horace de Vere's quarters, and had returned to
Sir Edward Cecil's quarters somewhat quarrelsome.   A ban-
tering remark of Herbert's, which would have given no offence
at another time, led to an angry brawl, followed by a challenge
to single combat, from which, however, Lord Walden was
dissuaded, apparently by his lady.

By the time he was forty-eight the second earl had become so
feeble that the king suggested to him, through Lord Cottington,

[1] The Earl of Suffolk's son-in-law.

chancellor of the exchequer, that he was no longer able to perform his duties as Captain of the Band of Gentlemen Pensioners and ought to resign. The earl took the hint badly. Was he to be turned out to grass after twenty years' service? he asked. He was not in fighting form just then perhaps, but, said he, he would wager that within a month's time he would be ready to play a set at tennis with His Majesty. The following Christmas he is described as contriving to hobble to court at the head of his band; but it was obvious to all that he was a broken man. In 1635 the king again called for his resignation, and this time it was submitted. His brother-in-law, the Earl of Salisbury, was appointed in his place.

After this the second earl made several unsuccessful attempts to regain office, no doubt because he sorely needed the emoluments; but he would have been unequal to the lightest duties.

In 1633 he lost his countess, who, after marrying at eleven and bearing nine children, died at the age of thirty-three. Her funeral certificate, preserved at the College of Arms, records that she died at the tower in Greenwich Park, of which the earl was keeper, on 19th August 1633,

whose noble corps were conveyed thence by water in a barge to Suffolk House in yᵉ Strand, neare Charing Crosse, yᵉ same being compleatly furnished and appoynted with all solempne ornaments of mourning befitting her honor and degree, where her said corpes contynued till Munday yᵉ 23ʳᵈ day of September following, at which tyme, about 10 of yᵉ clocke in yᵉ night, it was thence in a carriage couered with veluett, drawn by 6 horses, sett forth and adorned with Eschocheons and Shaferoones, being accompayned by most of yᵉ Nobles, of Lords and Ladyes in and about London, with other Knights and Gentlemen of quallity, in there coaches, who with much honor being directed by two Officers of Armes, yᵉ one bearing yᵉ Crowne and yᵉ other yᵉ Cushion of State, proceeded throught yᵉ Strand to Cheapside, and thence to Shorditch Church, where they tooke their leaues and departed, committing yᵉ said corpes to yᵉ care of yᵉ Lady Katherin, her eldest da. accompayned by other Ladyes, with yᵉ attendance of her owne officers and servants, who with great diligence and dutyfull respects waited on yᵉ same to Audley End.

Of the Audley End portrait of the second earl's lady the curious story is told that it was bought in an old Buckinghamshire manor house, where it was traditionally known as that of Elizabeth Home, wife of Theophilus, Earl of Suffolk, though how it came to the house no one knew.

Feeble as he was in his last years, Earl Theophilus seems to
have contemplated a second marriage, for in a letter to Sir John
Puckering from a gentleman who signs himself E. R., we find
'The Earl of Suffolk is shortly to be married to the Lady Leigh,
Sir Henry Leigh's widow of Oxfordshire. This lady is daughter
of the old Countess of Devonshire. I see the Earl at Court
crawling up and down; and my opinion is that a good caudle
would be better for his weak body than a lusty widow as she is.'
He survived until 1640, dying in May of that year at the age
of fifty-six.

Of the second earl's family, three—James, George, and Henry
—succeeded as third, fourth, and fifth earls of Suffolk. The
other son, Thomas, married and had a son, James, whose wife,
Charlotte Jemima Henrietta Maria, was a natural daughter of
Charles II by the Viscountess Shannon. The daughters will be
mentioned in a later chapter. Of his brothers—sons of the first
earl—Thomas, who lived to a great age and is the ancestor of
all Earls of Suffolk following the tenth, inherited the Wiltshire
estates of his mother's family and was created Earl of Berkshire;
Edward, the youngest, who was created Baron Howard of
Escrick in 1628, enjoyed with his brother, the Earl of Berkshire,
the sinecure office of farmer of His Majesty's greenwax until,
in 1650, he was accused of taking bribes from wealthy Royalists.
He was thereupon relieved of office, and in the following year
was sentenced to imprisonment in the Tower and a fine of
£10,000. On a plea of ill health, however, he evaded the
imprisonment and the fine was never exacted.

IV

THE THIRD EARL

JAMES HOWARD, third Earl of Suffolk and third Lord Howard de Walden, is a key figure in the history of Audley End because it was from a settlement made by him in 1687, that in 1747 the Suffolks were succeeded by the families to whom we owe all that has survived of the lord treasurer's palace. On the death of his father in 1640 Earl James succeeded to a heavily encumbered estate. The debts of the second earl are listed in two account books at the Essex Record Office,[1] which, while too confused to follow in detail, show clearly that the third earl acknowledged and undertook to pay off sums amounting to £55,000. When James I, the earl's godfather, said that the place was too much for a king but might do very well for a lord treasurer, he refrained from saying anything about the lord treasurer's descendants. The second earl had maintained a proud position and had used his influence at court to provide well for his family; but towards the end of his life he must have been as harassed by creditors as his mother had been. He would feel, no doubt, that so long as the Stuarts reigned the Howards might still expect office, and therefore that despite his debts Audley End might be kept in the family. A few years of court favour, he would argue, and the family fortunes would be restored. And as the third earl was only twenty when he succeeded in 1640, he could hardly be expected to realize how precarious the future was. His second godfather had been Buckingham. At the age of six he had been made a Knight of the Bath by Charles I. At nineteen he had been appointed to the command of a volunteer troop of horse for the king. But within a few years the House of Stuart had fallen, and its dependent houses with it.

Fortunately, when war broke out in 1642 the earl was still too young to have much of a political record. Fortunately also, he fell into line with most of his Essex and East Anglian neighbours in taking the parliamentary side, though he cannot have

---

[1] E.R.O. D/DBy. A.5 and 6.

37

lacked entirely the old high spirit of the Howards. Doubtless he was always a Royalist at heart. In any case, the Protector could hardly be expected to take a member of such a family on trust. So we are not surprised to find the earl, along with six other peers, being impeached in October 1647 for levying war against Parliament, and being imprisoned in the Tower for several months, particularly as his first wife was a daughter of Henry Rich, Earl of Holland, who was executed in March 1649 as a Royalist. Earl James, however, was released in June 1648 and allowed to resume his seat in the House of Lords. Prudently, he lay low, and spent most of his time quietly at Audley End, thus evading further suspicion and retaining both house and lands.

Like most holders of Audley End, the third earl served as lord lieutenant. He was appointed joint holder of that office for Suffolk in 1640, and sole holder by Parliament in 1642. But, unlike his father and grandfather, his interests were confined to the eastern counties—largely, no doubt, because Audley End was his only residence throughout the Commonwealth. Lulworth he had sold to Humphry Weld in 1641; his town house he sold for £15,000 to his brother-in-law, Algernon, Earl of Northumberland, whose name it bore until pulled down to make way for Northumberland Avenue.

Trimmer or not, at the Restoration Earl James was found on the king's side. He was earl marshal for the coronation, and in 1665 was appointed a gentleman of the bedchamber. Again the owner of Audley End was secure in a court appointment, but one that was hardly remunerative enough to enable him to resume the state of his ancestors and repair in his property the wastage of the war years. It had, however, the advantage of putting him in touch with the king, with the result that when Charles II complained that he was without a country house, because the palaces of the Tudor and Stuart monarchs had either fallen into decay or been demolished during the Commonwealth, the earl was able to offer him Audley End. It was suitable and convenient. Charles was delighted with it. He agreed to buy it for £50,000, of which £20,000 was to remain on mortgage, secured on the hearth tax in Ireland, and to leave the earl in possession of the whole of the estate with the exception of 283 acres of parkland. It was an excellent arrangement for both. The king gained what he required; the earl retained the remunerative part of his property, while shifting the enormous cost of maintaining the house on to the Crown. Moreover, when in 1667 the earl was appointed 'Keeper of the King's House at Audley End,' with Henry Winstanley of Littlebury as surveyor, he regained virtual control of the palace itself. And as the third earl's second countess, Barbara, eldest daughter of Sir Edward Villiers and widow of Sir Richard Wentworth, was the aunt of the king's mistress, Barbara Villiers, Lady Castlemaine, there was almost a family relationship between the king and the earl. Pepys [1] has the story of Lady Castlemaine, peeved at not being invited to a party given for the king and queen at the Duke of Buckingham's, running to her aunt Suffolk's, where, after railing against the royal party, she exclaimed: 'Well, much good may it do them, and for all that I will be as merry as they,' after which she went home and caused a lavish supper to be prepared.

We read again of the second Lady Suffolk in Pepys, who for 19th October 1663 writes: 'I hear that the queen did sleep five hours pretty well to-night, and that she waked and gargled her mouth, and to sleep again; but that her pulse beats fast, beating twenty to the king's or my Lady Suffolk's eleven; but not so strong as it was.' This was when the queen was so ill that she was shaved, had pigeons put to her feet, and received Extreme Unction. Pepys adds that the priest took so long over the business that the doctors became angry.

The earl himself has a distinguished place in our national history for his promptness in dealing with the powerful Dutch fleet, which under de Ruyter's command sailed up the Thames as far as Gravesend in the summer of 1667. He was then lord lieutenant of the county and governor of Landguard Fort, which he manned without a moment's delay, collecting his own retainers and pressing into the service every able-bodied man and boy from Newmarket to Harwich. He had little support from London, but when, in the first days of July, three thousand men landed at Felixstowe from the twenty-five Dutch ships that lay off the Whiting and Bawdsey Sands, and four hundred of them, carrying hand grenades and drawn cutlasses, with twenty-five-foot scaling-ladders on their backs, attacked the fort, the earl and his men repulsed them twice, the second time scattering them in such confusion that they were compelled to leave their gear behind as they ran. Pepys writes of the occasion on 3rd July 1667:

[1] 22nd July 1663.

Here I find all the news is the enemy's landing 3,000 men near Harwich, and attacking Landguard Fort, and being beat off thence with our great guns, killing some of their men, and they leaving their ladders behind them; but we had no horse in the way on Suffolke side, otherwise we might have galled their foot. The Duke of York is gone down thither this day, while the Generall sat sleeping this afternoon at the Council-table.

None of the official accounts pay adequate tribute to the earl for his part in the action—not unnaturally, perhaps, since to have acknowledged his vigour would have been to disclose the spinelessness at Whitehall.

Of the acquisition of Audley End by the Crown we have the account by Pepys, who is, indeed, almost a member of the family. His library is at Magdalene College, Cambridge, the college refounded by Audley, who ordained that his heirs, the possessors for the time being of Audley End, should be Visitors *in perpetuum*, and the *Diary* itself, brought into English by the Rev. John Smith, was first edited by the third Lord Braybrooke. The first reference to the house in Pepys is dated 27th February 1660. That day, he tells us, he and Mr. Bayton rode into Saffron Walden from Cambridge and put up at the White Hart. They were taken to Audley End by the innkeeper, and there, says Pepys,

the housekeeper shewed us all the house, in which the stateliness of the ceilings, chimney-pieces, and form of the whole was exceedingly worth seeing. He took us into the cellar, where we drank, most admirable drink, a health to the King. Here I played on my fflageo-lette, there being an excellent echo. He shewed us excellent pictures, two especially, those of the IV Evangelists and Henry VIII.

Seven years later, on 7th May 1667, Pepys paid a second visit, but, as Lord Braybrooke says,[1] 'he had in the interval seen more of the world, and become fastidious, travelling with his wife in a carriage and four.'

'Took coach,' he says of the second visit,

to Audley End, and did go all over the house and garden, and mighty merry we were. The house, indeed, do appear very fine, but not so fine as it hath heretofore to me; particularly the ceilings are not so good as I always took them to be, being nothing so well wrought as my Lord Chancellor's are,[2] and though the figure of the house without be very extraordinary good, yet the stayrcase is exceeding poor, and a great many pictures, and not one good one, in the house, but one of

---

[1] Braybrooke, p. 87.   [2] At Clarendon House.

Henry VIII done by Holbein; and not one good suit of hangings in all the house, but all most ancient things, such as I would not give the hanging up of in my house, and the other furniture, beds and other things accordingly. Only the gallery is good, and above all things the cellars, where we went down and drank of much good liquors. And indeed the cellars are fine; and here my wife and I did sing to my great content. And then to the garden, and there did eat many grapes, and took some with us; and so away thence well satisfied, though not that degree that by my old esteem of the house I ought and did expect to have done, the situation of it not pleasing me.

By the time of the second visit the long-drawn-out negotiations for the purchase of Audley End were well advanced. The first official reference to them is in the *London Gazette*, No. 39, 10th March 1666, which informs us that

On Thursday morning his Majesty, accompanied with his Royal Highness, and attended with several persons of quality, parted hence for Audley End, where he arrived that day at noon, with intention to spend the rest of the week in those parts, and to return hither on Monday, seeming much satisfied, as well with the noble structure of the house, as the pleasantness of the country about it.

Pepys knew what was afoot. He says: 'The King and the Duke are to go to Audley End tomorrow, in order to see and buy it of my Lord Suffolk.' And perhaps the town of Saffron Walden had some intimation of the earl's intentions, for the corporation spent £20 on a silver cup and cover, filled with saffron for presentation to His Majesty.

The third Lord Braybrooke was at pains to collect all the information available about Audley End as a royal palace, but it amounts to little. The *London Gazette* informs us that 'In the autumn of 1668, Charles II met the Queen and the ladies of her Court at Audley End, having been divertising himself for some time at Newmarket, and in visiting several forts and towns on the sea-coast.' The Walden churchwardens' book records that on 11th October following His Majesty attended matins at Walden church. Doubtless there were one or two other visits between 1666 and 1668, though the conveyance of the property was not, in fact, executed until 8th May 1669, when, as the deed recites, 'the King, upon his own personal view and judgement, had taken liking to the mansion called Audley End, with the park, out-houses, court-yards, orchards, gardens, stables, water-mills and appurtenances, as a seat fit for his Majesty's residence.'

The following year the New Palace, as the house was now called, rang with the voices of the Caroline courtiers, and Nathaniel Henshaw, an Irish physician and writer, a Fellow of the Royal Society, gives a vivid account of the queen and her ladies attending the fair near Audley End in a letter to Sir Robert Paston.[1] 'Last week,' he says,

there being a Faire neare Audley End, the Queen, the Dutchess of Richmond, and the Dutchess of Buckingham, had a frolick to deguise themselves like country lasses, in red petticotes, wastcotes, &c., and so goe see the Faire. Sir Bernard Gascoign,[2] on a cart-jade, rode before the Queen, another stranger before the Dutchesse of Bucking-ham, and Mr. Roper before Richmond. They had all so overdone it in their deguise, and look'd so much more like Antiques[3] than Country volk, that as soone as they came to the Faire the people began to goe after them. But the Queen going to a booth to buy a paire of yellow stockins for her swete hart, and Sir Bernard asking for a paire of gloves, sticht with blew, for his swete hart, they were soon, by their gebrish, found to be strangers, which drew a bigger flock about them. One amongst them had seen the Queen at dinner, knew her, and was proud of his knowledge: this soon brought all the Faire into a crowd to stare at the Queen. Being thus discovered, they, as soon as they could, got on their horses; but as many of the Faire as had horses got up with their wives, children, swete-harts, or neighbours behind them, to get as much gape as they could, till they brought them to the Court gate. Thus, by ill conduct, was a merrie frolick turned into a pennance.[4]

On 26th November 1670, on his way from Cambridge to London, the Prince of Orange, afterwards William III, stayed a night in the house he was later to own. He was described at the time as a 'well-countenanced man, with a handsome head of hayre of his owne.' His next visit was nineteen years later, in 1689, the year of the third earl's death, when he came as King of England.

But if accounts of royal visits are few, the palace was still one of the wonders of the realm, and as such had many curious and admiring visitors. In 1681, Ralph Thoresby found it 'the greatest house in England . . . a vast building or rather town, walled in.'[5] Edward Ward said: 'The magnitude of this house is reported to be such, that it is a day's work for a running

---

[1] Afterwards Earl of Yarmouth.
[2] Sentenced to death along with Sir George Lisle and Sir Charles Lucas after the surrender of Colchester, but reprieved because he was an Italian.
[3] Stage-players.   [4] *Ives Select Papers*, p. 39.   [5] *Diary*, vol. i, p. 65.

footman to open and shut the windows.'[1]   And Celia Fiennes, in 1697, wrote:

Thence we went to Audlyend 10 miles a house of the Earle of Sussex [Suffolk] which makes a noble appearance like a town, so many towers and buildings off stone within a parke which is walled round, a good River runs through it, we pass over the bridge; its built round 3 Courts, there are 30 great and little towers on the top and a great Cupilow in the middle, the roomes are large and lofty with good rich old furniture tapistry etc., but noe beds in that part we saw, there are 750 rooms[2] in the house; the Cannall in the midst of the parke look'd very fine its altogether a stately palace and was built for one of the kings.[3]

The reason for its neglect as a royal palace after the first few years is that Windsor was restored by Charles II and brought into use again.   So in spite of its thirty-two years under the Crown, the Earl of Suffolk must always have been regarded by his neighbours as their feudal lord, as his ancestors had been since the Dissolution.   But what all looked for in vain was an heir.   The earl had two sons by his first wife, Susanna, daughter of the Earl of Holland, both of whom died in infancy.   There were no sons by either second or third wife.   He had, however, two surviving daughters: one, Essex, by the first marriage, who married Edward, Lord Griffin, from whom the first Lord Braybrooke was descended, and a second, Elizabeth, by the second marriage, who married Sir Thomas Felton of Playford, Suffolk, page of honour to Charles II and afterwards treasurer of the household to Queen Anne.   From her was descended the second Earl of Bristol,[4] who came into half the estate after the failure of the male line at the death of the tenth Earl of Suffolk.

There is an account of the death of the second countess and her daughter, Lady Felton, in December 1681, in Luttrell's Diary. It runs: 'The countesse of Suffolk was seized with an apoplexy the 12th, and died the next day.   The lady Betty Felton, her daughter, was seized also with a fitt of the same the next day, and died of it.'   Later in the month, according to the same account, 'the countesse of Suffolk and her daughter, the lady

[1] *Works*, vol. ii, p. 231-2.
[2] An obvious exaggeration.
[3] *The Journeys of Celia Fiennes*, ed. Christ. Morris, 1947, pp. 63-4.
[4] Grandson of John Hervey, first Earl of Bristol, who by his second wife, Elizabeth, only daughter of Sir Thomas Felton of Playford, Suffolk, had issue eleven sons and six daughters.

Betty Felton, were carried through the citty in great state, attended with severall of his majesties coaches, and many of the nobility's, in order to their interment at Saffron Walden in Essex.'

Of the earl's third wife, Anne, eldest daughter of the Earl of Manchester, we have a charming account in a letter signed 'A. Stephens,' addressed to Abigail Harley on 12th April 1683. 'Lady Suffolk,' it runs, 'makes one of the rarest wives that ever I heard of, for her Lord, for the most part, with the gout and three score and six years old, is confined greatly to his chamber. She never stirs from him and admits very few visits if he be not so well as to see them.' Earl James lived modestly with his family at Great Chesterford throughout most of the fifty years of his rule, quietly paying off his father's debts and directing the affairs of his estate. The Commonwealth would keep him poor, but he appears to have been happy to live in retirement. His means, we may therefore assume, would be equal to his needs. And during the twenty-nine years from the Restoration in 1660 to his death in December 1688 he would see his fortunes rise steadily from the uncertainties of the post-war years to the security established by the Revolution of 1688. It is true that he did not live long enough to appreciate the full significance of what happened in 1688; but he had witnessed the steps that led up to it. As a quiet reflective man, he had doubtless realized that feudalism as his ancestors had known it in their castles and manor houses had gone for ever. The new race of tenant farmers among whom he had lived, and with whom he had associated, had increased in prosperity throughout his lifetime, for it was the steadily rising rentals made possible for landowners by the growing wealth of the farmers that enabled the gentry to assume the strong position they held under William and Mary and continued to hold under the Georges.

The earl's tenants, too, were benefiting from the rise in prices, and many of the buildings still to be seen on the estate date from this period. According to Gregory King the average income of a temporal lord of Charles II's time was £3,200 a year. Earl James's income was double that figure. In a sense he was making the best of two worlds, because more than £2,000 of his income in the closing years of his life came from the Seal Office. He was thus enjoying both the traditional or pre-war source of aristocratic income and the new or post-war source that derived from rentals. For all that, large as Earl

James's income was by modern standards—taking into consideration the difference in money values—it would be small in comparison with the pre-war incomes of the first Earl of Suffolk and the fourth Duke of Norfolk, with their staffs of retainers, several of whom may well have had salaries of a thousand a year, to say nothing of their armies of servants. But it is extremely difficult—perhaps impossible—to strike a balance between the economics of such as he at the beginning of the century and that at the end. At the end they could no longer afford the scores of servants they had believed essential to their well-being at the beginning, any more than we of the twentieth century can afford the houses we thought essential at the beginning of the present century. But such were no longer necessary. As a result of the growing prosperity of the farmers in north-west Essex, the labouring people had ceased to be dependent on the Great House to the extent they had been. And from the earl's point of view the hordes of servants he had known in boyhood had been a relic of the feudalism which depended on the maintenance of private armies. With the nation's peace secured by a central government there was no need for noblemen to command such power, and it had been slowly ebbing from them. But if they were sensible enough to adjust themselves to the new conditions life could be as rich as ever. The new that was gained could compensate for the old that was lost. So while Earl James is not a spectacular figure he is an important one in being typical of the wiser kind of landowner of his own generation.

Let us look at his account books for the last complete year of his life.[1] They show that his total income was £6,558; his expenditure, £3,989. His capital was therefore increased in that one year, and it was not exceptional in this, by £2,569. The last statement of account is endorsed: 'Examined by mee this 10th Nov: 1688, Anne Suffolk,' followed in a very shaky hand by the earl's 'I do allow of this accompt, Suffolke.' The rents total £2,575, of which £1,234 came from Walden, £303 from Littlebury, £431 from Great Chesterford, £84 from Little Chesterford, £131 from Newport, and £199 from Wendens. His rents of assize brought in £211, and the land in his own use was assessed at £101. From sales of timber he derived £183; from courts £82; from 'Casuall & Forraine Receipts' £1,257. These would have been sufficient for the life he lived; but he

---

[1] E.R.O. D/DBy. A.1-4.

had that other source of income, the office of the Privy Seal, which raised him to a state of affluence. In the year 1687–8 it produced £2,145 19s. 7d.

On the other side of the reckoning we have the payments:

	£	s.	d.
To my Lady	300	0	0
To Miss Felton	66	0	0
Annuities	150	0	0
Gifts and Charity	127	10	2
Rents	459	17	11½
Rates and Taxes	42	1	4
'Diett and Acchate'	1,136	12	9½
Stables and Liveries	669	16	10½
Fees and Wages	458	4	6
Repairs and Ornament	186	4	6
Husbandry	121	5	1
'Necessaryes and Extraordinaryes'	271	0	11½
	3,988	14	2

Each year, of course, began on Lady Day, and rents were normally paid half-yearly as they are to-day. The rents of assizes, or fixed rents, were for the seven manors:

	£	s.	d.
Walden	81	3	8½
Littlebury	25	7	4
Great Chesterford	30	14	11
Little Chesterford	7	5	3
Newport	20	12	8
Wendens	31	0	6
Hadstock	14	18	3

The receipts for 'Lands in my Lord's Use' were two sums from his bailiff: £94 9s. 0d. for barley and £7 5s. 6d. for grass. The total of the 'Casuall & Forraine Receipts' was made up from these items:

		£	s.	d.
Mar. 25	Rents from this Accomptant on the Last Year's Accompt as appears	424	3	4
May 3	Recᵈ for a young Chestnutt Mare sold	15	0	0
7	Recᵈ for a young Bay Horse sold into Sussex (beside 10d. given)	39	10	0
June 6	Recᵈ of Mr. Hudleston for a Bay Gelding (besides 10d. given to his man)	29	10	0
24	Recᵈ of ye Widdow Symonds for a Bolting Mill		12	0

			£	s.	d.
Oct.	11	Rec^d of Liev^l Hebb for 5 mares (besides a Padd Mare, & twenty shillings to his man)	74	0	0
Nov.	5	Rec^d of Mr. Turner for a Bay Horse (besides 10d. given to his man)	34	10	0
	14	Rec^d for an old Limbeck		15	0
Jan.	7	Rec^d of Liv^l Hebb for a young Bay Horse (besides 10d. to his man)	26	7	6
	10	Rec^d of Mr. Nelson for a young Bay Horse	30	0	0
	16	Rec^d of Mr. Nettervill for some things at Suffolke Street House	4	10	0
Feb.	8	Rec^d for Old Copper, brass & pewter sold at Audley End	6	17	0
		Rec^d of Wm. Patch a fine upon renewing a lease	5	0	0
	28	Rec^d of my Lord Jermine for ye Liberty of St. Edmunds Bury	550	0	0
Mar.	3	Rec^d for Old Lead sold at Audley End	7	12	4
	24	Rec^d of my L^{ds} Perticular Money resting due one of his years Accompt now ended	9	11	0

Total of Casuall & Forraine Receipts £1,257 18 2

What, we wonder, was the name of Liev^l, or Liv^l Hebb?
Had he a Christian name as attractive as that of Phenenna
Browne, who paid his £1 0s. 6d. regularly in Walden, or was it
simply Oliver?

My lady received her allowance in three sums of £100 each
in June, October, and February. Miss Felton's allowance,
apparently, was for pin money, and also to pay her maids. The
£150 'annuities' was, in fact, one annuity only. It was paid to
George Howard, his brother, who succeeded him as fourth earl.
The 'Gifts and Charity' items include regular allowances of £10
and £4 a year; £6 10s. 0d. quarterly to John Harvey for the
Audley End poor; £2 'for a boy whose legg was broke';
Christmas boxes to tradesmen's servants, £4 4s. 6d., and £5 at
Christmas for the Audley End poor; and the same sum to the
overseers for the Walden poor. The most interesting item,
however, appears against the date March 13th. It is 'To a
Breefe for ye French Protestants as per Acct^d. £10.' This was
evidently for the relief of refugees affected by the Edict of
Nantes.

The 'rents' paid by the earl include £250 a year to a Mr.

E

Angier for 'House Rent'—presumably for the town house, sums
to the vicars of Walden, Littlebury, Great and Little Chesterford, Wendens, and Ashdon for tithe composition; £20 a year
to the poor of Newport 'for ye pond'; £1 9s. 10d. at Michaelmas
'To ye Shreife of Essex, for ye King, for one year's Vicontell
Rents or Certaintyes.' Under 'Diett and Acchate' we have such
items as:

	£	s.	d.
For Sea Coals and Charges inning them	40	9	4
For Scotch Coales	38	12	6
To Mrs. Wheeler for ye Carters feast	14	16	1

A 'travelling coach' bought on 1st June of that year cost
£80 12s. 6d., and the cost of maintaining the earl's coaches and
coach horses amounted to £300 a year, about half the total cost
of his 'Stables and Liveryes.' Wages cost him £458 4s. 6d. that
year. The steward had £120; Mrs. Wheeler, the housekeeper,
and John Disell, the cook, had £20 each. Others receiving
relatively large salaries, but whose duties are not specified, were:
Mary Durrant, £24; and three—Mr. Lones, Mr. Tough, Mr.
Lovett—receiving £20 apiece. A Mr. Watson had £15; Mr.
Lones, 'a year's fee as baylif of ye Manors,' a further £13.
Then come the chaplain, Mr. Cooper, with £10, and £10 each
to Edward Corbie, groom; John Harvey, bailiff; and Robert
Rogerson, gardener, which seems to suggest that these three
were regarded as equal in status. James Ayrey, the butler, was
only slightly above them, with £11. William Howse, the
coachman, had £7; the postilion, the porter, and three footmen
had £5 each. The names of these servants are of no special
interest; but John Metcalf, the porter, was almost certainly a
Yorkshireman, and so, in all probability, was Edward Corbie,
the groom.

'Repairs and Ornament' included £118 13s. 6d. on repairs at
Audley End Almshouse, a large item in 1687. In the list of
'Necessaryes & Extraordinaryes,' Daniel Malthus is entered as
receiving £6 19s. 0d., Mr. Levesque, 'chirugion,' £10, two
items relating to the earl's failing health. Another interesting
item is: 'Disbursements in goeing ye bounds of Walden
£4 4s. 0d.'

One item that would have worried the earl a good deal if he
had still been responsible for the upkeep of Audley End was
the unpopular hearth tax of 2s. for each hearth, imposed in
1662 and continued until the first year of William and Mary.

The Great Hall

There were one hundred and twenty-nine hearths at Audley End.[1] He missed that, as he missed so many other expenses connected with the upkeep of a great house.

The importance of his fifty years' rule, then, is in the building up of the estate. With the single exception of 1677 for Newport, there is a complete series of court rolls for the period 1660–80 for the manors of Chipping and Brook Walden, Wendens Ambo, Littlebury, and Newport, and in addition a composite roll for Great Chesterford and Hadstock, 1677–80, and Little Chesterford, 1678–80. The courts, which were held annually in autumn up to 1675, and afterwards in spring, were presided over by the chief steward, Richard Newman, or his very capable deputy, William Lyngwood, with up to seventeen jurors. Normally there were about thirteen jurors for the annual courts, and about four for the special courts summoned as required to deal with emergency business. The procedure was simple and businesslike. All the old military accompaniments had ceased with the great Land Act of the Restoration, and it is interesting to see a new pattern developing. The first business was to present absentees, who were fined threepence. Then deaths were presented and the business of the court began in earnest. To take the 1661 court at Chipping Walden as a typical example, we find Antony Pennystone paying fines ranging from 5s. to £9 to be admitted to the four properties owned by his father, who had died since the last court was held. Eight other admissions to property followed, six by descent and two by purchase. Six proclamations for heirs to claim property were made next, and in two of these the properties were seized on the lord's behalf, three proclamations having been made without any one appearing. Such procedure as this was normal; but what is worth noting is that in 1660 long lists of persons swearing allegiance to the king were read out.

Another duty of the jurors was to elect certain officers. This was done at irregular intervals during most of the period, with the terms of office tending to become shorter as time passed. Constables and pinders—the officers who impounded the stray cattle—were appointed in 1665 for all the manors covered by the records, and at Newport, apparently the most enterprising of the manors, a hayward, sealers of leather, and tasters of bread and ale were also elected. After 1676, when the first of the spring courts was held, elections recurred every two years, and

[1] E.R.O. Q/R. Th.1.

it is worth noting that in Chipping Walden, which had three constables, one was nominated by the lord of the manor, two by the town.

Petty nuisances, such as walls and fences out of repair, ditches in need of scouring, and similar offences, were dealt with at these manorial courts, and also offences against regulations that were more in the nature of by-laws, particularly in connection with the common fields. Orders were frequently made for balks that had been ploughed up to be restored. Cattle were not allowed in the common meadow, or 'le broome,' from 15th March to 'the usual time.' They were to be kept off the stubble for fourteen days after harvest commenced, and sheep were to be kept off for a further six days. There were any number of regulations of this kind, although practically all of them seem to arise out of William Lyngwood's spring court of 1676. At all events, little is heard of such offences before that date.

There are instances of special privileges. At Newport, any one turning out sheep or pigs on the stubble within fourteen days of the parson finishing his harvest forfeited 40s. for each offence. At Chipping Walden it was the poor who enjoyed a special privilege. No one was permitted to put cattle upon the highway to graze except twenty poor persons named by the treasurer, and six or eight of the company or fraternity of the town of Walden.

The timber sales remind us of the woodland rights possessed by the lord of the manor, and the jurors of courts-baron were frequently called upon to adjudicate on the cutting down of timber on waste land. All suits, of course, were made to the earl as lord of the manor, and we have seen something of the income he derived from them.

The third earl was the last to enjoy both peerages held by his grandfather, which had different remainders because the Howard de Walden barony was by writ, the Suffolk earldom with ordinary limitation. Consequently the former continued to be vested in the issue of his own body, while the latter descended through his uncle's offspring until the death of the tenth earl, and is now in the descendants of his uncle Thomas, of Charlton, Wiltshire. It has thus no present connection with Audley End. Nor did any of the third earl's descendants enjoy his wealth. After his death the profits of the Seal Office were no longer available to the family, and the dowager countess continued to enjoy the income from the estate throughout the lives of the fourth and fifth earls, both of whom she survived. In 1706 her receipts were £1,150, her payments £316.[1] The woodlands had twelve years' growth, so they yielded £160 that year, otherwise the accounts were normal. The fourth and fifth earls may well have envied her. She was far richer than they were.

[1] E.R.O. D/DBy. A.368.

V

THE LONG DECLINE

'SEVERAL YEARS AGO,' wrote Horace Walpole to the Countess of Ossory in 1783, 'when Lord Strafford and I were at Lord Thomond's, we walked to Walden Church and were shown in a vault there the coffins of eleven Earls and Countesses of Suffolk that had died since that time.' There were, in all, ten earls of Suffolk at Audley End between the creation of the earldom in favour of the builder in 1603 and the dispossession of the heir to the tenth by two descendants of the third in 1747. Of most of them there is little or nothing to be said. The first three are important. The sixth was a man of mark in his day, who added the barony of Chesterford and the earldom of Bindon to the family titles. There are interesting stories to relate of the lives of the eighth and ninth. But when we think of Audley End in relation to the rest of them we can only agree with Defoe, who on seeing what he describes as 'the ruins of the once largest and most magnificent pile in all this part of England,'[1] said it was built by and decayed with the noble earls of Suffolk. Indeed, when the last of them died the mansion was almost beyond repair.

When returned to the Suffolks by the Crown in November 1701 it would already be far gone, and indeed no money changed hands. The property was conveyed to the fifth earl by William III on condition he surrendered all claim to the two-fifths of the original purchase price of £50,000 still unpaid. As the mortgage for this amount was secured on the proceeds of the hearth tax in Ireland, which was about to be repealed, the earl had Hobson's choice. He could not do other than accept. And small as the price of repurchase was, it is extremely unlikely that the property could have been sold to any one else for as much, which means that in less than a hundred years the value of the palace that cost—according to the builder's own statement—£200,000 to build and furnish had fallen to £20,000.

The third Lord Braybrooke tells us of a tradition that the

[1] *A Tour through England and Wales*, Everyman edition, vol. i, p. 88.

king 'took away many valuable articles from the house, for which the family never received any remuneration; and especially the tapestry.' The place from which a large piece was removed can be seen in the Tapestry Room. Mr. H. Avray Tipping, however, in describing the house for *Country Life* in 1927, draws attention to an entry in the Great Wardrobe accounts, which, as he says, suggests that the king was dealing with his own property and under no obligation to pay for what he removed. The entry is for 1671, and refers to 'Hangings and other Wardrobe Stuffe now at *Audley End* to be bought of the Right Hono^ble the *Earle of Suffolke* for his Maties Service.' If they were, in fact, bought in 1671, there was obviously no need to pay for them again thirty years later.

The third, fourth, and fifth earls were sons of the second, and this 'hat-trick' succession, if the term may be allowed, was repeated when three sons of the fifth succeeded in turn as sixth, eighth, and ninth earls. George, the fourth earl, married twice, but died without issue. As he held the estate for between two and three years only, there is little to say of him. Nor is there much to say of the fifth, who ruled for eighteen years, except that he held a few minor appointments, such as that of Commissary General of the Musters in Charles II's reign.

The first important reference to him occurs after the defeat of Waller at Roundway Down in Wiltshire on 17th July 1643, when Malmesbury was put under his command. He fortified and held it for the king until it fell to Colonel Massey. Fifty years later, after he had succeeded to the earldom, we meet this same Henry Howard in an account by Luttrell which relates how a packet from Holland was attacked by two French privateers and sunk after a gallant action in which several Frenchmen were killed. The captain and a few others were captured, but most of those on board were drowned, 'among which,' says Luttrell, ''tis thought is the Earle of Suffolke who was expected.' The rumour, however, was false.

We may assume that the fifth earl spent little time at Audley End during the eight years he owned it, and that during his lifetime the process of decay continued unchecked. He was, of course, well advanced in years when he inherited the estate. He was sixty-five. And he was seventy-five when he recovered possession of the house. But if there is little to say of him it is none the less interesting to see him, as we have seen the others, against the background of his period and of the history of his family. He was born in the last year of the first earl's life. He had therefore known the palace in all its glory. He would often have heard his father and two brothers discuss it as a liability, and can have experienced little pleasure when the burden of it fell on himself. His, we may say, was the period of disillusionment, and in his person the Suffolk line appears to have put away ambition for a generation. Macky, in his *Characters*, says that the fifth earl was 'A Gentleman who was never yet in business, loves cocking, horse matches, and other country sports.' Earl Henry, perhaps, had at last paid heed to the counsel of his great-grandfather, the fourth Duke of Norfolk!

But if the fifth earl's children had been of the same mind as he there would be no mansion at Audley End to-day. Fortunately they were not. The fifth earl married as his first wife the daughter and heiress of Andrew Lord Castlestewart, an Irish peer, and without doubt this infusion of Irish blood into the Howard strain accounts for certain unpredictable elements in the characters of her offspring, the sixth, eighth, and ninth earls. So after the death of the fifth earl at his wife's seat in 1709 the pulse of life again began to quicken at Audley End.

Henry, the sixth earl, who had been created Earl of Bindon and Baron Chesterford during his father's lifetime, was a man of more than common ability. He was Commissary General of the Musters—his father's old post—from 1697 to 1706, sat for Arundel from 1695 to 1698, for Essex as a Knight of the Shire in 1705, became First Commissioner of Trade and Plantations, or President of the Board of Trade, in 1717, and generally played the part that was expected of him, first as heir, and afterwards as head of a great house. But it was neither for his ability nor for his political services that he was raised to the peerage before his father's death. It was in order that he might take up the most illustrious office associated with the Howard name, that of earl marshal. In the Audley End archives, under date 1705, there is a document [1] addressed from the Duke of Norfolk to Queen Anne, which begs leave to draw Her Majesty's attention to the fact that the duke, being a Roman Catholic, is not qualified to act in that office, and praying her to approve, under her Privy Signet, the appointment of his cousin, Henry Howard, to act in his stead, 'at the desire of the Right Honourable Henry, now Earle of Suffolk, being aged and infirm,' who had, of course, a

[1] E.R.O. D/DBy. F.3. See Appendix.

prior claim. The queen gave her consent, and in Luttrell's Diary, under a date for April 1707, we find: 'This day the Earl of Bindon, Earl Marshal of England, open'd his commission in the Painted Chamber and adjourned to the Heralds' Office.' This means that on that date Lord Bindon held a court of chivalry, according to the rules laid down by Edward III, with the lord high constable and himself as judges. These courts of chivalry were military in character and tried military offences, but their main function was to pronounce judgments on disputes concerning rights to bear arms and questions of heraldic distinction. Perhaps their most interesting cases were those in which delicate questions of personal honour were involved. When Lord Bindon sat in 1707 he was attended by the highest noblemen in the kingdom, by the king's officers of arms, as well as by proctors, doctors of civil law, and all the usual officers of the court.

In 1714 the sixth earl became lord lieutenant of Essex, and in July of the following year received orders prompted by the preparations then being made for the Old Pretender to land in the country, which recited: 'Whereas there is open rebellion in Scotland and other divers places, the Lords Lieutenant of the Counties are to raise the Militia Regiments under their command forthwith and secure all Papists and other traitorous persons without fear or favour.' Thus throughout his short life he was a public figure and a man of influence. He was also a man of family. By his first wife, Penelope, daughter of the Earl of Thomond, he had four sons and one daughter. After marrying as his second wife Henrietta, daughter of the third Earl of Beaufort, the widow of his first wife's brother, who also died before him, the sixth earl died at the age of forty-five in September 1718.

In his *Sir John Vanbrugh*,[1] Laurence Whistler tells us that the sixth earl, as earl marshal, tried to get Vanbrugh made a Knight of the Garter. Besides being an architect and a dramatist, Sir John was a herald of note, and it was in this last capacity that he became an intimate friend of the earl, who, says Laurence Whistler, engaged him to carry out a restoration of Audley End. This was in the last year of the earl's life, at the time Vanbrugh, who had designed his palaces for the age of magnificence which he believed to be dawning, was at the height of his fame. Blenheim, which he hoped would inspire others

[1] Cobden Sanderson, 1938, p. 243.

to dreams of almost equal splendour, was nearly completed. He wrote to a friend at the time:

I met John Conyers there [at Blenheim] on Thursday last, with several virtuosos with him. He made mighty fine speeches upon the Building, and took it for granted no subject's house in Europe would approach it, which will be true, if the Duke of Shrewsbury judges right in saying there is not in Italy so fine a house as Chatsworth, for this Blenheim is beyond all comparison more magnificent than that. My Lord Carlisle has got his whole garden front up, and is fonder of his work every day than other. The Duke of Shrewsbury's house [1] will be about half up this season. My Lord Bindon is busy to the utmost of his force in new moulding Audley End, and all the world are running mad after building, as far as they can reach.

Laurence Whistler suggests that Vanbrugh had a blind spot towards Jacobean architecture, and had therefore no respect for the great palace of the Suffolks. The truth is that, as Nikolaus Pevsner pointed out in the *Architectural Review* for February 1950, Vanbrugh was probably more sympathetic towards Elizabethan and Jacobean style than any one else of his time. Its flair for magnificence was in keeping with his character. That he did not carry out the proposed restoration of Audley End was undoubtedly due to the sixth earl's premature death and to the seventh earl's youth, and still earlier death at the age of twenty-eight, four years after succeeding. We know that he did not lose interest in the family when the sixth earl died because in a letter written by him to the new earl, Charles William, on behalf of himself and his friends, he urges the young earl to come to London quickly and try to secure for himself his father's post as earl marshal. Vanbrugh, it is said, had been chosen to write this letter as the man who had 'most credit' with the new earl.

Vanbrugh's intentions for Audley End were thus frustrated, and all he could do was recommend, about 1721, the destruction of all the buildings round the Great Court, most of which by this time were ruinous. This he was allowed to do. In their place he built brick walls, with two lodges, which have since been demolished, at the north and south ends of the west front. The only constructive thing he did indoors was to extend the Great Hall, which had always been too short for good proportions, and to provide at the far end of it two staircases and a screen similar to those at Grimsthorpe.

[1] Heythrop, designed by Thomas Archer, Vanbrugh's imitator.

Staircases with steps supported by a wall had recently come into use when Audley End was built, but were not introduced here. The original stairs were of the newel type still found at the rear of the house. Mr. Pevsner, in the article quoted a moment ago, has a most interesting comment to make on the ceiling above the Vanbrugh staircase, which had previously been regarded as original Jacobean work. He says: 'I have never been able to reconcile these wilfully shaped stars with what Jacobean ceiling designs I know, and would thus tentatively submit that we possess here a Vanbrughian paraphrase of the Jacobean style.' He admits that it might plausibly be suggested that the ceiling belongs to the period of Jacobean restoration carried out by the fourth Lord Howard de Walden, first Lord Braybrooke; but points out that the pattern is 'incomparably bolder' than that of other ceilings of eighteenth-century date. To his illustration of this ceiling he adds:

The staircase was renewed about 1720 and has been attributed for good reasons to Vanbrugh. But it had not so far been recognized that Vanbrugh also redesigned the plaster ceiling. This in its imitation Jacobean pattern and with its unmistakably early eighteenth-century detail, is the earliest example of a Jacobean Revival ever traced.

The more we compare this work with other ceilings in the house, the more convinced we become that Mr. Pevsner is right.

Of the destruction of the Great Court we have a vivid note by William Cole, the antiquary friend and correspondent of Horace Walpole, whose manuscript notes are in the British Museum. He says:

I saw that noble house much decreased when I went to Mr. Butts' school at Walden; I remember going there on an evening to see the buildings taken down, and the noise of the lead being flung off the top of the house to the ground, struck my imagination so much that I have since thought it no unlike scene to what might have been seen all over the kingdom at the end of King Henry VIII's reign.[1]

Charles William, the seventh earl, like several other heirs to the earldom, had wrongly styled himself Lord Walden before succeeding. He was page of honour at the coronation of George I, and at his father's death became lord lieutenant of Essex. No doubt he would have held other high offices if he had not died so young. His wife, Arabella, was the daughter of Sir Samuel Astry of Henbury in Gloucestershire, whose family

[1] Braybrooke, p. 92.

is extinct and whose seat is demolished; but Ethel M. Richardson, in her book on the Howard family, *The Lion and the Rose*,[1] tells us that in the old churchyard at Henbury there is a gravestone to 'Scipio Africanus, negro servant to the Right Hon[ble] Charles William Earl of Suffolk and Bindon, who died the 21st of December, 1720, aged 18 years.' On the footstone are the lines:

> I who was born a Pagan and a slave
> Now sweetly sleep, a Christian, in my grave.
> What though my hue was dark:
> My Saviour's sight
> Shall change this darkness into radiant light.
> Such grace to me my lord on earth has given,
> To recommend me to my Lord in Heaven,
> Whose glorious second coming here I wait
> With saints and angels Him to celebrate.

In the same book a passage is quoted from the *History of Court Fools*, referring to the Earl of Suffolk's fool, or jester, Dicky Pearce, who was buried in Berkeley churchyard, Gloucestershire, where an epitaph, said to be written by Dean Swift, preserves his memory:

> Here lies the Earl of Suffolk's fool,
>   Men called him Dicky Pearce;
> His folly served to make folks laugh
>   When wit and mirth were scarce.
>
> Poor Dick, alas! is dead and gone;
>   What signifies to cry?
> Dickys enough are left behind
>   To laugh at by and by.

The seventh Earl of Suffolk died on 9th February 1722; his countess on 23rd June. But he held the estate long enough to complicate the succession by settling it [2] after the death of the countess on the younger of his two uncles, Charles Howard, passing over Edward, who, of course, succeeded to the earldom, and to whom he left a mere hundred pounds a year. He even went so far as to provide in his will for remainder of the estate to the Effingham branch of the family. It was an extraordinary arrangement, though there was perhaps little to choose between in the two uncles. Charles was a knave and Edward a fool—though no jester. In these conditions Charles William, named after both, may have thought the estate safer with the knave!

[1] Vol. ii, pp. 380–1.   [2] E.R.O. D/DBy. E.5.

The result of this action was that when the seventh earl and his countess died without issue, Charles immediately took over both house and estate, and in doing so gained custody of all the family papers—settlements, deeds, and writings of every kind. But the new earl's lawyers could not be expected to allow this state of affairs to remain unchallenged. And the earl himself, though of feeble intellect, was not unfamiliar with court proceedings. It was he who made the spectacular appearance in court during the trial of Lord William Russell to impeach the evidence of his kinsman, Lord Howard of Escrick, and who figured again at the trial of Algernon Sidney for the same purpose. Later in life, in January 1724, he was himself tried by his peers for improperly selling protections from arrest, and was committed to the Tower. Earl Edward was an odd character. His nephew may have thought that he would not have brains enough to see that he was being defrauded by the new settlement. Charles also may have counted on this. If so, they had failed to reckon with the lawyers. Whatever his own feelings Edward was persuaded to contest the will.

But to do this access had somehow to be gained to the documents already held by Charles. This was achieved by inducing Edward to prefer a bill in the High Court of Chancery, praying that Charles might be required to set forth his own claim. When this was done the lawyers' suspicions were confirmed because Charles produced no deed or settlement made between 1650 and 1714, though several were known to have been made during that period, in particular, as the family discovered later, the important settlement made by Earl James in 1687, on which the future of the house was subsequently found to hinge. This defect was pointed out, and Charles was peremptorily ordered to produce and set forth all deeds and writings of every kind relating to the house and estate, now in his custody or power. As expected, he refused, and in consequence the estate was sequestered.

But Earl Edward was too poor to continue the litigation for long, and it was plain to the lawyers that the estate itself would not at this time bear a heavy financial burden. So after four years of suits and controversies Edward, on 10th June 1725, improperly entered into articles of agreement with his brother, whereby Charles was to bear all costs and charges, but to retain the estate and mansion so long as he paid, or caused to be paid, £1,200 a year out of the rents and profits to Edward, subject to a proviso that nothing in the agreement should bar the male issue of the earl, who was then, and remained, a bachelor. It was further agreed that if Edward should marry a peer's daughter who brought with her a portion of £6,000 a suitable settlement should be made.

But though Charles agreed to this he made no arrangements for charging the estate with either the £1,200 required annually or the immediate legal costs. Nevertheless, he always said he was willing to have such arrangements made, and finally a Bill was brought before Parliament to enable him to sell or mortgage part of the estate for that purpose. At this stage, however, it was pointed out that the Bill was highly prejudicial to the earl —in the first place because, if passed, it would have the effect of assenting to the settlement made by the seventh earl, and in doing so would destroy any claim the present earl might have to his £1,200 a year, or, indeed, to any part in the estate. In other words, it was argued that the earl's right was to all or nothing, and that the Bill was bad because it sought to condone the action of Charles in entering upon the estate, and to justify him in possession.

Meanwhile Edward had probably grown tired of the whole affair. No doubt he would have been a happy man if he could have had his £1,200 a year and been allowed to live in peace with his friends and his books. He was a dreamy, studious creature, who fancied himself as a poet. Horace Walpole, in *Noble Authors*,[1] describes him as a nobleman 'with great inclination to versify, and some derangement of his intellects.' He goes on to say: 'The executors of this Lord conferred some value on his works by burning a great number of the copies after his death. Indeed, the first volume is not without merit, for his Lordship has transplanted whole pages of Milton into it, under the title of Elegancies.' Earl Edward's *Musarum Deliciae* is advertised in the book as containing 'essays upon pastoral ideas supposed to be written above two thousand years ago by an Asiatic poet who flourished under the reign of the Grand Cyrus.' The contents include such themes as 'Daphne Bathing in a Fountain,' 'An Epistle to Harmoniae,' 'To Almeria with a Basket of Fruit,' with similar Arcadian conventions, and the general tone of the collection is to be found in the opening sentence: 'How pleasant was the life of an Arcadian Swain! How undisturbed from care and trouble did the peaceful

[1] Vol. ii, pp. 119–20.

The East Wall of the Great Hall, looking North-east

Shepherd live, whose short pilgrimage thro' this Sublunary Globe was one entire course of blest security, perfect ease, and virgin innocence?' Such a state of life might well appeal to the vexed holder of an empty title, whose brother had deprived him of his estate, and whose lawyers would not allow him to go in peace with the comfortable allowance that had been offered him in lieu of the property.

The verse which follows is artificial and conventional, but not without charm. 'Corinna Dressing at her Toilet' is a promising title and produces some delightful images:

> In various curls and sundry annulets,
> Her paper'd locks she with her fingers sets;
> Her necklace she upon a ribbon strung,
> And in her ear her saphire pendants hung.

All very romantic and appropriate for a bachelor, no doubt, although, perhaps, not every one would accept the noble earl's assurance that:

> When the charming maid puts on her stays,
> She goddess like her radiancy displays.

The enigmatic Earl Edward completed his own pilgrimage 'thro' this Sublunary Globe' in 1731, leaving Charles to inherit the title and enjoy the undisputed possession of the estate. But it was still heavily burdened with debts. So heavily indeed that an Act [1] was passed empowering Charles to raise money by sale or mortgage for their payment. There was already a mortgage of £5,000, with accumulated interest, on the house, the park mill, and the lands belonging to them, contracted by Henry the sixth earl and Charles William, then called Lord Walden, during the sixth earl's lifetime. In addition, the seventh earl had contracted debts on his own account amounting to £8,855 as soon as he came into possession. Earl Charles was being pressed continually for payment of these long-standing debts, to say nothing of his own, and was therefore obliged to seek the Act empowering him to raise the necessary funds.

The charges made on the estate by these later earls must have come near to ruining it. One of the most revealing documents relating to money in the Audley End archives [2] concerns a dispute between Henry, the tenth earl, son of Charles the interloper, and a Miss Baggs. It appears that in 1686 the Earl

[1] E.R.O. D/DBy. E.5 and D/DBy. T.17.   [2] E.R.O. D/DBy. L.1.

of Thomond charged his estate with £8,000 as a portion for
Lady Penelope, his daughter, who married in 1691 Henry, afterwards sixth Earl of Suffolk.   In 1704 Henry, at this time known
as Lord Walden, borrowed £1,500 at 6 per cent interest from
John Baggs, Esq., and assigned to Baggs as security the £6,000
of his wife's dowry still outstanding, covenanting both for
himself and his heirs.   In July of the following year he borrowed
from Baggs a further £900 at the same rate of interest and on the
same security.   Baggs then died and his widow claimed the
money.   But even after succeeding to the estate in 1709 the
sixth earl was still unable to pay, and from that time to his
death in 1718 he continued to remit small sums of money to
Mrs. Baggs, which makes it clear that he was unable to free
himself of this comparatively small debt to the end of his life.
When he died intestate over £2,000, in fact, remained unpaid,
and as Mrs. Baggs died in the same year, her daughter claimed
the money from Earl Charles William, who was no more able
to pay than his father had been.   So this long-standing debt
came to the ninth earl, and eventually to the tenth and last of
the line, and it seems extremely unlikely that Miss Baggs ever
did get the money, because the solicitor who examined the
matter on behalf of the ninth earl expressed the opinion that
the security originally given to Mr. Baggs was the debt due to
Henry, afterwards sixth earl, from Lord Thomond's estate,
not his expectation of the Suffolk estate.   Since Mr. Baggs
accepted that debt as security his executors must stand by it.
Whether the earl received the £6,000 from Lord Thomond or
not, it was certain that at his death he left no personal estate
whatever, and therefore, in his opinion, there was nothing from
which the sum could now be claimed.

Such then were the fortunes and financial embarrassments of
the earls of Suffolk.   From the time when Audley End was
built, it seems clear that not one of them, with the single exception of the third earl while living at Great Chesterford and not
at Audley End, was ever out of debt until Henry, the tenth and
last, restored the estate to solvency by marrying Sarah, the
daughter of a wealthy brewer named Thomas Inwen, in May
1735.   So of the original Audley End the truth is that not one
of its ten Suffolk owners could afford to live in it.   The lord
treasurer's palace was always a white elephant.   But while this
is a fact, it must not be taken at its present-day value.   It is
doubtful whether any of the ten earls would be as disturbed by

this insolvency as a nobleman of our own day would be by a relatively small unsecured overdraft on his bank—if, indeed, such an overdraft would now be allowed! Money was not in the seventeenth and early eighteenth century the dominant factor that it later became. It was only with the ascendancy of men of the Thomas Inwen class that rank began to go cap in hand to capital, and eventually to be controlled by it. So our tenth earl is again a representative figure, as so many of his predecessors had been—representative because they had not had character enough to master their environments, and had therefore been at the mercy of the prevailing circumstances of their succeeding generations. The tenth earl did what so many did at that time, he saved himself from bankruptcy by marrying money.

The tenth earl's marriage settlement is of considerable interest. The transition from the old aristocratic attitude of sublime disregard for economic facts to the new materialism can be traced most clearly in the evolution of the marriage settlement, which steadily increased in importance during the eighteenth century until it became standardized.[1]

Sir William Temple, in *An Essay on Popular Discontents*,[2] wrote in 1750: 'Within less than fifty years, the first noble families . . . married into the City for downright money, and thereby introduced by degrees this public grievance which has since ruined so many estates by the necessity of giving great portions to daughters.' Sir William's dating, however, is deceptive. The first merchant to buy his way on the grand scale into the aristocratic families of England was Sir Josiah Child, who died in 1699, and from whom a considerable proportion of our present-day nobility are descended. He saw that the old landed families had become impoverished during the civil wars while he had been making a fortune. He saw also that they still had great influence. And he bought that influence for himself by arranging powerful marriages for his children and grandchildren. Others followed suit. As to the second part of Sir William Temple's statement, what he meant was that as the city merchants had been prepared to give up to £50,000 to gain for themselves a son-in-law of exalted birth, the landed gentry had been obliged to raise similar sums if they were to bid in the same market.

[1] See H. J. Habakkuk, 'Marriage Settlements in the Eighteenth Century,' *Trans. Roy. Hist. Soc.*, 4th series, vol. xxxii, 1950.
[2] *Miscellanea*, part iii, p. 269.

F

To do so they had been compelled to mortgage, and often to ruin, their estates.

But while Sir William is putting the date of the first of these marriages too late, he is correct in attributing this custom as an evil to the eighteenth century. It was under the Georges that the great Whig families became infected with Hanoverian pride, and in order to maintain their magnificent establishments mortgaged their estates in haggling over the marriages of their sons and daughters. But this intermarrying with merchant families had at least one useful consequence. As a result of it, marriage settlements came to be regulated in a businesslike manner, with dowries fixed on an agreed scale, according to social position. Before the eighteenth century there had been complete confusion in that both dowries and provisions for younger sons had varied without rhyme or reason. The new regularity was all to the good, because it meant that fewer estates were now eaten up by lawyers over will and settlement disputes.

In the marriage of the tenth earl with the daughter of Thomas Inwen there was nothing to be gained for Sarah but the title. There was no influence worth speaking of and the family home was a ruin. So presumably the £25,000 [1] she brought with her was for the title alone. The earl himself cannot have been worth much! Of this sum £18,000 was used to discharge existing mortgages, and the remaining £7,000 went to the earl, who had been brought up largely by his rascally father and had known little of his mother, Henrietta Hobart, of whom there will be much to say in the next chapter. In consideration of this dowry there was to be a charge of £1,600 a year on the revenues of the estate for the benefit of the countess, to secure which Inwen, who was member of Parliament for Southwark at one time, had the estate assigned to himself, his administrators and assigns, a proceeding that was quite invalid since the earl was only a life tenant; for when he died intestate and without issue in April 1745, ten years after the marriage, it was found that he had neglected to suffer a recovery.[2] Of his last illness the story is told by the third Lord Braybrooke that years afterwards Thomas Pennystone, the steward, used to relate with pride how he rode express to London in the middle of the night to fetch Sir Edward Hulse, a leading physician of the day, to

[1] E.R.O. D/DBy. E.7.
[2] The legal term for the process by which entailed estate was commonly transferred from one party to another.

attend the earl. Changing horses once only, at Epping, he made the journey of forty-six miles in three hours, five minutes, calling at Bishop's Stortford on the way to order sets of horses for the doctor's carriage.

At the tenth earl's death the Suffolk title passed to Henry Bowes Howard, fourth Earl of Berkshire, great-grandson of the first Earl of Suffolk, the builder of Audley End, and both the Berkshire and Suffolk titles have continued in his descendants. Seven years after the tenth earl's death his widow married, as his second wife, Lucius Charles Cary, seventh Viscount Falkland. She continued to draw her £1,600 a year from the estate; but the second Earl of Effingham, in accordance with the terms of the will of Earl Charles Edward, entered into possession.

Thus the Audley End line of the Suffolks broke, and with the passing of the last, at the age of thirty-eight, we see how far the tide of their prosperity had ebbed since the time when, at the fall of Somerset, Archbishop Abbot wrote in a personal memoir: 'King James, for many insolencies, grew weary of Somerset, and the kingdom groaned under the triumvirate of Northampton, Suffolk, and Somerset.' [1]

[1] Rushworth's *Historical Collections*, vol. i, p. 456, 3 Chas. 1.

VI

LADIES OF THE HOWARD FAMILY

I F SEVERAL OF the first ten earls of Suffolk tend to
be either shifty or shiftless, the same could hardly be said
of their ladies.   Theirs are the high lights, if not always
the honours, from Margaret, mother of the first earl, and
Katharine, his wife, to Henrietta, the ninth earl's countess and
George II's mistress.   It was Audley's daughter who brought
the estate to the Howards, and we shall see in a moment that
it was another daughter of the house, Elizabeth, Countess of
Portsmouth, who brought it to the Griffins and Nevilles.   It is
not uncommon, perhaps, for daughters to be more devoted than
sons to their ancestral homes; but no English house can owe
more than Audley End to its ladies.   Nevertheless, they have
had—and deserved—as many curses as blessings.

Of the daughters of Thomas, the first earl, Elizabeth, the
eldest, married as her first husband William Knollys, Earl of
Banbury, and as her second, Edward, Lord Vaux of Harrowden.
Of her, apparently, all that has been thought worth saying is
that 'she was not as bad as her next sister.'   Her infidelity in
marriage was the original cause of the long litigation that led
up to the case of the Banbury Peerage.   But what a sister
Frances was !   She was a girl of ten when the new reign brought
such influence to her father.   At thirteen she was married to
Robert Devereux, Earl of Essex, the son of Elizabeth's favourite,
a youth of fourteen, from whom she was separated immediately
after the wedding so that he could return to the Continent and
resume his education.   But in spite of the hastiness of the
marriage the king and his courtiers combined to celebrate the
union of these two great houses with all the pageantry that
London could muster.   Ben Jonson and Inigo Jones produced
The Masque of Hymen for the occasion, contriving a dance in the
shape of the bridegroom's name, with the maskers in white
heron plumes, while all the jewels and ropes of pearls that the

city could afford were worn by the ladies.   The king himself presided and joined in the merriment.   But there was one alarming and prophetic feature.   Eight of the principal noblemen of the day issued from a richly illuminated globe in the allegorical figure of a man, then drew their swords and threatened to interrupt the marriage rite.   They were announced as the Perverse Affections.

The person whom these subversive spirits were to infect was the king's favourite, Robert Carr,[1] who seven years later married the countess, after the first marriage had been dissolved on the ground of non-consummation.   The course of the Essex divorce case is well known.   Justice had no part in it from first to last. In order to establish the countess's alleged virginity a court of female inquisition was held; but the lady examined was not the countess, about whose chastity no one who knew her could have any illusions.   The king himself ordered that her place at the examination should be taken by a Miss Mounson, the daughter of Sir Thomas Mounson, a young lady of undoubted innocence.   The court was thus able to find as directed, and with its finding before them, the judges of the ecclesiastical court were subsequently able to give judgment in the countess's favour, and to annul the marriage.   Carr was then created Earl of Somerset, so that in marrying him Lady Essex should not lose rank, and on St. Stephen's Day 1613—by which time the bride was twenty—in the presence of the king, the queen, the Prince of Wales, and all the most eminent persons in Church and State, the couple were married in the chapel at Whitehall, then of course a royal palace.   The whole business was as farcical as it could possibly be.   Both weddings took place on the same day of the same month, in the same place, with the same king to give the bride away and pay the expenses, and the same dean of the chapel—a bishop of Bath and Wells—to recite the rigmarole.   To complete the farce, Lady Essex was married with her long and beautiful hair hanging loose, which was held to signify virginity.   And so well did she conduct herself that a friend of her first husband said that those 'who saw her face might challenge Nature of too much hypocrisy for harbouring so wicked a heart under so sweet and bewitching a countenance,' adding 'that she had grown to be a beauty of the greatest magnitude in the horizon of the Court, and every

---

[1] His portrait as Earl of Somerset, K.G., believed to be by Mark Gerard, hangs in the dining-room at Audley End.

tongue grew an orator at that shrine.' It was of this marriage that Donne wrote:

> Then from those wombs of stars, the Bride's bright eyes,
> At every glance a constellation flies,
> And sows the Court with stars, and doth prevent,
> In light and power, the all-eyed firmament.
> First, her eyes kindle other ladies' eyes,
> Then from those beams their jewels' lustre rise;
> And from their jewels torches do take fire;
> And all is warmth, and light, and good desire.

Of the feasting he wrote:

> ...the tables groan as though the feast,
> Would, as the flood, destroy all fowl and beast.

Nine days later, when the couple were entertained at Merchant Taylors' Hall by the lord mayor and aldermen of London, there was a torchlight procession through Cheapside, followed by a feast, a wassail, two masques, and a play, that kept the company away from their beds until three o'clock next morning.

The wedding presents included a basin and cover of silver gilt from the chief justice, Sir Edward Coke, and a pot of gold from his lady. The bishop's wife provided the bride's cake.

Less than three years later, in May 1616, these same courtiers and nobles who had sung epithalamiums for the wedding assembled in Westminster Hall to hear the earl and countess answer upon their arraignments for the crime of having murdered in the Tower, Sir Thomas Overbury, a friend of the bridegroom, who had disapproved of the wedding. It was then disclosed that the countess, while married to her first husband, had bought from an astrologer named Dr. Forman philters to chill the love of Essex for her and to kindle that of Carr. Among other objects procured for this purpose were puppets, enchanted papers, a piece of human skin, and a black scarf covered with white crosses. The countess pleaded guilty, and sentence of death was passed on her; but in pronouncing it the lord high steward, Lord Chancellor Ellesmere, said: 'Since the Lords have heard with what humility and grief you have confessed the fact, I do not doubt they will signify so much to the king, and mediate for his grace towards you.' While imprisoned in the Tower, Lady Somerset gave birth to her only child, who was given the queen's name. The story is told of the countess that while waiting for the child to be born she placed her hand on herself and said: 'If I were rid of this burden it is my death that is looked for, and my death they shall have.'[1] The child in question was the Lady Ann Carr who married William Russell, Earl of Bedford, and by him had a family of three daughters and seven sons, one of whom was the Lord William Russell who was accused of complicity in the Rye House Plot.

Green refers to Frances Howard as 'the most profligate woman of her time.' Perhaps she was; but it is some mitigation to reflect that the king as well as her parents were anxious that she should marry Carr. Probably the evil genius in this affair, as in so many others that brought distress to the Howards of Elizabeth and James, was the Earl of Northampton, who, says Horace Walpole,[2]

addicted his services to the Earl of Somerset, and became a chief and shocking instrument in that lord's match with Northampton's kinswoman the Countess of Essex, and of the succeeding murder of Sir Thomas Overbury. Northampton, the pious endower of hospitals, died luckily before the plot came to light; but his letters were read in court . . . not all, for there was such a horrid mixture of obscenity and blood in them, that the Chief Justice could not go through them in common decency.

The advantages to himself and to his beloved nephew, Thomas, the bride's father, of the match would be plain enough to Northampton, and to promote it he was gambling, as he had gambled before in promoting a marriage, with the lives of his own kinsfolk.

Catherine, third daughter of the first Earl of Suffolk, married William Cecil, second Earl of Salisbury and builder of Hatfield House, and by him had seven sons and five daughters.

Of the daughters of Theophilus, the second earl, Catherine, the eldest, married Lord Aubigny, the younger son of the Duke of Richmond and Lennox, said to have been 'a young man of great promise,' whose life was cut short. He fell at Edgehill, where he is believed to have been shot by one of his own men. Shortly afterwards Lady Aubigny obtained from Parliament a pass to interview the king about her husband's affairs, and went for that purpose to Oxford. As she was about to withdraw from the royal presence Charles entrusted her with a small box, saying that 'it much concerned his own service, and that he

[1] *State Papers Domestic*, 1616, 17th Nov. No. 296.
[2] *Noble Authors*, p. 151.

wished her to carry it with great care and secrecy, until a gentleman should call to her ladyship for it.' This precious box fell
into the wrong hands and brought to light the Waller plot.
Lady Aubigny was imprisoned for her complicity, and would
have been put to death if she had not escaped to The Hague with
Lord Newburgh, as ardent a Royalist as herself, whom she later
married. The story of this spirited lady is told by Clarendon,[1]
who describes her as 'a woman of a very great wit, and most
trusted and conversant in those intrigues, which at that time
could be best managed and carried on by ladies, who with less
jealousy could be seen in all companies: and so she had not been
a stranger to the most secret transactions with the Scots.'

Another of the second earl's daughters, Elizabeth, married,
as his second wife, the tenth Earl of Northumberland, who
bought Northampton House in the Strand and gave it his name.
She lived to be ninety-seven. A third married the Earl of
Orrery, and the youngest, Frances, married Sir Edward Villiers,
a half-brother of the Duke of Buckingham. From her are
descended the earls of Jersey. This second Lady Frances
Howard was governess to the Princesses Mary and Anne,
daughters of James II, and successively queens of England. To
her husband, who was knight marshal of the household,
Charles II granted the palace and manor of Richmond. His
sister, Barbara, married his wife's brother James, the third Earl
of Suffolk, as his second wife.

It was of Lady Margaret Howard, who married the Earl of
Orrery, that Suckling wrote the lines:

> Her feet beneath her petticoat
> Like little mice stole in and out,
>   As if they feared the light.
> And O, she dances such a way!
> No sun upon an Easter Day
>   Is half so fine a sight.

She also was a noted beauty of her day, but unlike her aunt
and grandmother she was as good as she was lovely. A contemporary says of her that she was of 'unaffected piety, love of
her Lord, and sweetness of temper.' And a portrait in the
possession of the Earl of Shannon shows how admirable an
index her features were to such a character.

Sir John Suckling's poem was in celebration of her wedding.
He describes the scene at Suffolk House—not yet Northumber-

[1] *History of the Rebellion*, new ed., vol. v, p. 292.

land House—and engagingly relates that the bride's finger was
so thin that the ring would not stay on it. He sings, with the
charming spontaneity of his best verse:

> Her cheeks so rare a white was on,
> No daisy bears comparison
>   (Who sees them is undone);
> For streaks of red were mingled there,
> Such as are on a Katherine pear,
>   The side that's next the sun.
>
> Her lips were red, and one was thin,
> Compared to that was next her chin,
>   Some bee had stung it newly.
> But, Dick, her eyes so guard her face,
> I durst no more upon them gaze,
>   Than on the sun in July.

All these were daughters of the earls of Suffolk. Of the
countesses of Suffolk the most renowned was Henrietta, wife of
the ninth earl, who, while Mrs. Howard, became the mistress
of George II, and a lady of note in the society of her day.
Alexander Pope introduces her into his *Moral Essays* as Chloe,
the name Lord Peterborough gave her:

> She speaks, behaves, and acts, just as she ought,
> But never, never reached one generous thought.
> Virtue she finds too painful an endeavour,
> Content to dwell in decencies for ever. . . .
> She, while her lover pants upon her breast,
> Can mark the figures on an Indian chest;
> And when she sees her friend in deep despair,
> Observes how much a chintz exceeds mohair.

The portrait appears to be less of a caricature than most of
Pope's, for Mrs. Howard was as different from the romantic
conception of a royal mistress as the king was from that of a
royal lover. In any case, the only woman George II ever loved
devotedly was his wife. He took a mistress because he thought
it the proper thing for a prince to do, and the queen, no doubt,
was glad to be relieved of his company for a few hours daily.
She approved of Mrs. Howard because she found her sensible
and respectable. If she were removed, the queen feared, the
king might very well fall into worse arms. Apart from her
natural good sense and restraint, Mrs. Howard was about forty
when George became king, while he was forty-four.

Henrietta Howard's was a tragic life. The more we read of her the more we pity her. She was the daughter of Sir Henry Hobart of Blickling Hall, Norfolk, and her husband was the Charles Howard whose acquaintance we made in the last chapter, the rascal described by Lord Hervey [1] as 'a wrong-headed, ill-tempered, obstinate, drunken, extravagant brutal younger brother of the Earl of Suffolk's family.' Lord Chesterfield said 'he was sour, dull, and sullen,' and thought the marriage 'unaccountable, unless from a certain fatality which often makes hasty marriages, soon attended by long repentance and aversion. Thus they loved, thus they married, and thus they hated each other for the rest of their lives.' This unhappy pair were legally separated, as we shall see, in 1728.

As a third son, Charles was not at the time of the marriage expected to succeed to the earldom. His income must have been very small indeed, and Henrietta's portion of £6,000, £4,000 of which was settled on herself and her heirs, was not sufficient to keep them out of debt. In 1710, therefore, partly to escape from their creditors and partly to try to make the acquaintance of the future sovereign, they went to live in Hanover. By this means they hoped to gain positions at court when the Elector of Hanover should come to the English throne as George I. It is said that when they arrived in the new country they were so poor that Mrs. Howard sold her hair in order to raise money to entertain the Hanoverian ministers to dinner. Hanover, however, gave them little—though Mrs. Howard was taken into the future queen's service for a short time—and after three years they returned to London, living for a time as Mr. and Mrs. Smith in poor lodgings in the Golden Square neighbourhood, where Mrs. Howard did her own house-work and attended to her husband and child, whom nobody, it seems, suspected of being the future ninth and tenth Earls of Suffolk. After such an experience it is little wonder that she expressed herself in her *Reflections upon the Married State* somewhat tartly:

August 29, 1716.

What is the Marriage Vow? A solemn contract where two engage. The woman promises duty, affection and obedience to the man's commands, to guard that share of his honour reposed in her keeping. What is his part? To guide, to protect, to support and govern with mildness. Have I performed my part in word and deed? How has

[1] *Memoirs*, vol. i, p. 54.

Charles answered his? In no one article. How guided? To evil. How protected and supported me? Left destitute, wanting the common necessaries of life; not always from misfortunes, but from choice. What (from justice as well as from humanity, nay, even from his vows) ought to have been mine, employed to gratify his passions. How governed? With tyranny, with cruelty, my life in danger.

Then am not I free? All other engagements cease to bind, if other contracting parties fail in their part. Self-preservation is the first law of Nature. Are married women then the only part of human nature that must not follow it? Are they expected to act upon higher principles of religion and honour than any other part of the creation? [1]

She points out the folly of a woman enslaving herself to her inferior, but disclaims any thought of revenge, arguing that as Charles has been her husband so long, to dishonour him in public would be to dishonour herself. In other words, she cannot expose the wretchedness of his life without making public the wretchedness of her own.

Mr. and Mrs. Charles Howard parted about 1717, while Charles's brother, the sixth earl, was still alive, and as First Commissioner of Trade and Plantations was a prominent figure in the State. At this time there would still seem little likelihood of Charles succeeding to the title, and he was despised by every one. A letter written to Henrietta, threatening to take legal action against her if she did not return to him at once, and complaining that her treatment had twice endangered his mind, shows what a weak, vindictive creature he was. Henrietta had no difficulty in replying to so foolish a threat. His object, as every one knew, was to extract money from the prince, who was already showing marked favour to Mrs. Howard, although she was not known to the public as his mistress until about 1720. But in spite of the prince's interest, Charles was not easily subdued. In his blackguardly threats, usually made when he was more than half drunk, he had one ally, the king, who enjoyed nothing better than tormenting his son and embarrassing his daughter-in-law.

For ten years Charles Howard continued to pester his wife with these vulgar demonstrations until, in the autumn of 1727, he made so bold as to enter St. James's Palace and there succeeded in reaching the princess herself, in whose household Mrs. Howard was officially employed. Lord Hervey had the whole story from Caroline many years later. According to this,

[1] Add. MSS. 22627, f. 13.

Howard came blustering into her Royal Highness's presence
when she was alone, loudly demanding his wife, and shouting
that if he could not take her by force from the palace he would
waylay her while driving, and would drag her from the
princess's coach if need be.   Caroline confessed that she had
been horribly frightened, but had bravely dared him to try.
'What added to my fear,' she confided to Lord Hervey, 'was
that, as I knew him to be so brutal as well as a little mad, and
seldom quite sober, so I did not think it impossible but that he
might throw me out of the window . . . but as soon as I had
got near the door, and thought myself safe from being thrown
out of the window, *je pris mon grand ton de reine, et je disais* I would
be glad to see who should dare to open my coach door and
take out one of my servants; *sachant tout le temps qu'il le pouvait
faire s'il le voulait; et qu'il aurait sa femme, et moi l'affront.'*   With
that she bade him an imperious good day.

   The date of this dramatic appearance of the aggrieved husband
has been confused in various accounts of it.   In *Walpoliana*,
Horace Walpole is made to date it as late as 1731, while in the
Reminiscences he writes as though it occurred about 1717.   The
correct date is undoubtedly 1727.   Croker, in a footnote to
Hervey's *Memoirs of the Reign of George the Second*, says:

A large original correspondence on this subject is extant, from
which it appears that the differences and personal separation between
Mr. and Mrs. Howard took place about 1717; that early in 1727 Mr.
Howard, who was in the King's family, obtained the commands of
His Majesty—ready enough to displease and affront the Prince—to
remove his wife from the Prince's service.   It was at this juncture
that the carrying her off by force was in contemplation, and that
she was removed to Richmond.   In the meanwhile George I died,
and a negotiation was begun or continued for a legal separation,
and it was in this state of the case that, sometime in the autumn of
1727, the interview of Mr. Howard with the queen must have taken
place.   See the whole story in the biographical notice to the *Suffolk
Papers.'*

   In those last few weeks of George I's life Charles played all
his master cards.   He was firmly lodged at Audley End, but
was being pressed for the £1,200 a year that he had agreed
to pay his brother Edward, the eighth earl.   His wife, now
the most influential lady in the land after the queen, was his
only asset.   The old king failing, he turned to the Archbishop
of Canterbury, who may hardly be thought a fitting companion

for such a man.   But the archbishop [1] was obviously afraid of
a public scandal at this point.   He did not altogether accept
Howard's story, but he strongly disapproved of his wife being
in the royal household, and on terms of intimacy with the man
who was about to be crowned king.   So he took up Howard's
case,[2] somewhat to the amusement of those who knew how
matters stood at court.   It ought, however, to be said that the
archbishop's fears were not entirely without foundation.   If
Charles had in fact been bold enough to go to law, it is most
probable that at this particular time his wife would have been
ordered to return to him, king or no king.

But both the king and Mrs. Howard knew well enough that
what Charles really wanted was not his wife, but her price.
And the figure he might be silenced with was an annuity to
cover the one he was engaged to pay to his brother Edward.
Understanding this, with characteristic stupidity the king
actually sent old Lord Trevor along to the queen to suggest that
it would be better if she, and not himself, made Howard an
allowance of £1,200 a year.   Her Majesty, not unnaturally,
thought they were asking rather much of her.   She did not see
why she should both keep the king's trulls—*guenipes* was the
word she used—under her roof and pay their husbands too!
The king, therefore, agreed to increase his allowance to Mrs.
Howard from £2,000 a year to £3,200 so that she, the wife,
could pass on the £1,200.   This arrangement made, 'Mrs.
Howard,' wrote Gay to Dean Swift on 28th March 1728, 'is
happier than I have seen her ever since you left us, for she is
free as to her conjugal affairs by articles of agreement.'

Mrs. Howard's literary friendships, which were so remarkable
for a woman who had nothing whatever of either the muse or
the blue-stocking about her, ripened at Twickenham, where
George built for her (at a cost of approximately £12,000) a
Palladian villa, Marble Hill, between Richmond Bridge and
Orleans House.   Lord Burlington superintended the decorating,
Pope and Lord Bathurst laid out the grounds, Gay and Arbuth-
not organized the household, and Swift is said to have nominated
himself as custodian of the wine cellars.

What did these people find so fascinating about the lady?
That she was sensible and pleasant all agree; but brilliant men
do not as a rule lose their heads to a woman because of her
remarkable capacity for keeping her own.   She herself was

[1] William Wake.   [2] Wake, enclosure with Add. MSS. 22627, f. 30.

certainly not clever, let alone brilliant. She was pretty and kind in a negative sort of way, but she was neither beautiful nor generous hearted. 'Her countenance,' said Lord Chesterfield, 'was an undecided one, and announced neither vivacity, nor dullness.' Perhaps it was her equanimity that appealed to the wits of that over-sharpened age. She could always be relied on to prick their intellectual bubbles with a well-timed commonplace.

Her value for the king is more easily explained. She was the one woman his testiness could never disturb. However disagreeable he might be Mrs. Howard was always unruffled; however ridiculous he was she was always sensible and quite unaffected. Few of those who studied her knew what she had been through in her early married life, and what mastery she had over herself. Here at last, she must have felt, was security. It was worth more than the rest of them knew.

When the eighth earl died on 22nd June 1731, and the miserable Charles succeeded as ninth Earl of Suffolk, Henrietta was promoted to a position at court more befitting the rank of a countess. She at once became groom of the stole to the queen, succeeding in that office the Duchess of Dorset, who had held it since 1727. This office is usually combined with that of mistress of the robes, and requires attendance at court on formal occasions only. Lady Suffolk, however, was still allowed to live at St. James's. Of her change in status she wrote to Gay from Hampton Court on 29th June 1731 that she had kissed hands for the place of mistress of the robes, and added: 'Mr. H. took possession of body and goods [the late earl's], and was not prevailed upon till yesterday to resign the former for burial. Poor Lord Suffolk took so much care in the will he made, that the best lawyers say it must stand good. I am persuaded it will be tried to the utmost.'[1] She had good reason for this opinion. The eighth earl had left all he possessed, which cannot have been worth more than two or three thousand pounds, to Henrietta herself, with the Duke of Argyll and Lord Islay, old friends of hers, as trustees,[2] believing no doubt that this would be the best way of saving it for the benefit of her son, who would eventually become tenth earl and owner of Audley End.

[1] Add. MSS. 22626, f. 53.
[2] Lady Pembroke to Mrs. Clayton, 1st July 1731 (Thomson, *Memoirs of Lady Swindon*, vol. i, p. 233).

In later life Lady Suffolk became hard of hearing, and after twenty years the king grew tired of being tied, as he said, to a deaf old woman. The countess had experienced more than one uncongenial tie; but in 1733 she was released from the most irksome. That year the ninth earl died, and his countess, by this time about forty-five, became free to remarry. Her opportunity came two years later in an offer from the Hon. George Berkeley, who had little to commend him, but was evidently the best that offered. When Lady Suffolk told the queen—during the king's absence in Hanover—that she had a mind to marry George Berkeley, Her Majesty was both surprised and annoyed.

'My good Lady Suffolk,' she pleaded, 'you are the best servant in the world, and, as I should be most extremely sorry to lose you, pray take a week to consider of this business, and give me your word not to read any romances in that time, and then I dare say you will lay aside all thought of doing what, believe me, you will repent, and what I am very sure I shall be very sorry for.' [1]

Lady Suffolk was probably wise in providing for her future in this way. We may be sure that she knew perfectly well what she was about. It was unusual, to say the least of it, for a queen to be so put out on seeing the king's mistress leave court, but George II's company was not easily borne. No woman would want him all to herself. Lady Suffolk, by her sweet nature and good sense, had done more than any one else to make life with such a king bearable for his family. Moreover, the queen had never had much cause for jealousy, for however much he had denied it, she had always known that she had the king's love, and that he relied on her more than on Lady Suffolk. What had the king and Lady Suffolk counted for in affairs of state? They had never known the power exercised so long by the queen and her dear Sir Robert Walpole. For Her Majesty, then, she had been a person of great convenience. Of what she had been to the wits and poets of her day their own records speak. For the rest, Lord Hervey, who was of the opposite faction at court and therefore not predisposed in her favour, may speak. He says: 'Good sense, good breeding, and good nature were qualities which even her enemies could not deny her; nor do I know any good or agreeable quality which those who knew her more intimately would not as readily allow her. She was civil to everybody, friendly to many and unjust to none: in short,

[1] Hervey, vol. ii, p. 185.

she had a good head and a good heart, but had to do with a man who was incapable of testing the one or valuing the other.' Though no longer in the public eye she had another forty years of life to give to her friends, by whom she was greatly loved in her old age, as well as being much valued for her remarkable memory and clear, unbiased knowledge of the generation she had known so intimately. She died on 26th July 1767, aged eighty-six. By this time her only son, the tenth Earl of Suffolk, had been dead for twenty-two years, and Sir John Griffin Griffin was established at Audley End.

The Stables from the South-west

VII

THE DISPOSSESSION

THE DISPOSSESSION of the tenth earl's heir by three descendants of the third earl in 1747 began in a curious way. We have seen that when the tenth earl died intestate and without issue in 1745 Thomas, second Earl of Effingham, took possession of house and estate on the strength of a deed dated 31st March 1721, by which Charles William, the seventh earl, after suffering a recovery of his estate, had resettled it on the earls of Effingham and their heirs male in the event of there being no heirs male of himself or of his two uncles, Edward and Charles Howard, the eighth and ninth earls. If the seventh earl had been entitled to make such a resettlement Lord Effingham's claim would have been firmly based; but the Countess of Portsmouth, one of the three living descendants of James, the third earl, was advised by her solicitor, John Sanderson, that this was doubtful. In looking through a bundle of old legal papers for something suitable for his boy to copy 'by way of practice,' Mr. Sanderson had come across the rough draft of a settlement apparently made by the third earl on 31st March 1687, in consideration of his marriage with the eldest daughter of the Earl of Manchester, which, if authentic, would destroy the validity of the later document. In the third earl's settlement it was provided that if there should be no male heirs of himself or his brothers, the fourth and fifth earls, there should be remainder to himself in fee, which meant that the seventh earl, as grandson of the fifth, was only tenant for life and thus had no power to create an entail.

It was indisputable that the last in the male line of descent from the third earl was the tenth, and at his death on 22nd April 1745 Mr. Sanderson began his inquiries. On the 25th of the same month he wrote to Lady Portsmouth informing her that he had heard on good authority that Lord Suffolk had died without making a will. He had heard also that an Act had been passed in the first year of the present reign for the sale of part of the estate to pay off certain debts, and that there was a suit in

Chancery ready for hearing in which the late earl, his countess, and her trustees, together with the Earl of Effingham, sought a ruling on some point of difference. He continued: 'And I am told that the settlement made by Earl James, and all the settlements made since that time, are set out and fully appear in the pleadings.' He therefore advised her ladyship to allow him to obtain copies of this, for, he said, 'I very well remember that the dispute between the late Earl's father and uncle [1] arose upon the settlement made by Earl James, whether the remainders limited by that settlement were well barred by the recovery in the year 1721.'

Another of the descendants of Earl James, Lord Hervey, afterwards second Earl of Bristol, wrote to Lady Portsmouth on the 30th of the same month that it was being said in London that he and she were entitled in equal shares to some part of Lord Suffolk's estate. He repeated Mr. Sanderson's story, but added to it a rumour of another settlement made by the third earl, which would bar the countess and himself until the Berkshire line of the Howards died out. He was informed,[2] he said, that the seventh earl was empowered to levy fines, suffer a recovery, and make a further settlement, which he did in 1715, and according to this report Lord Effingham's claim must rest on the 1715 settlement. But, continued Lord Hervey, as most of the estate was then out in jointures or dowers, that settlement would appear to be invalid. Charles William, however, according to the report, was informed of this, and made another settlement in 1721 or 1722, with the same limitations as before as regards Lord Effingham, excluding his elder uncle, Edward, and leaving the estate to his younger uncle, Charles, the father of the earl who had recently died.

Lord Hervey then went into the long suit in Chancery between Edward and Charles, which ended in an agreement being made between them by which Charles, in consideration of Edward's quitting his claim to the estate, received £1,200 a year.[3] The lawyers, he reported, were arguing that if there had not been some flaw in the seventh earl's settlement Edward would not have given up the whole estate for £1,200 a year. It seemed probable that there was such a flaw; but even so, he and the Countess of Portsmouth could not yet be sure whether they or Lord Berkshire, now eleventh Earl of Suffolk, would benefit. Meanwhile Lord Effingham had taken possession, and the

---

[1] The ninth and eighth earls.   [2] Wrongly.   [3] See pp. 59, 60.

Dowager Lady Suffolk had most imprudently handed over to him all the documents they would require for any claim they might make.

On the same day Mr. Sanderson wrote to the countess mentioning the same doubts about the seventh earl's recovery, for, he argued, if it had not been bad why did Charles Howard, afterwards ninth earl, allow the estate to be sequestered for a long time rather than produce the title deeds which, if valid, would have established his claim? He refused to do so, in Mr. Sanderson's opinion, because with them he would have had to produce the settlement made by Earl James in which Edward, the eighth earl, was clearly the remainder man. The late earl, he confirmed, certainly did not make a recovery.

The next exciting move came with a letter from John Craster, a barrister employed by Lady Portsmouth as counsel, dated 8th May 1745. It begins:

Madam, Late last night I received my Lady Suffolk's bill to make good her jointure. It contains three long family settlements, and several other conveyances, and there are so many manors and estates comprised in each settlement, and those limited to different persons and users, that it is impossible upon one perusal to form a clear conception of the title. But this much I think appears, that a considerable part of the estate depends upon the settlement made by Earl James in 1687.

Mr. Craster was writing after a first perusal, and said that he found the matter very complicated; but as he understood it Earl James had intended the estate to continue with the title, and had made his brothers, George and Henry, and his nephews, Henry, Edward, and Charles, tenants only for a period of ninety-nine years. So none of these could suffer a recovery. In a settlement made in 1715, on the marriage of Charles William, afterwards seventh earl, such a recovery was purported to be made, but it could never have been valid. Charles William had evidently discovered this, for in 1721, after the death of the sixth earl and, what was no less to the point, after the death of Ann, the third earl's widow, who had long survived her husband and had enjoyed an income from the estate, Charles William had suffered another recovery to include her jointure lands. If this recovery also should prove void, the final limitation in the third earl's will—all other limitations to the heirs male being spent—would become operative, namely, the limitation in favour

of his own heirs in fee. These heirs were the Countess of
Portsmouth, her sister (Mrs. Whitwell), and Lord Hervey. If,
however, the seventh earl's recovery were to prove valid Lord
Effingham would be entitled to the estate.

On further consideration this appeared so improbable that the
three descendants of the third earl were advised to exhibit a
bill of complaint against Sarah, Countess Dowager of Suffolk,
Thomas, Earl of Effingham, and others, 'being seized in fee of
and in the manors lands and tenements hereinafter mentioned
of the yearly value of £4,000 and upwards,'[1] and so forth.
They claimed that as Henry, the tenth earl, had never suffered a
recovery to bar the remainder of 1687 they were now entitled
to the estate, and on 16th October 1747 judgment was pro-
nounced in their favour. But their victory was not complete.
The mansion, mill, and park were excluded, because when the
1687 settlement was made these were Crown property and were
not in the earl's hands. That part of the estate, therefore,
which had been recovered from the Crown by the fifth earl
must be excluded. The Earl of Effingham was fully entitled
to this.

Meanwhile the Countess of Portsmouth, the dominant person
in these proceedings—and just how dominant she was we shall
see presently—had not been idle. With the concurrence of
Lord Hervey she had employed a friend of the family, William
Vachell of Great Abington, a colonel in the Coldstream Guards
and a justice of the peace for Cambridgeshire, to examine the
estate. This Colonel Vachell, who was obviously a man of
the highest integrity and very able, had special claims on the
countess. He belonged to an ancient Berkshire family and
was evidently an intimate friend of the countess's first husband,
the eccentric Henry Grey of Billingbear, who by his will dated
1732, and proved in 1740, made him ultimate residuary legatee
of his large estates, conditionally upon Vachell taking the name
of Neville. But, as we shall see in the next chapter, this and
other intentions of Mr. Grey had to give way to those of his
strong-minded wife. Colonel Vachell, however, appears to
have managed the Billingbear estates for the countess until her
death in 1762. Apparently he presented to the Waltham St.
Lawrence living in 1758.

William Cole, the antiquary, thought highly of 'the worshipful
Colonel William Vachell,' and referred to him as 'my most

[1] E.R.O. D/DBy. E.7.

worthy friend.' This, then, is the gentleman upon whom we must rely for our information about the Audley End estates at this juncture.[1]

On 10th August 1746 Vachell wrote to Lady Portsmouth that he had spent considerable time in the Audley End and Saffron Walden neighbourhood and was now fairly familiar with the state of affairs in those parts. There appeared to be about £1,100 in hand, including woodlands. The steward, Mr. Pennystone, seemed to be an honest man. He had, of course, his enemies, as most stewards had, however just; but Colonel Vachell personally was very impressed by him. 'I have taken pains,' he says,

since my appointment, to enquire his character. All agree he is a very judicious man in country affairs, that he is a man of substance, and honest for anything my informers knew to the contrary. There are few stewards that have not their own interest more at heart than their master's, and they all have it in their power to save to themselves. Your Ladyship sees there is an absolute necessity that there must be a steward. . . . Pennystone may indeed suck some honey from lands in hand; and where to find a man that will not is beyond my skill.

The colonel did not misjudge his man. The Pennystones had a long connection with Audley End, and the son of the colonel's man must have been steward for about fifty years when he died in 1802.

Vachell reported that tenants had never known where they stood with the late earl, that he had promised and forgotten his promises, and generally that he had not enjoyed much confidence in the district. That being so, it was of the greatest importance that whatever was done now must be done in earnest. Perhaps the chief cause of dissatisfaction had been that all tenants had been tenants at the earl's will, and had enjoyed no security. Colonel Vachell suggested that leases should be granted with covenants for repairs, and as far as possible that the present tenants should be kept, as, according to Mr. Pennystone, rents were paid with such regularity twice a year that it was very unusual to have £30 in arrear. The best farms, however, stood engaged for payment to the Dowager Countess of Suffolk's jointure to the tune of £2,500 a year, a life interest which the lord chancellor upheld in his judgment in favour of the claimants.

[1] Collection of letters in Lord Braybrooke's possession.

Colonel Vachell was in due course appointed receiver of the estate on behalf of the Countess of Portsmouth and Mrs. Whitwell on the one hand, and Lord Hervey on the other, between whom they were to be divided in two equal lots. The appointment was to be from Lady Day 1747 to the Michaelmas following, and the estate was run as a unit under his direction, with Thomas Pennystone as land steward, until 22nd December 1753, when a deed of partition was signed, dividing the estate equally between the second Earl of Bristol, as Lord Hervey had become on the death of his grandfather in 1751, and the Countess of Portsmouth and Mrs. Whitwell. For the purpose of this division the estate was valued, and it was found that the Walden part was practically equal to all the rest. Such difference as there was could be removed by adjusting the woodlands. Essex had always been a well-wooded county, and the northwest had long been famous for its oaks. But the later Earls of Suffolk had made several great falls, so in 1753 there was very little large timber for sale. Moreover, a considerable quantity was needed for repairs if the estate was to be put into good order.

But what of the house? Without the estate it was of little use to any one, particularly as it was in a state of extreme dilapidation. When the Countess of Portsmouth first visited this home of her ancestors she may well have recalled the lines in one of Shakespeare's sonnets:

> When I have seen by Time's fell hand defaced
> The rich proud cost of outworn buried age,
> When sometime lofty towers I see down-razed,
> And brass eternal, slave to mortal rage. . . .
> This thought is as a death, which cannot choose
> But weep to have that which it fears to lose.

The schoolchildren of Walden and Audley End used to play in the ruined gallery, and Lord Effingham had thoughts of selling the house for conversion into a silk factory. The windows were broken, much of the furniture had been removed by the Dowager Countess of Suffolk and sold. Demolition was considered; but prospective buyers who came down from London shook their heads when they learned that there was no navigation nearer than Bishop's Stortford or Cambridge. To dismantle such a house would cost a great deal, and little could be sold in the vicinity.

But in spite of its condition the Countess, though childless and comparatively old, was determined to buy Audley End, and to restore it to something of its former glory. She therefore instructed Colonel Vachell to enter into negotiation for its purchase, and he at once began making tentative inquiries. There had, he discovered, been a valuation of the materials of the house made some years earlier when the tenth earl had considered demolition. It gave: Stonework, £1,201; Glass, £97; Iron locks and latches, £289; Lead, £3,339; Bricks about house and fence walls, £905; Wainscot, £280; Partitions and boards, £1,166; Outbuildings, £657; Movable goods, £50; making a total of £7,984. The park timber was valued at £1,115, the 283 acres of parkland at £6,367, the mill in the park at £600, bringing the total up to £16,066. This was rather more than the £15,000 rumoured to be the sum Lord Effingham had said he would accept—which in the colonel's opinion was still far too much, even though it included presentation to the mastership of Magdalene College.[1] The colonel pointed out: (1) that the stone in general was no better than clunch; (2) that the outdoor marble would crumble to pieces on being taken down; (3) that much of the glass had been broken since the Suffolk valuation; (4) that the locks and latches item was absurd unless something else was included, as these alone could not be worth more than a third of the stated amount; (5) that lead valuing was pure guess-work; (6) that the value set on the brick was ridiculously high, having regard to the cost of cleaning and carting away the rubbish. As for the wainscoting, this had now gone out of fashion and if offered for sale would be a drug on the market, wall-paper being so much cheaper. The timber he thought over-valued because of late years high winds had played havoc with windows and roofs, with the result that snow and rain had done much damage. The outbuildings might be sound enough, but the movable goods referred to had probably been removed already. On the other hand, admitted the colonel, the Suffolk estimate was made when money carried 6 per cent interest, and consequently when land was at a lower value, which meant that although the building was now worth less, the land was worth more.

On 14th July 1751 Colonel Vachell wrote to Lady Portsmouth that he was informed that a Mr. Ware, a plumber, and a Mr. Phillips, a builder, had valued the house for its materials at

---

[1] See p. 12.

£3,750. The lead, which every one agreed was the most important item, even though its purchase was speculative, was put at £1,752 in this new valuation. In reporting this Vachell draws the countess's attention to something that he must have had in mind from the beginning, but had been careful to keep to himself, namely, the farm buildings, the materials of which were far more marketable than anything about the house, which from a commercial point of view was getting a disproportionate amount of attention. He says:

I have taken the liberty in a former letter to acquaint your Ladyship that from the situation of Audley End Park, certain profits must arise. It's the great road for Welsh and Scotch Black Cattle, besides vast quantities of sheep to the feeding grounds of the County of Essex. An estate so enclosed and so situated is rarely to be met with, and therefore is certainly of greater value than any farm in the county.

From the outset there had never been any doubt about Lady Portsmouth's determination to have the place. There was only the question of price, and her ladyship's indebtedness to Colonel Vachell is clear enough. He must have saved her thousands of pounds, and this, there is every reason to believe, she acknowledged. Finally, on 9th September 1751, the price was agreed at £10,000, of which a little over half was for the 283 acres of parkland, £547 for timber, £444 for the mill, which, with 500 head of deer in the park, the presentation to the Mastership of Magdalene College, and other perquisites, left little more than £3,000 for the house and its outbuildings.

Audley End had now reached the lowest ebb of its fortunes. The place that cost £200,000 in 1616 was valued at little more than £3,000 in 1751, which shows how little can have been spent on maintenance. But the tide was about to turn. The original Audley End had been built largely to satisfy the ambition of one countess, the new Audley End was to achieve the ambition of another.

VIII

ELIZABETH, COUNTESS OF PORTSMOUTH

ONE OF THE difficulties in sorting out the Audley End families is that they change their names so frequently. We first meet the Countess of Portsmouth as Mrs. Grey, following on the death of her first husband, Henry Grey—or Neville—of Billingbear, Berkshire, who was also her cousin. Henry Grey's father, Richard Neville, had married the daughter of Lord Grey of Werke, at one time Governor of Barbados, and the son of the marriage had been required to take the grandfather's name. Henry and Elizabeth Grey had no children; but Grey had a nephew, the son of his sister Catherine, whose husband was an auditor of the exchequer named Richard Aldworth, and naturally this nephew was brought up expecting to inherit the Berkshire estates of the family at his uncle's death. But he and other interested parties had not reckoned with the widow, Aunt Elizabeth!

News of his uncle's death came to Richard Neville Aldworth [1] from that loyal friend of the family, John Sanderson, their solicitor, who in September 1740 [2] wrote: 'Your aunt immediately sent for me and the will, which was made in the year 1732. . . . I am sorry to tell you that you have no immediate provision made for you. The Lights [3] and his whole personal estate of every kind whatsoever is given absolutely to Mrs. Grey and she is made sole executrix.' The real estate was left in trust to Mrs. Grey for life, and after her death to Richard and his heirs, on condition they dropped the name of Aldworth and assumed the name of Neville. If Richard should die without issue the estate went next to John Griffin Whitwell, [4] his wife's nephew, on the same condition; and if both nephews died

---

[1] Father of the second Lord Braybrooke.   [2] E.R.O. D/DBy. C.1.
[3] The lighthouses at Orford, Suffolk, and Winterton, Norfolk. E.R.O. D/DBy. C.1.
[4] Afterwards first Lord Braybrooke.

without issue it went to William Vachell, who received an annuity of £100 under the will and repayment of £5,936 borrowed from him by Grey on two mortgages. John Sanderson got £20 a year by the will.

Mr. Sanderson felt keenly the unfairness of withholding the estate from Richard, and evidently believed the will had been made under pressure from the autocratic aunt. On 4th October 1740 he wrote: 'Tho' your uncle seldom spoke of you lately without tears in his eyes, yet he had not courage to add a codicil to it [the will] in your favour, tho' there was one ready in a friend's hand to have offered if he had shown the least inclination.' It is only fair, however, to say in the widow's favour that she had, as the will[1] itself stated, brought a considerable portion to her husband at marriage.

Grey had made Richard an allowance during his lifetime and had treated him in every respect as his heir. Now everything depended on the goodwill of Aunt Elizabeth, so Richard—or Dick, as we may call him—anxiously awaited her pleasure, while Mr. Sanderson and other friends stood by, watching his interests as carefully as prudence would allow, and missing no opportunity of speaking a word in his favour. On 9th October Mrs. Grey wrote the dutiful letter so eagerly awaited, and we can imagine Dick's trembling fingers as he opened it. It was a most touching epistle.

'Dear Dick,' she wrote,

this is the third time I have attempted to thank you for your very tender and affectionate letter, but my tears flowed so fast it was impossible to proceed, and though I know the same difficulty will attend me now, and ever must when I am obliged to touch on a subject that makes me the most unhappy of my sex, yet I am determined to be no longer silent, lest you should impute it to want of affection or regard for you, tho' I hope you know me too well to think that possible, for indeed, my dear, no person now living has a greater share of my affections than yourself, and I flatter myself our friendship will be reciprocated when time, I hope in God, will make us less unhappy than we are at present.

Here I am in this once dear and delightful place,[2] which now appears a desert to me, and all that used to contribute to my health and pleasure now aggravates my miseries; but I'll have done, and not add to your affliction by mentioning my own, which is as great as human nature can support.

[1] Berkshire Record Office. D/EN. F.21.
[2] Billingbear, Berkshire, always a dearly loved home to the Nevilles.

This is all very moving, of course; but Dick, who was twenty-three at the time and wishing to marry and settle down, received, from acquaintances of both, letters which show how others regarded the matter. They show also how interested these young men were in wills and entails and settlements and what-not at this time. Harry Bulkeley—afterwards Viscount Bulkeley—for example, wrote in unprintable terms from Lincoln's Inn about Grey's spinelessness, before launching out in the manner of a budding politician on 'the plan of our most glorious Revolution,' meaning, of course, the revolution of 1688 which put him and his class in control of the land and its government. A William Sturrock wrote more calmly:

When first I heard the news at Paris of your disappointment, it quite struck me, and I immediately concluded, either your uncle knew not your merit, or an artful woman hindered him in his last moments from reflecting on it. Dear Dick, this last is the case of many an honest man, who to avoid wrangling and debate at such a critical juncture, may be brought to do anything, even to the prejudice of those he loves best. You are in the right to caress her without showing the least resentment.

This last sentence hints at Dick's perfect diplomacy. In those days diplomacy was learnt not as a theoretical subject, but in the Mr. Squeers manner. Dick did, in fact, become a distinguished diplomat, and it may well be that he learnt his profession the hard way by his perfect self-possession in dealing with his formidable aunt. So successful was he in disguising his natural feelings that we find John Sanderson writing to him as jubilantly as legal etiquette would permit: 'So far as I am able to judge of Womankind, you are in high favour with your aunt. She read me part of your letter on Mrs. Neville's death, and about your uncle's debts, and I plainly saw by her eyes that she was well pleased with the compliment you paid her.'

The liveliest letters dealing with this melancholy episode came from Charles Churchill, who in 1746 married Horace Walpole's half-sister, Lady Mary Walpole. He was the son of Sir Robert's crony, General Churchill, by Mrs. Oldfield, the actress. At the time of his uncle's death Dick was living in the household of Francis Calandrini, First Syndic of the Republic of Geneva, whose daughter, Magdalen, he married, and Churchill writes gallantly:

Pray assure Mad[elle] Calandrini in a particular manner of the great esteem we have for her, and how much we are her very humble servants. Our compliments to all the knights of Arthur's round table. . . . Pray my compliments to Madame Jallabert and wish her joy from me of her son's coming so happily into the world. *Entre nous* he ought to be confounded ugly.

A few months later, following the announcement of the heart-broken lady's new marital adventure, upon which she embarked within a year of her first husband's death, Churchill rises unprintably to the dangled bait. But let us hear the news from Aunt Elizabeth herself. On 2nd June 1741 she writes to Dick:

And now, my dear Dick, as you have on all occasions my sincere affections and good wishes, I hope I shall have yours on an event on which all my future happiness depends. I told you in my last that if I changed my situation in life it should not be to your disadvantage or my own discredit, and I believe you will think I have kept my word when I tell you my next letter may probably be signed Lymington. The lord of that name [1] is here now, and desires me to assure you of his friendship, and that he will write to you very soon. I have a house full of company, so you will excuse me if I only add the assurance of my being unalterably your very affectionate aunt.

The faithful John Sanderson also wrote to Dick to tell him of the proposed marriage, referring to the bridegroom as having a 'universal good character,' and seeming to be 'an exceeding good-natured gentleman,' who might turn out to be a great help to them in guiding the mettlesome aunt. He slyly slips in the information that Lord Lymington had settled £1,500 a year on her ladyship for life, and she the same sum out of the Lights on himself for life, which meant that the survivor benefited by that sum. Charles Churchill's opinion of the matter is nobody's business now, but it is amusing to find him referring to Mrs. Grey as 'an old Bitch that I hope the Devil will damn to all Eternity.'

No doubt Mrs. Grey was genuinely fond of Dick, though she never doted on him as she did on her own nephew, John Griffin Whitwell, whom she made her heir. Nor can she have foreseen that belated justice would be done to the Nevilles by that nephew when he, also having no family, made the son of Dick Neville his own heir. The two nephews were devoted friends throughout their lives, and in spite of what he might have felt about his aunt, Dick brought up his own son to respect this great lady of the family, and even to love her. It is clear from correspondence that she always expected to be treated

[1] John Wallop, Viscount Lymington, created Earl of Portsmouth 1743.

as head of both the Aldworth-Neville and Whitwell-Griffin families, and to be kept informed of their progress. Thus we find her writing to Dick in April 1755:

I cannot omit returning dear Mr. Aldworth my thanks for the constant and particular account he was so good to give me of his dear little people in their late indisposition, on whose account, except yourself, I am sure nobody had more anxiety, nor more sincerely congratulates you on their recovery, than I do. Pray kiss the little things for me, but you must excuse me if I desire Dick may have two.

In 1817 the boy who was to have two kisses, by this time second Lord Braybrooke and a distinguished figure in the society of his day, endorsed this letter: "'Tis nearly sixty-two years since Lady Portsmouth's two letters were sent on my recovery from inoculation, then thought a great risk.' Inoculation was evidently the indisposition referred to.

Snippets from voluminous correspondence may give a wrong impression of any facts involved; but nothing can so well convey the general tenor of a period, or a social group, than browsing among old letters. And one never goes far in letters of the Jane Austen period without coming upon references to fortunes. Here, as I turn over this Neville correspondence, my eye catches such bits as (1772): 'Lord Hinchingbrooke is to be married to Lady Mary Poulett, the Duke of Bolton's daughter, with £36,000 down. If the Duke should not have a son she will be entitled to an estate of five or six thousand a year.' Such titbits as that would be found in practically every letter written by persons of quality at the time, communicated as fussily as similar titbits were by the ladies in *Cranford*, who, it will be remembered, used to run into Miss Matty's with the latest gossip. News of weddings and elopements might well be followed by such intimations as what the king thinks of such and such a preacher; how he likes Mademoiselle Heinel and which of the two, *Israel in Egypt* or *Jephtha*, pleases him the better; or such wicked remarks as: 'They say the Duchess of Cumberland is all gravity and dignity. She must be strangely altered from what I knew her formerly in her maiden state. I then had the honour to be of several parties at Vauxhall with her Royal Highness.'

It is among such company that we see Lady Portsmouth, an imperiously typical figure of her age—haughty, calculating, ambitious, and, though childless, planning to rebuild the home

of her ancestors.   But to the house itself: among papers found
there when the countess acquired it was a letter addressed from
Worksop Manor by James Scott, who had evidently been consulted by the tenth Earl of Suffolk as to what should be done
with the mansion.   It is dated 23rd February 1745 and informs
his lordship that the most ruinous part is the east range, the
part that contains the Long Gallery, which had been so much
admired by visitors, and so highly praised by a long succession
of writers.   The cost of restoring this range would be great,
and Mr. Scott says that 'upon the whole I imagine your Lordship will incline to the taking that part down.'   He adds: 'I
cannot find the least advantage in taking down the part which
contains the Hall, especially as it affords your Lordship the two
best rooms in your House, the large parlour and Fish room over
it, and wants but little repairs in comparison with the Gallery
part.' [1]

Mr. Scott advised the demolition of the entire range containing the Long Gallery, and, in order to give what remained
a finished appearance, that the fronts of the south and north
wings should be faced up with stone taken down, 'putting in
such real windows as your Lordship shall chuse to have in them,
and preserving some regularity with blank windows.   I would
take down those two Towers over the Staircases, hip back the
roofs of the wings, and continue round the ballustrade, which
will be a good finishing, and appear regular and handsome.'

Mr. Scott then considered the question that was to exercise
the minds of the countess and her nephew as well, that of
restoring communications in the mutilated building.   He says:

It follows next that there be an arcade or covered way across the
court from wing to wing, and that the communications be reconciled
quite round the court, for which there can only be two ways.   One
is the taking of a passage from the rooms quite through, and the
height of the storey, opening the spaces which now contain the
windows into arches, which will give a strong light into the rooms.
Or altering the windows into arches, placing the light to these rooms
in the circular part of the arches, and make a low covered way quite
round the court, by which means not one of the rooms will be
diminished in size.

He was of the opinion that the materials in the range to be
removed would practically pay for the alterations suggested.

The idea of taking down the Long Gallery had been turned

[1] Portsmouth letters in Lord Braybrooke's possession.

over in the mind of more than one earl. Colonel Vachell found an estimate which he thought might even date from a time earlier than that of the removal of the Great Court, that is to say, from the sixth earl's time. But most notes concerning this work belong to the tenth earl's time. Thus we find Cole, writing in 1744, saying:

The present Earl of Suffolk deeming Audley End much too big for his estate, I heard him say, while I was at his house this winter, that he had a design of making it much less, by pulling down either the Hall or the Gallery, but that he did not know which to take away, there being inconvenience in doing either, and it would be a pity to do it, for though the Gallery is the most incomparable room of the sort for length, breadth, and height, the Hall is equally grand, though not so big; so I hope my Lord will alter a resolution which everyone is concerned about.

Nothing was done about this by the Suffolks, so it was left for the Countess of Portsmouth to begin the work of demolition and restoration at Audley End, which her nephew completed after her death. In its early stages this was directed by Thomas Phillips, a London builder, who supervised the dismantling of the gallery immediately after purchase. There are a number of bills connected with the work still extant.[1] From them we learn that the removal of the whole wing cost the countess £363, and that 62 tons 28 lb. of its lead was sold to Edward Ives at £12 15s. 6d. per ton in April 1753. Other materials sold include: 401 feet of timber to Admiral Byng at Potton at 8d. per foot; 4½ tons of lead to Admiral Byng at Wrotham Park at 14s per foot, which amounted to £49. Mr. Flowers of Walden bought all the old panelling and the floor-boards from one room for four guineas, along with 87 feet of timber at 8d., 100 feet of paving at 3d., 396 yards of old wainscot at 6d., making a total of £14 1s. 0d.

These accounts make sad reading if we pause to reflect on the former splendour of the gallery that was being demolished, and the scenes it had witnessed, particularly while Charles II and his court were there, or while Pepys was examining its furnishings with the critical eye that was all too often diverted to ogle the ladies. Tales of the Long Gallery were told in Saffron Walden long after its removal, and may be to this day. The third Lord Braybrooke relates that a Mrs. Mapletoft, who died at a great age in 1803, used to tell her family how the schoolchildren of

[1] E.R.O. D/DBy. A.364.

her young days played there, and how if a pin was dropped at one end the sound could be heard at the other.

The pictures that Pepys saw in the Long Gallery had evidently been removed by the third earl, because we find them bequeathed in 1720 by Anne, his widow, to her niece, Lady Charlotte Montagu. The portrait of Henry VIII referred to in the *Diary* was among them, as also were portraits of James I and his queen, of Charles I and Charles II. In view of this bequest of the third earl's widow we may reasonably doubt whether the Long Gallery at Audley End was ever used by the family after the house was returned to the fifth earl by William III in 1701.

The Chapel would be in no better condition:

> Shorn of its glass of thousand colourings,
> Through which the deepened glories once could enter,
> Streaming from off the sun like seraph's wings,
> Now yawning desolate.

The nature of the work undertaken by Mr. Phillips on the Countess of Portsmouth's behalf in the early 1750s shows in more practical terms how dilapidated the property was. The roof was extensively repaired, new guttering and bearers fixed; beams were spliced and irons fixed to secure them; staircases required many new steps, and so forth. Plasterers' work done for the countess by William Wilton amounted to £223; glaziers' work to £190. The old quarry glass in what was then the best apartment—the one next the pond—was releaded, and, where necessary, squares of the 'best Ratcliff Crown glass' were fitted. Mr. Phillips was not to be envied in his task.

Having saved the house from demolition the countess's next object was to safeguard its future, and this, of course, she did by stimulating pride in the place in the mind of her heir, John Griffin Whitwell—who had changed his name to Griffin on succeeding to his uncle's estates in 1749—as doubtless she stimulated pride in her other home, Billingbear, in the mind of her late husband's nephew, Richard Neville Aldworth. Thus she had two spirited and accomplished young men waiting on her favours, to say nothing of her connections by the Portsmouth marriage, all of which must have been extremely gratifying to her. In describing George III's coronation we find Horace Walpole giving a vivid impression of the old lady towards the end of her life. 'My Lady Harrington,' he says,

covered with all the diamonds she could borrow, hire, or seize,

Elizabeth, Countess of Portsmouth, *c.* 1720, after C. Jervas

and with the air of Roxana, was the finest figure at a distance; she complained to George Selwyn that she was to walk with Lady Portsmouth, who would have a wig, and a stick—'Pho,' said he, 'you will only look as if you were being taken up by the constable.' She told this everywhere, thinking the reflection was on my lady Portsmouth.

Incidentally Lady Suffolk — Henrietta, the ninth earl's countess—was there, and as Horace had helped to dress her hair he was particularly interested in her appearance.

Finally, by her will dated 9th June 1759 and proved in 1762,[1] Lady Portsmouth cleared up the complications of her life and resolved more than one of its many discords. Nevertheless, the two nephews who came into estates by her passing continued to regard her with the utmost veneration. She had been the dominant figure in their lives.

The countess gone, her will became, as it were, the law and the prophets to the family. Let us learn how it affected Richard Neville Aldworth in his own words: [2]

Aug. 14th, 1762.

Dear Fan,

This Evening we open'd the Will with which I have no Reason to be dissatisfied, for she has left me the Goods and Furniture in & about Billingbear, except Plate, Linnen, *Books, & all the Pictures* which are not mark'd with the Name of Grey or Neville. However, tho' by this Means I lose almost all the Good & valuable Pictures & the Deer Cattle & Arrears of Rent of course go to her Sole Executor, Sr J. Griffin, yet in the great Point of all, she has show'd me, not only Justice, but Affection. If Sr John dies without *Sons* the Lights descend to me, & my Sons, then they go to Mat & his Sons, and then to Mary. The Essex Estate goes as it should do, to Mat, after Griffin, but that as well as the Lights, skips next to Mary, with an Annuity in that Case, of £300 to Elisabeth. You will observe Mad^{me} de Welderen is not mention'd, nor is she in the whole Will but to confirm the £200 a y^r settled on her upon her Marriage. What a fall is here? All her Expectations vanish'd into Smoke, for not a shilling does she get by the Will either in Possession, or Reversion. My Lord gets a Pearl Necklace, & the House in Town. Mrs. Whitwell £100 pr. An. Elis. £50. Mary £50. Young Savile £50. Besides these Annuities she has left three legacies. To Young Capt. Savile £1000. To Mary £5000 if she marries with the Consent of Ld P. & Sr J. G. & £50 to Mrs. Watts. She does not mention a Soul more that I remember either Friend, or Servant; tho' poor Mrs. Dunn certainly merited a Legacy. I must not omit a friendly noble Act of Griffin's. It seems she had bought a little Ground joining to Billingbear Park, which

---

[1] E.R.O. D/DBy. T.11/1.   [2] E.R.O. D/DBy. C.2/7.

H

she leaves in my Option to have upon paying Sr John 2$\overset{£}{1}$0. the purchase money.   Griffin instantly says her only Reason for not giving it me herself, was that He might, & insists on making Little Dick a present of it.   In short He is a fine honest Fellow, & I am glad since thro' old Grey's Folly I have been a sufferer, so good a Man is better'd by it.   She loved no Soul but him, & after him I seem to have been as well with her, as any one not excepting her own dear Lord.   Another Good from this is that I shall certainly get another Peep at you all before I leave England, which I do not think even this Contingency will prevent my doing very suddenly.   You therefore may expect me every Day, after tomorrow, when I must dine with the D. of B. & (?) Sec Palmer by Griffin's Appointment at Night.   God bless my Fan & Dick.   honest Ned & Miss Mainwaring.   & as for honest Fan she's not forgot in my Prayers I assure Her.

R N A alias
R N

Endorsed:

To Mrs. Goudet at Stanlake
near Twiford
Berks.

From
R N Aldworth.

A week later he wrote: [1]

Old Broadstreet, Aug. 21st, 1762.

My Dear Fan,

I always write to you with Pleasure, but particularly So, when I can tell you good news, to your Heart's Delight.   I am much better off at Bill. than I thought.   The Deer are mine, & the Rent from Lady Day, of all the Farms let upon Lease which I believe as well as hope, they all are.   This already makes an Addition of £600 but what will be your Joy & Miss Manwaring's when you know the Soap & Candles are mine too Tho' I did not know this, my good Lady did.   She is to be carried to Bill on Monday, & buried the next day at Waltham.   I have wrote to Watts to omit nothing that can Show my Respect towards her Memory, & I know he will obey me with Pleasure. What I have to add, is really an Acquisition; I have got the Reversion of my Jamaica Place for my Dear Boy, & long, long may he live to enjoy it.   The Inclosed is from Griffin to him, & I dare Say will make him happy.   Tell the Dear Fan, & him, with my best Love to them Both, I don't quite despair of having another Game at Romps with them, & honest Ned, before I leave England.   The D. of Marlborough marries Lady Caroline next Monday.   The D. of B. goes down with them to Woburn on Tuesday, & Stays there till the End of the Week. I may possibly therefore embrace you All again before I Set out, but

[1] E.R.O.   D/DBy.   C.2/8.

this I shall know by Tuesday Night, & of course you will know it on Wednesday. Y^rs Most Sincerely

RNA alias
RNN.

The generous spirit shown in these letters by Richard Neville Aldworth, now Richard Neville Neville, towards the countess's beloved John Griffin Whitwell, now John Griffin Griffin, was fully returned by the other. The two had become as brothers to each other, and if possible an even greater love, as we shall see presently, was to ripen between John Griffin Griffin and Richard Neville Neville's son, who eventually became the second Lord Braybrooke, and from whom all the subsequent Lords Braybrooke are descended. The details of the will need not concern us. The important points so far as Audley End goes are that the mansion and most of her property was left to John Griffin Griffin and his heirs, on condition that each and every one of them should take the name of Griffin, and that if the immediate heir should die without issue, it went to Richard Neville Neville, who in that event would be required to change his name to Griffin, a name to which he had no right whatever, because he had no descent from the Griffins—and for that matter he might reasonably have protested that Neville was the nobler name.

In framing her will,[1] the dominant principle in the countess's mind was that there should be as little division of her estates as possible. She was obliged to divide them between the two nephews, but she clearly hoped that they would eventually come into the hands of the heir of either the one or the other—as they did—and she made specific provision for that happening.

The last important bequest was the right to appoint the Master of Magdalene College, Cambridge, vested in the owner of Audley End, which she bequeathed to George Jennings of Newsells in the county of Hertfordshire, and William Harvey of Chigwell in the county of Essex, and their executors, administrators, or assigns for the space of ninety-nine years upon trust to present Barton Wallop upon the first vacancy, after which the presentation was to be vested, as hitherto, in the owners of Audley End.

Thus the old abbey at Audley End, which had known so many godly fathers and not-so-godly sons, found in Elizabeth, Countess of Portsmouth, a very strong-minded godmother.

[1] E.R.O. D/DBy. T.11/1.

IX

SIR JOHN GRIFFIN GRIFFIN

FOURTH LORD HOWARD DE WALDEN

WITH SIR JOHN Griffin Griffin, who became fourth Lord Howard de Walden and first Lord Braybrooke, we leave the ruined courts of the original palace and see the house squarely as it stands to-day. He held the estate inherited from his mother and aunt for thirty-five years, rebuilt the house, put the land into order, and left on the neighbourhood the ineffaceable impress of his character and influence. So what happened between 1762 and 1797 must be studied in detail. And it is worthy of such study, because again we have a representative figure at Audley End, though one who was in all respects different from the earls of Suffolk who had lived there. From first to last Sir John was a man of the highest integrity, who took himself and his life seriously, and seemed born to occupy an exalted position in the courtly society of his day. Though not, perhaps, a colourful character, he was, according to his lights—and to the lights of his generation—an entirely admirable one. There was no wayward shadow of genius about him. He was orthodox, conventional, punctilious, and therefore typical of the greater part of the ruling class of his age, the age that gave us such immense national prestige—and prestige, be it said, was very dear to Sir John's heart.

The Griffins were an old family. According to papers at Audley End [1] they appear first about 1200, when a Sir John Griffin of Gumley in Leicestershire and Weston in Northamptonshire married a Favell of Weston. Braybrooke, Northamptonshire, the most important seat of the family, came to them late in the fourteenth century by marriage with a Latimer, a descendant of the John de Latimer who acquired it by marrying the daughter of its Norman holder in 1232. At the death in 1569 of the

[1] E.R.O. D/DBy. Z.41.

last in direct succession, the property fell to a nephew, Edward Griffin of Dingley, solicitor-general to Henry VIII and attorney-general to Edward VI, Mary, and Elizabeth. From him was descended Sir John's great-grandfather, the Edward Griffin who married the third Earl of Suffolk's daughter, Lady Essex Howard.

The family was Royalist, and at the Restoration Edward Griffin was given the lucrative office of treasurer of the chambers, previously held by both his father and his maternal grandfather, Sir William Endelle. But in 1688 he incurred the nation's displeasure by attaching himself to James II, whom he accompanied into exile, and by whom he was created Baron Griffin of Braybrooke. The honour, however, was only to be enjoyed in exile, for when he returned to Britain it was to take part in the abortive attempt to invade Scotland, where he was taken prisoner, tried, and sentenced to death. And though the sentence was never executed he remained a prisoner until he died in the Tower in 1710.

Inevitably the first Lord Griffin's Jacobite sympathies kept the family in obscurity for some years. But the Countess of Portsmouth's pride being what it was we might have assumed that by her time this unfortunate episode was forgotten. Yet it cannot have been, for when Sir John came into the property he knew surprisingly little about his family, and asked his mother, old Mrs. Whitwell, to write down all she could remember. She, a loyal subject of King George and withal a Protestant, seems to have been sensitive about her grandfather's misdeeds, as she thought them, for she describes her record as a 'melancholy account,' and offers it not to stimulate family pride in her son, but as a warning. Nevertheless, she assures him, 'Your pedigree will show you that you are a Gentleman of Ancient Descent, that your ancestors have been often well matched.' Even so, she adds, if he is wise he will rely for success in life on his own endeavours, and not count too much on his pedigree.

According to Mrs. Whitwell's account Braybrooke Castle had been sold by her grandfather in Cromwell's time to pay his composition. But this, she says, was only a temporary set back, for at the Restoration 'all was Prosperity and sunshine, a good estate, a good place, & my Grandfather in a retired way of living (for such incomes) must soon retrieve.'

She then relates how her father, the second Lord Griffin, who married a daughter of Judge Rainsford,[1] applied himself to court, and being 'a handsome, accomplished young man' was well received there.   In addition he had from his father an income of £500 a year, on which he lived 'gentilely,' not being one of the king's more extravagant cronies.   And so life continued for him until the 1688 revolution compelled him to go into retirement and live quietly on his exiled father's estate at Dingley.   His son, the third Lord Griffin, Mrs. Whitwell's brother, was by no means a credit to the family.   Macky, in his *Characters*, describes the first Lord Griffin as 'a great sportsman and brave; a good companion.'   In a copy of the book in the British Museum there is a marginal note by Dean Swift informing us that 'His son was a plain drunken fellow.'   But by son, no doubt, the dean means grandson, for that seems to be a fair enough description of the third lord, whose weakness for the bottle resulted in most of the family property falling into the hands of an astute attorney named Thomas Peach.   Mrs. Whitwell apparently refers to her brother's excesses in a charming letter [2] in which she says:

Fearing I should be prevented writeing next post, and not daring to trust to the Merchant (whose multiplicity of busines might probably be an excuse) I think it convenient to let you know that on Sunday my Lord left us,[3] after having been pretty well warmed on Saturday night at my neighbour Mr. Hunt's.   I can't omit telling you that he raised half the town when he came home with hollowing &c.   Mr. Whitwell, knowing him well, thought proper to run before him, & gott into bed before his Lordship could call for more drink.   How he contrived to be so forward I can't guess, for Mr. Whitwell was perfectly sober.   I own I was in pain for my own and neighbours' windows, a set of merry people, with his Honour their commander, having lately broke most of the windows between Mr. Peach's and Doctor Farrel's, not excepting the latter.   Everybody must acknowledge the justice sets good examples.

How the Countess of Portsmouth must have resented her brother's behaviour!   Not, perhaps, because the justice, as Mrs. Whitwell put it, set such a 'good' example, or broke Lawyer Peach's windows after a drunken orgy, but because he allowed the lawyer to get hold of so many of his title-deeds.   In short, she would resent her brother's failure to preserve intact the family fortune much more than his failure to preserve the family

[1] There is a portrait of Sir Richard Rainsford in the dining-room at Audley End.
[2] E.R.O.   D/DBy.   F.30.   [3] She writes from Oundle.

dignity.   No one took the squire's drunken bouts very seriously
in the middle of the eighteenth century.   We can imagine,
therefore, how she would impress upon her nephew and heir
that it was his duty to restore the family, whose name she was
so determined he should bear, to something of its former
affluence and glory.   That being so, we may well ask what was
the state of affairs in the principal home of the Griffins at this
time.   We have seen how ambitious the countess was to restore
Audley End; what of Dingley?   Of the inside, anyhow, we get
a vivid impression from a letter written after the death of the
third Lord Griffin in 1742.
   'After a long search,' says the writer,

I at last found the Portrait of James Earl of Suffolk thrown with
most of the Family Pictures into the Lumber Room, but dressed in
the same manner you describe, in armour, with a General's Truncheon
in his hand.   What family pictures are in the house are as follows:
   In the Bed Chamber below stairs is the picture of Lady Essex
Howard.   In the Drawing Room, a head of James, father of the late
Ld Griffin, another of Judge Raynsford.   In the Parlour are your
grandmother, daughter of Sir Richard Raynsford, and one of Miss
May.   In the Lumber Room, a prey to spiders and all manner of
filth, is a picture of the first Ld Griffin in his Robes, and another of
him done in his younger years, in a Roman shape.   One stands upon
a Casque, & the other on a Seymeter.   In the same place are the
portraits in full length of two ladies, which us'd to hang at the west
end of the Great Hall, the one has a China Jarr, the other a Bead
Necklace in her hand, but no labels to distinguish their names.   A
full length of the present [late?] Lord Griffin.   The late Ld Griffin
deliver'd into my Hands, not long before his death some very curious
miniature pictures in crayons, one of Bishop Latimer, King Charles
the First, and Second, the rest family pieces.   These I sent to Town,
and had them fram'd & gilt, & glassed in a very elegant taste; but
Mr. Peach taking the advantage of my absence, being at Norwich for
Orders, got possession of the House, seiz'd all Ld Griffin's effects, my
own Cabinet, in which were these valuable Pictures.   If I can by any
means recover them, they shall be at your service; but I believe that
will never be in his life time.

   But the affairs of the family were soon on a different footing
when Sir John, at the age of thirty, became head of the family,
married, and by Act of Parliament changed his name from
Whitwell to Griffin.   His bride was Anne Mary Schutz, a grand-
daughter of the great Baron von Schutz who came to England
with George I, and would undoubtedly have been one of the

first to receive an English peerage if such honours had not been barred by the Act of Settlement. The baron had two sons. Augustus, the elder, was equerry to George II when prince, and afterwards master of the robes and privy purse. Prince William of Orange is said to have been in love with his daughter—who married Baron Grovestein—while she was maid of honour to his wife, the Princess Royal, eldest daughter of George II. Sir John's bride was the daughter of the baron's second son, Colonel John Schutz. It was thus a marriage of considerable influence, and must have given great satisfaction to the Countess of Portsmouth, who doubtless arranged it.

Although at the time of Sir John's marriage the Countess of Portsmouth was still in her prime it was then that she made him her heir, and by the marriage settlement [1] secured to him and his descendants the whole of her share in the Audley End estate, subject, of course, to the £1,600 a year chargeable for the benefit of the Dowager Countess of Suffolk. The bride's portion was £8,000, which was not, perhaps, as much as Sir John, with his considerable prospects, might have commanded; but the political and social value of the marriage would be carefully assessed by the family lawyers on both sides. At all events, the countess's hand is very prominent in the settlement, and she would be a hard bargainer. That Sir John was her grateful and loving nephew is shown in everything he says of her both then and afterwards, and not least in the last note of all, written thirteen years later in recording her death on 13th August 1762. 'I have just suffered,' it runs, 'the loss of the best Friend Man was ever blessed with, by the Death of Lady Portsmouth.'

First and last Sir John was always the soldier. He could have followed no other career with comparable success. Nor would he have been likely to choose another. He was vigorous and forthright, a man of action; above all he was a man of his own day and generation, and, as we see reflected over and over again in the literature of the age, war to the eighteenth century was not only heroic, it was progressive. To be a soldier was to be a man of enterprise as well as a man of spirit. So inevitably we find Sir John adopting a military career and distinguishing himself at every step.

In 1744 he obtained a commission in the 3rd Regiment of Foot Guards, and served in Flanders under the Duke of Cumberland until the peace of 1748. In 1747 he was made captain.

---

[1] E.R.O. D/DBy. T.10/1. 1748.

In 1756, at the beginning of the Seven Years War, he was aide-de-camp to the king, and served as such in the early campaigns of that war.   In 1758 he became major, and the following year colonel of the 50th Regiment of Foot.   Two years later he was appointed major-general to all forces, horse and foot, and in the same year colonel of the 33rd Regiment of Foot. Everything continued to go well with him in his various campaigns until, while serving at the battle of Campen under the Hereditary Prince of Brunswick, he received a gunshot wound above the knee and was disabled for several months.   As a result of this injury he was obliged to receive his commission as lieutenant-general in 1761 by proxy.

Sir John was made a Knight of the Bath shortly before George III's coronation in 1760, and the summons which he received from Lord Effingham, as earl marshal, to attend for that ceremony at the Court of Requests in the Palace of Westminster on Tuesday, 22nd September, by eight o'clock, in the full habit of the Order, has been preserved.[1]   What makes it especially interesting is that on the back Sir John has written a memorandum, which besides being valuable for its own sake shows how popular and respected he was already among the knights he had joined so recently.   Here it is:

The Knights of the Bath walk'd immediately before the Privy Counsellors in the Procession.   They claim'd a Right of Table to dine in the Hall, & the Right was allow'd by the Lord Steward (Lord Talbot) but there not being Room for as many People of different Professions & Dignities to dine in the Hall, as the Lord Steward wish'd for, the Knights of the Bath consented to dine above Stairs with the Lord Steward at his own table with the Officers of State, who attended his Majesty at his Dinner; but to keep up their Privilege of table & Precedency over the Judges, the two youngest Knights of the Bath there present, did dine at the table in the Hall & were at table placed by the principal Herald between the Privy Counsellors & the Judges.   I took this Memorandum at the time & at the Request of some of the oldest of the Knights of the Bath.   J. G. Griffin.

When peace returned in 1763, and he had celebrated the victory of British arms by erecting in his grounds at Audley End a Grecian temple after a design by Robert Adam, Sir John turned his mind to politics, and a letter from Pitt,[2] addressed from Hayes on 28th October 1763, shows that he already commanded respect in that quarter.

[1] E.R.O.   D/DBy.   C.8/23.   [2] E.R.O.   D/DBy.   C.8/30.

'Dear Sir,' writes Pitt, now Earl of Chatham,

I receiv'd this day the honour of your very obliging letter of the
27th from Audley End, and am extremely flattered with the wishes
you are so good as to express of having some conversation together
before the meeting of Parliament.   As you mention that next week
wou'd be a convenient time for you, I will take the liberty to propose
Tuesday morning next at Eleven, in Jermyn Street.   I wou'd not have
ventured to name so near a Day, if you had not encouraged me to do
so by saying that notice the day before wou'd be sufficient.   Shou'd
this happen to be inconvenient to you, I beg you will name any time,
and I will, with great pleasure, come to Town to have the honour of
meeting you.   I am with sincerest esteem and consideration &c.
    Lady Chatham and my Sister join in all compliments to you and
Lady Griffin, to whom my respects.

But we must not imagine that Sir John was receiving these
respectful compliments for his own sake only.   He was then
sitting in Parliament as member for Andover, a seat he held
by the interest of his uncle, the Earl of Portsmouth, who had
immense territorial influence in the West of England.   Indeed
Sir Lewis Namier, in *The Structure of Politics at the Accession of
George III*, mentions this very case in discussing the political
influence of the large landowners at this time.[1]   So Chatham,
no doubt, had Portsmouth in mind when he made his bow to
Griffin.
    The first Lady Griffin died in 1764, but—as was not unusual
in that age—her place was quickly taken by another.   So we
have a letter from Chatham dated 21st April 1765, congratulating
Sir John on his engagement to be married to Katherine, daughter
of William Clayton of Harleyford, Buckinghamshire, whom he
married on 11th June.   Of his first marriage we know little;
but of the happiness that his second wife brought him there is
everywhere at Audley End the most charming evidence.   Both
marriages were childless, but apart from that one disappointment both Sir John and his lady continued to pay loving tribute
to each other throughout their thirty years together.   The
second Lady Griffin must have been in all respects a most
gracious lady, and after the hectic and irresponsible life of the
Suffolks at Audley End it is with joy indeed that we reflect on
the house, not only restored to something of its former
magnificence but the scene of so much happiness.

[1] Footnote, pp. 130–1.

And now Sir John formed an ambition to complete the restitution of his family by calling from abeyance the Howard de Walden title, last held by his great-grandfather, James, third Earl of Suffolk. It was a perfectly normal ambition for a man of his wealth and attainments. There must have been as many gentlemen of substance aspiring to baronies under the second and third Georges as there had been aspiring to baronetcies under the first James, and perhaps almost as many who obtained them. 'Who is there now,' wrote Egerton Brydges,[1] 'that has not seen his neighbour, originally his equal or his inferior, dressed up in robes of ermine, and converted into an hereditary senator?'

Since 1762 Sir John might be thought to have had a triple claim. He had family, he had estate, and he had a house that had always been held by a peer. So in the August of 1766 we find him writing to Chatham:[2]

My Lord,
    The Friendship your Lordship has so often and so kindly expressed for me, at the same time that it induces me to flatter myself you'll pardon the trouble I am giving you, it encourages me also to hope your Lordship will continue to me your Protection in promoting my request.
    My situation, my Lord, both as to Family and Circumstances is sufficiently known to you, and I am ready to persuade myself your Lordship will not blame, nor think my ambition ill plac'd if with the Fortune that is deriv'd to me from my ancestors I should earnestly wish to share some of their Honours.
    That I am sensible that any success I may meet with must flow entirely from your Lordship's goodness to me, yet it becomes me to say a word or two in Favour of my Request, that it may not appear very unjustifiable, either to the king or to your Lordship.
    I have had a Peerage, my Lord, so very near me, as that it died with my own uncle, the late Lord Griffin. I have besides an undoubted joint claim with Lord Bristol to the Barony of Walden, as your Lordship may see by the enclosed paper I trouble you with: added to this I am possessed of a family Place and Estate by lineal Descent, that from the Dissolution of the Monasteries to my Time, has ever had a Peer for their Owner.
    Although the ancient Barony of Walden would on many Accounts be far more eligible to me than a new Creation, yet as I have some Reason to believe Lord Bristol would not willingly depart from his

[1] *Reflections on the late Augmentations to the English Peerage, 1798.*
[2] E.R.O. D/DBy. C.8/72.

claim, so I should think myself extremely happy, and highly honoured by y^r Letter.

Presuming on your Lordship's partial Friendship for me I have thus ventured to trespass upon your Patience, and lay my Wishes at your Feet. . . .

Lady Portsmouth intended preferring this Petition to the late King about eleven years since; but the Attorney General of that time giving it as his opinion 'that the king's reviving it in Lady Portsmouth would carry it to the heirs of her body only,' and would not carry it to my mother and her heirs preferable to the other coheir, made her decline taking any further steps in the affair.

Chatham, whose letters to Sir John were always fulsome in general terms but extremely guarded in particular, replied [1] that he was not yet sufficiently acquainted with His Majesty's intentions concerning the making of peers to make any promises at present. There had been many applications, he said, and he had reason to believe that the king would not easily be moved. He would, however, keep his friend's wish in mind, and take advantage of any occasion that arose for putting it forward, but at the moment he could not advise pressing the claim. The words were evasive. Others were advanced while Sir John, with better claims than most of them, was left to cool his heels in the Commons for a further eighteen years.

It is possible that a new creation would have been simpler; but undoubtedly Sir John had set his heart on the Howard de Walden title, and undoubtedly Lord Bristol, in whose heirs it now continues, refused to withdraw his own claim. Obviously it was a more suitable title than any other he might have chosen. Elizabeth had been notoriously mean with her new creations, and only four of her peerages had been by writ. They were those of Cheyney, Compton, Norreys, and Howard. The baronies of Hunsdon, St. John, Buckhurst, and Burghley had been by patent. Of the four by writ, that of Cheyney was extinct, while Compton was in the Earl of Leicester, and Norreys in the Earl of Abingdon. Sir John's claim to the Howard de Walden title was therefore of more than common interest, and he continued to make his ambition known until, in May 1784, the grant was made. In his final and successful petition to the king for its revival, he wrote: [2]

Your Majesty's petitioner most humbly entreats your permission to offer some few observations for your Royal consideration that he

[1] E.R.O. D/DBy. C.8/74.   [2] E.R.O. D/DBy. L.2.

trusts may in some measure induce your Majesty not to think the less favourably of his case.

That he is of a very ancient and respectable family seated in Northamptonshire several centuries past.

That in the 5th of Henry VI one of his Ancestors, from whom he is lineally descended, was found to be the next heir-general of the whole-blood to Thomas Lord La-Warre, but that the said King Henry VI did confer the said Barony (on account of the entail of the estate) on Reginald West of the half-blood, in preference to your petitioner's ancestor, John Griffin, who was heir of the whole-blood; which is quoted on different occasions by the best authorities and in Collins's collection of arguments on claims of Baronies by Writ.

That your petitioner is the immediate representative and heir-general of the Griffin family.

That he is from the Alliance on which he founds his claim descended lineally from Thomas Duke of Norfolk. . . .

Lastly that the Griffin peerage, Baron of Braybrooke in Northamptonshire, came so near to your petitioner as to expire in his own uncle.

In short, he made his humble submission to the king not to set out his claims to the barony in question, which experts would put, but to show of his family that:

Their race was not of yesterday, or lately brought to passe,
Of old it was, and know they shall whence its beginninge was.

On being granted succession to the Howard de Walden barony [1] Sir John received what he described as 'a very handsome and obliging letter from the Corporation of Andover,' the seat he had held as a Whig by the Earl of Portsmouth's interest for so many years, and to which he had recently been re-elected for the sixth time. But though he had sat so long as a Whig it is to be noted that in the Lords he usually voted with the Tories.

Meanwhile he had been steadily scaling the military ladder. In March 1766 he had been appointed to the command of the first troop of the Grenadier Guards, which, incidentally, were then mounted, in conformity with the current practice of arming one troop out of every cavalry regiment. In April 1788 he was appointed colonel of the 4th Dragoons. Finally, at the age of seventy-eight, he became field marshal.

[1] E.R.O. D/DBy. L.2 and 3.

But perhaps the appointment that pleased him most was that to the lord lieutenancy of Essex, which, like the peerage, came in 1784. With that he must have felt that he had at last taken his place with the most illustrious of his ancestors, as indeed he had in popular esteem, for at this time he enjoyed, both as man and landowner, the respect of tenants and neighbouring gentry to a degree unequalled by either former or later owners of Audley End, and with good reason. The Lords Braybrooke of the Neville family have had, as they have merited, the respect of the county in full measure; but it was Lord Howard who pulled the society of the region together after its loss of cohesion under the Suffolks, and who thus became the dominant figure in the reconstituted estate and great house. The builder of the first Audley End had been more ambitious, and for a short time more powerful; but he had never been able to consolidate, with the result that at the end of his life he could not sit back as Lord Howard could, to reflect with complete satisfaction and composure of mind on what he had done, both for his tenants and for himself.

But what, we may ask, of his more intimate personal life? Of this we know little. He was too busy a man to have much leisure for the cultivation of the refinements of social life. In public and private he was always the outspoken soldier, valued for his integrity and simple goodness. The gentler lights that play about his portrait are from the affection of his family, his wife, his mother, and his sisters. Of his mother, a serene, homely figure, he spoke always with gentle affection, while of Mrs. Whitwell's joy in her family—joy that not one of her nine children was to know—there are many tender expressions in her letters, particularly in two that came to Sir John at her death in 1769. Her will, so different from her sister's, is chiefly concerned with personal things. It is couched in the simplest terms, but, she says, 'as I am so happily convinced of the perfect unanimity that subsists between my dear children, I'm persuaded that no disputes will arise between them from any incorrectness that may appear in this sheet.' She desires that her wearing apparel may be given to her maids, mentioning by name Peggy Tindalle; but her laces are not to be given away, and the maids are not to have new gowns. 'Some little remembrance' is to be given to Mrs. Webber, 'as I've desired her assistance to my maids.' And so she runs on, closing with an expression of her gratitude for the affection of her family, and her happiness in their love for each other. In her last note to Sir John [1] we can almost hear her voice:

My dear Son,

As in my Will, my Funerall is left to your discretion. I must request that it may be done in the most private manner, and that Mr. Chipchase in this street may serve it. I desire the little bell only may ring, and that only for a few minutes. I should not dislike being laid in St. George's burying ground and to be deposited as early as possible in the morning of the fourth day after my decease. If this seems absurd to you, my request will be your justification. I make no doubt of your flying up (if you are not in Town) to poor Betty's assistance.

I can't sign this without telling you once again how happy you have always made me, by the most dutyful, tender, and generous behaviour to your affectionate mother, Anne Whitwell.'

Mrs. Whitwell was not a clever woman with her pen, so it has seemed desirable to modify her spelling and punctuation in this last note. Here, while we are glancing at this bundle of faded letters, is one from Sir John himself, not yet Lord Howard de Walden, which is so characteristic of the man that it must be given in full.[2] It is addressed to his dear friend, Richard Neville Neville, the Dick Neville (Aldworth) who was kept waiting so long for his uncle's estate, and whose son was to succeed Sir John at Audley End as second Lord Braybrooke.

Audley End. Jan: 17. 1773.

Indeed, my dear Friend, if Lady Griffin did not keep up a pretty constant Correspondence with my Cousin Fanchen, I should have blush'd to have told you I am now going to thank you for y'r kind Letter of ye 18 of last September—which, however, had I attended Parliament, I should not have thus delay'd writing to you—tho' you have a much better Scribe in Jemmy Hayes on Parliamentary Business than you could have in Me. Instead of that Wrangling House, we have laugh'd & danc'd away the Time very chearfully on our own, with several kind Friends, & I assure you often wish'd you among us: We often drink your Health & am glad to find you are so much the better for it. . . . I think you have indeed made a much wiser Choice in returning this Winter, where you so happily experienc'd your Health ye last, than in having taken the Naples Track—from where I have had ye Pleasure of hearing twice from my Friend Dick,[3] who seems very happy—& is I suppose by this Time at Rome. He'll tell

[1] E.R.O. D/DBy. T.11/1.   [2] E.R.O. D/DBy. C.3/28.
[3] Richard Aldworth Neville, afterwards second Lord Braybrooke.

you perhaps I am not quite so idle as you may think me. . . . You are very kind in ye Concern you express for us on ye Loss of ye sweet little Girl that both my Wife & Self had really a fix'd Affection for. She indeed suffer'd more than I did. Our Friend ye Col: still lives, tho' with every Mark of Infirmity & old Age; in Truth its melancholy to see old Friends in so helpless & deplorable a State: not so with an old Tenant of mine, above 80 years of Age, who was seiz'd last Month in very severe Weather towards Night, as he was returning home from Market, with a Diziness in his Head which oblig'd him to dismount & lay an hour or more on ye wet & cold Ground 'till Relief came towards him. He was taken up in a Cart & carried home—was for many Days to Appearance in a dying State: he rallied however surprisingly & is again as well as he has been for many years. This is ye Man too that you have heard me speak of, who has had five Wives. By his last, whom he married at about 70 years of Age (himself I mean) he has Three or Four very fine & healthy Children: Neither of ye four first ever brought him Any—& now, lest you sh'd hear it unfavorably from other hands, I am to inform you I have had a very Providential Escape from a bad Fall I had almost Three Weeks since in hunting. My Groom's attention & Resolution was I really believe of infinite Consequence. The shock I receiv'd from ye Fall made it necessary in ye opinion of those that were by, that I should be blooded. He undertook it without ever having blooded a human Being before, & did it well & effectively & I hope I am now so well that I shall feel no future ill Consequence from it.

I have only Room left to say that Lady Griffin, with her sincere Comp^ts to you all, will very soon answer y^r D^rs' Letter. We take it for granted you have heard Lady Cornwall has a D^r—but you may not know perhaps (which however is ye Case) that her Estate is thereby equally secure to S^r: George's Family as if it had been a Son —Adieu, Yrs. J. G. G.

There was nothing of the Chesterfield or Walpole about Sir John as a correspondent. He did not practise letter writing as an art. But his letters clearly reflect the healthy, manly life he lived, the steadfastness of his character, and the forthrightness of his relations with others. His world was made up of soldiers and sportsmen, of politicians and country parsons, and equally of gamekeepers and land stewards. As for the ladies, they were his wife, his sisters, and the wives of his friends. There might be a haughty countess or two as acquaintances in the background, a bishop's lady, and the wives of neighbouring squires. Doubtless he knew the wives of all his tenant farmers, and gave them a nod and a smile when they dropped him their curtsies. There were no Molly Lepels (Lady Hervey), and

Sir John Griffin Griffin, Fourth Lord Howard de Walden,
First Lord Braybrooke, 1719–97

certainly none of the brilliant ladies who could hold a *salon* entranced with their conversation, as so many of this particular generation were able to do.   He was essentially a simple, kindly, home-loving man; but a man of great force of character, whose two lifelong passions, springing from pride of race in him, were for reclaiming the lost dignities and estates of his ancestors, and for rebuilding the ancestral home.

X

THE REBUILDING

SO LONG AS the sovereign remained the source of all political and social power it was inevitable that with the advent of a new reigning house every ambitious nobleman should present himself, his family, and his fortune in the light most favourable to himself and most flattering to the king. And there could be no better way of doing this than by encasing himself in a magnificent dwelling, furnished with the most luxurious appointments he could afford. When this happened with the Stuarts the original Audley End was built. When the first George arrived the Howards were impoverished. But Sir John lost no time in catching up with his contemporaries under the third George. And in doing so he had the benefit of their examples. Under the Georges, as Miss Gladys Scott Thomson has shown in her books on the Russells, the three Whig dukes, Devonshire, Portland, and Bedford, rebuilt their houses and entered upon their period of greatest power. But they had advantages not enjoyed by Sir John. The wealth of landowners generally was accumulating steadily at this time by the sale of leases, as land advanced in value to keep pace with the nation's mounting prosperity. The wealth of the Whig dukes, and of others with them, came chiefly from their ownership of property and commercial interests in the new industrial towns, and more particularly in London itself. Sir John had none of this. There was no mineral wealth at Audley End. But he was nevertheless a rich man, and well able to compete with many of nobler rank and larger estate than his.

But if political considerations were paramount in this widespread desire for display, there was also a universal desire for brighter, healthier, and sweeter dwellings than any that had satisfied the less elegant seventeenth century. We have seen that by the time Sir John reached Essex the eighteenth century was half spent. By then the movement that found its most ambitious expression through the genius of Vanbrugh had become subdued. Though the wealth of the nation was increasing, it was already being more widely distributed, and the mode of life of the aristocracy had been modified accordingly. There were smaller retinues of servants than formerly. The plans of houses had been improved and at the same time simplified. Awkward steps leading in and out of rooms, low ceilings, unlighted staircases, and windows that let in neither light to show up the cobwebs nor air to dispatch them, had given way to lofty rooms ordered in storeys, each with an accepted use, and with large sash windows to bring the joy of daylight indoors. And this newly discovered indoor light was so much appreciated that ways were sought of increasing it. For this purpose white plastered ceilings became general. They reduced the dust and deadened the noises from the floor-boards above. And as delight in good plasterwork increased, it developed a delicacy of treatment in keeping with the elegance of the age.

These two—a pardonable wish to attract notice and a natural desire for comfort and convenience—would be in Sir John's mind when he embarked upon the rebuilding of Audley End in 1763. But an even stronger motive was the family pride that determined so much of his thought and action. The work extended over the rest of his life, but it was concentrated in two waves, and we have his own word for it that he spent altogether £100,000 in laying out the park and converting the rambling old palace of the Suffolks into what was substantially the house as we see it to-day. Even if this rebuilding of the home of his ancestors had not been a passion with him he would still have had much of it to do. If Suffolk neglect had not made this essential, the Countess of Portsmouth's eagerness had. What she had begun would have had to be rounded off in some way, and she had not been particularly wise in her work. The third Lord Braybrooke says [1] Sir John had 'ample cause to regret the precipitation with which his aunt had acted.'

As to the manner of the rebuilding, it was clearly Sir John's ambition to do this in the spirit of Pope's *Epistle to Lord Burlington*:

> To build, to plant, whatever you intend,
> To rear the Column, or the Arch to bend,
> To swell the Terrace, or to sink the Grot;
> In all, let Nature never be forgot. . . .
> He gains all points, who pleasingly confounds,
> Surprises, varies, and conceals the Bounds.

[1] Braybrooke, p. 94.

Consult the genius of the Place in all;
That tells the Waters or to rise, or fall;
Or helps th' ambitious Hill the heav'ns to scale,
Or scoops in circling theatres the Vale;
Calls in the Country, catches op'ning glades,
Joins willing woods, and varies shades from shades;
Now breaks, or now directs, th' intending Lines;
Paints as you plant, and, as you work, designs.

His impulse was not artistic.   There is no evidence of his being affected by any of the movements of the age, and he had nothing of the dilettante about him.   Though a kinsman of the Herveys he was of a different turn.   Consequently there is nothing unique about the work of Sir John at Audley End.   It is not, shall we say, one of the houses that no student of architecture can afford to miss.   The outstanding characteristic of both the rebuilding by Sir John and of the restoration by the third Lord Braybrooke in the next century was their concern to keep the new in harmony with the old.   Even experts have difficulty in dating the structural work.   So although it was restored at the the time when the wealthy Whigs of the eighteenth century were employing the prolific artists and architects of the age to build for them, there is little in the building—which is not to say in the decoration—that can be traced to individual hands.

It was, perhaps, fortunate that when Sir John began to rebuild in 1763 the Palladian movement had run its course, though we may doubt whether it could ever have appealed to him.   In its more ambitious flights it would probably appear to him pretentious and un-English.   On the other hand, we may feel that he would admire William Kent's work.   Though there is nothing in his letters to show that he was interested in architecture as such, there is much to show that he liked to see his property in good order.   As we should expect from such a man, he was always methodical, and we can imagine him examining accounts and estimates carefully before making decisions.   But above all he would want an Englishman's home in an English setting, and the fine sweep of a 'Capability' Brown landscape would be much to his taste as a sportsman and a man of the open air.   Hitherto the gardens at Audley End had been formal.   They had been designed, like the old monastic gardens, as places for retirement—outdoor extensions of the house, with avenues along which the lord and his lady could saunter unseen from bowling green to cherry garden, and from trim parterre to green arbour furnished with statues and seats placed as carefully as were the tables and chairs indoors. As early as 1712 Joseph Addison had written in praise of naturalistic gardening in the *Spectator*; but it was William Kent who, in Horace Walpole's words, 'leaped the fence, and saw that all Nature was a garden.'

Sir John was not the man to desire seclusion. His statues were not set up behind yew hedges; they were on hill tops. And whichever way we look to-day we see something personal to him, showing how delighted he was by the new lay-out. In 1763, the first of 'Capability' Brown's three years of planning at Audley End, he built, as we have seen, the circular temple west of the house, to commemorate the victorious ending of the Seven Years War. Over the Cam, broadened and deepened, is the three-arched bridge designed, like the temple, by Robert Adam and completed in 1764. To the north is the obelisk erected in 1774 in memory of the Countess of Portsmouth. The entrance gateway with the Howard crest was restored in 1786. And if we go northward towards the site of the abbey mill we cross what was once Sir John's Elysian Garden, traces of which remain. Here also is the Palladian bridge and tea-house built by him in 1783. Finally, in 1792, on an eminence to the east of the house he built a Temple of Concord—twenty Corinthian columns supporting a panelled ceiling and friezes with figures in low relief—to commemorate George III's recovery from his 1789 illness. And it was near this that Lady Howard, before leaving the beloved home after her husband's death, added a last memorial in the shape of an urn to commemorate Lord Howard himself. On the pedestal supporting the urn were inscribed these lines, selected and perhaps partly composed by the Bishop of London:[1]

> O thou most loved, most honoured, most revered,
>   Accept this tribute to thy memory due;
> Nor blame me, if, by each fond tie endeared,
>   I bring once more thy virtues into view.
>
> These lovely scenes thy memory shall restore;
>   For thee the silent tear be duly shed;
> Beloved through life, till life could charm no more,
>   And mourned till recollection's power be dead.

But his biggest job was with the house itself. Accounts of

[1] The second stanza is from the Dirge in *Cymbeline*, by Collins.

work carried out for him by bricklayers, masons, statuary
workers, slaters, carpenters, joiners, plasterers, and every other
kind of craftsman almost have been preserved. They are most
precise in their detail.[1] Work was begun in May 1763, and for
June we have payments for deals, etc., for scaffolding. From
June 1763 to 31st December 1764 over £200 was spent for
items including stone from Eversden quarry, cleft stone, Ketton
and Burwell stone, ashlar and clunch, as well as on four loads
of pantiles from Holland, presumably for farm buildings. The
stone came by water to Cambridge, and was brought from there
in estate wagons. The bricks were made on the estate—a
hundred and ninety thousand between June and November 1763,
and between forty and fifty thousand a month during July,
August, and September.[2] Of payments to men engaged in the
work we begin with £259 for brickmaking in May 1763; £196
to Mr. Johnson the smith between May 1763 and the end of
1764. During the same period £150 was paid to Mr. Jackson
the carpenter, £196 to Mr. Ward the bricklayer, in addition to
£127 for bricklayers' measured work. More than £1,300 went
for masons' work, £86 to Mrs. Morgan for ironmongery, £50
to Mr. Wade the glazier, £130 on account to Mr. Rose for
plasterers' work, and £275 for lime, etc. One of the most
interesting items in this period is that of £30 14s. 0d. to Mr.
Edwards 'for loss sustained by stopping the mill,' which was
probably a sound move. The surrounding land is low, and the
inevitable flooding would almost certainly be aggravated by the
mill dam. It is common knowledge that much good land was
ruined in this way. But such items show that the rebuilding
of the house and the laying out of the grounds by 'Capability'
Brown proceeded together. And when we think of the scope
of the undertaking we can hardly be less than amazed that Sir
John should have been able to attack on so broad a front within
a year of the countess's death. That he did so is proof of both
the depth of his pocket and the force of his character. Here
obviously was the potential general—a man well able to direct
large-scale operations.

The range of the work undertaken at one time continues to
amaze us throughout 1765. There must have been a whole
regiment of men engaged here throughout these two years.

[1] E.R.O. D/DBy. A.259.
[2] Brick-making continued on the estate until the beginning of the twentieth
century.

Thus we find one mason busy for thirteen days at three shillings a day putting up twelve feet of the old balustrade for Sir John's approbation, and working out a cornice to go under this; while from 30th April to 15th May 1764 the gateway opening on to the London road was being taken down and renewed. £20 was paid for fosse walls next the road; £11 15s. 10d. for a fence wall north of the front court, reckoning the brickwork at 25s. a rod. Then renewals were required on the west front, where the rainwater head beside the north porch is dated 1766, while indoors there were workmen everywhere, particularly in the library, then on the ground floor, the galleries, the arcade, and the housekeeper's apartments.

It is true that much of the indoor work was required at once if the place was to be lived in with anything approaching comfort. The destruction of the east range of the inner court by the Countess of Portsmouth meant that there was now no proper communication between the north and south ranges except through the Great Hall. Along the back of this she had built an open arcade, which was quite inadequate, so Sir John was obliged to build above this a new gallery, with a passage above that on the second floor, thus connecting the two original staircases at the back of the Great Hall to serve the three floors. At the same time he rebuilt the eastern ends of the north and south ranges. Altogether, therefore, the house acquired a completely new aspect from the east, though one closely in keeping with the rest of the building in architectural style.

The most badly conceived part of this first restoration was in the service apartments. The original domestic offices had been removed by Sir John Vanbrugh, and the new ones could not conveniently be accommodated in the main block. Sir John was therefore constrained to erect them to the north, in a range detached from the main building. Even so, it is difficult to understand why they should have been placed so conspicuously and so inconveniently. Later a yew hedge was grown to conceal them; but they must long have detracted from the appearance of the house. Their detached position, however, may have saved the mansion, for the original offices were destroyed by fire in 1881 and had to be rebuilt.

There is much in these accounts that would interest a student of building methods and costs, and any one who knows the house intimately would enjoy running each item to earth, as it were, though he might well find this more difficult than would appear likely at first glance. The great quantities of timber purchased could disappear anywhere. It might be thought that particular items, such as chimney-pieces, would be easily recognized. They are not, because they have so often been moved from one room to another, particularly during the third Lord Braybrooke's time. A note made in January 1764 shows that a chimney-piece was taken down in the library and put up in the 'North Room.' Another note says: 'Altering chimney-piece that we're taking down in Sir John Griffin's study next to the Mount Garden and to be put up in the North Room next to the stairs.' These chimney-pieces, of which there are several beautiful examples at Audley End, are particularly interesting because several of them were designed by Robert Adam. In this first wave of building Adam designed chimney-pieces for the Great Parlour, the Library, and the Great Drawing Room. Unfortunately, none of these rooms can be recognized to-day by those names. They were then on the ground floor of the south wing. At this time the 'Parlour' evidently had a marble chimney-piece, which was subsequently moved to the bake-house.[1]

In 1763, on 6th October, ten tons of Westmorland slates at 60*s.* a ton were bought, apparently from the quarry. Then the following year we find: 'Nov. 8th and 15th, Seven Ton of Westmoreland slates from Bedford House at £3 15*s.* 0*d.* £26 5*s.* 0*d.* Paid for weighing and loading ditto slates   15*s.* 0*d.*' This, apparently, is an instance of noblemen trading with each other for their mutual convenience. Transport was still difficult, and we find that the slates came up from London by water. There are numerous references to materials being conveyed on Ware barges, and it is evident that Sir John had his receiving place in London at the Vine Inn, which is mentioned frequently.

Freestone ashlar was paid for at the rate of 6*d.* a foot; moulded freestone at 9*d.*; moulded work on hardstone at 1*s.* Timber and deals came from a Mr. Cator's, but where his place of business was is not indicated. He received substantial sums in payment during these years—£255 11*s.* 6*d.* in 1763, £228 19*s.* 4*d.* in 1764, and so forth, and it is interesting to note that the flooring boards were imported. The building up of the Royal Navy had played havoc with the country's timber.[2] Wainscots came from Messrs. Eeles & Bond. Most of the expert craftsmanship, such as the carving of chimney-pieces, bases, capitals,

[1] E.R.O. D/DBy. A.365.   [2] See *Annals of Agriculture*, vol. xviii, p. 34.

and ornamental work in stone, was done in London, and some of the most interesting work of this kind is charged for in John Moore's accounts.   Thus in 1764 we have:

Jan. 4th

	£	s.	d.
To 13 ft. 6 in. of veined slabb for a chimney-piece at Audley End @ 5s. per foot	3	7	6
To a Dorick column statuary marble chimney-piece for the library at Audley End, deducting the black coverings. N.B. It will be found in the Estimate	111	14	3
22 ft. 1. Cube Portland to the four circular stone for the bridge @ 2s. 6d. ft.	2	15	$1\frac{1}{2}$
To carving and masoning two circular stones with the crest and motto at £4 10s. 0d. each	9	0	0
To two with the date and other decorations @ £2 10s. 0d.	5	0	0
To carving a fifth stone with a crest	4	10	0

May 7th

	£	s.	d.
To 144$\frac{1}{4}$ days two masons working at Audley End at what they were ordered @ 3s. a day	21	12	9
To 207$\frac{3}{4}$ days two polishers @ 2s. 6d. a day	25	19	$4\frac{1}{4}$
To 59 weeks 2 days lodging for four men @ 1s. per week	2	19	4
Travelling for one mason to and from Audley End, 80 [1] miles @ 5s. per 20 miles	1	0	0
Ditto for another to go down		10	0
For 160 miles two polishers to and from do. @ 3s. 6d. per 20 miles	1	8	0
56 ft. 1. of veined marble slab for four chimney-pieces @ 5s. per foot	14	0	5
0. 9$\frac{1}{2}$ cube of the best statuary marble without spot for a Gothick moulding round a chimney-piece for the Fish Room [2] @ 40s. per foot	2	9	$5\frac{1}{4}$
15 ft. 5. running of enriched moulding; the one bead-string, the other a dentrical drops between the spaces, the dentrical enrichments with a pearl at the end of each, together @ 15s. per foot	11	11	3
15 ft. 8 in. of veined marble for the Gallery @ 5s. per ft.	3	18	4

Slaters' work by William Thomas included Westmorland slating over the arcade, or long gallery, and the kitchen offices along with old Welsh slating, both at 11s. 6d. a square, while

---

[1] i.e. from London and back.   [2] i.e. the Saloon.

sundry expenses include a charge for the slaters coming and going from London. One item, 'Returning home three days myself, two days a man,' sounds like holidays with pay, but the charge was, of course, for travelling only.

Robert Wheeler, the joiner, had a large bill for general repairs, in which appears the item: 'New steps to the staircase at the south end of the gallery, £6 12s. 8d.' His biggest job was the making of new window frames and the fixing of new wainscot. Samuel Wade, the glazier, followed with new glass, new lead on the library in the south wing, sash weights, and so forth, bringing his account in 1764 up to £429 11s. 9d. Then came the painter, and his work included three coats to the screen in the Great Hall. The plasterers were also busy as early as 1763–4 with such work as an ornamental ceiling to the new gallery and arcade, repairs to most of the older ceilings, 413 ft. of Gothic ornament on walls (£20 13s. 0d.), 271 ft. 8 in. architraves frame on walls (£7 18s. 5½d.), No. 8 Ionic Antique Capitals to pilasters, and No. 8 bases to ditto. The total was £311 15s. 4½d.

Large sums were spent annually from 1763 to 1766; but the accounts for this period are not as clear as those for the second great wave of improvements, that of twenty years later, which coincided with Sir John's elevation to the peerage. William Ivory, who was not, apparently, a member of the distinguished Norwich family of architects,[1] was in charge of the work and kept detailed accounts,[2] which show payments amounting to £1,258 in 1784, £3,621 in 1785, and £2,370 in 1786. From this time to the end of his life Lord Howard spent approximately a thousand pounds a year on maintenance, with such occasional capital additions as a keeper's house, built in 1787 at a cost of £304, and a new laundry, which cost £223. In the same year appear items for Purbeck stone and paviours' work, amounting to £138, mahogany (£11), and gilding (£35), which were probably in connection with the construction at that time of a new family vault in Walden church, for which occurs the specific entry: 'For building the entrance to the new vault at Walden Church, £85 17s. 3d.'

In 1788 he spent £39 10s. 0d. on fanes, etc., to the six turrets. In 1790 there was considerable work done to the park and gardens, on which over £540 was expended in the following year.

[1] See Stanley J. Wearing, F.R.I.B.A., *Georgian Norwich: its builders*, 1926, pp. 40–1.
[2] E.R.O. D/DBy. A.261.

But it was indoors that most of the work was done after 1784, the year of Sir John's elevation to the peerage.   During the years 1784–6 he spent £4,121 in improving his indoor amenities and beautifying his principal apartments.   During the next three years—and by this time he was in the late sixties—his exceptional expenses continued at the rate of about a thousand pounds a year, principally for furniture, and when we see how much could be bought for a thousand pounds in the seventeen-eighties we realize that these are very substantial sums.   The furniture bills for 1786, for example, amount to £1,285.   There was a special reason for this enriching and refurnishing   With the grant of the peerage Sir John had achieved his great ambition; he now hoped that he might be honoured with a royal visit, and it was in preparation for such an event that he redecorated his state rooms and particularly the Saloon, the most beautiful room in the house, which was done, as the inscription in the north-west corner records, as a kind of thank-offering:

Henry VIII A.D. 1539, granted the Monastery of Walden, on the scite of which this house now stands, to Lord Chancellor Audley. Elizabeth A.D. 1597, by special writ, summoned to Parliament Thomas Lord Howard de Walden, in the next reign created Earl of Suffolk. He built this house A.D. 1616.   After many reductions it descended to Sir John Griffin Griffin, K.B., confirmed Lord Howard de Walden George III A.D. 1784.   He, among other additions and alterations, refitted (the ceiling excepted) this Saloon, to commemorate the noble Families through whom, with gratitude, he holds these Possessions.

Thus, as the Great Hall is pre-eminently the room of the Earls of Suffolk, the Saloon, reached by ascending Sir John Vanbrugh's staircase, is pre-eminently the room of Sir John Griffin Griffin in the fullness of his stature as fourth Lord Howard de Walden.

The ceiling of this fine apartment is original and may be dated about 1615.   Fishes, dolphins, and other aquatic subjects are represented in the plasterwork of its thirty-two panels, and it is from these that the Saloon takes its family name of the Fish Room.   Pepys, as we have seen, remarked on his second visit that the ceilings at Audley End were not so fine as those at Clarendon House, built in 1665; but the great interest of the Saloon ceiling, which may be compared with the library ceiling at Blickling, the home of Henrietta, the ninth earl's countess, is mainly historical.   It illustrates the development of plaster-work from the heavy three-dimensional style, inherited from the Tudor woodcarvers, to the light and elegant two-dimensional work of the Adam period, so well exemplified elsewhere in the house, and indeed in the same room. Here we have the pendants to remind us of the earlier vaulting, yet with moulded beams of the Tudor form giving place to the strapwork borders characteristic of James I's reign beautifully modelled in low relief and drawn down at the points of intersection to form pendants. In order to appreciate what this elaborately ornamental plasterwork meant when it was introduced to England we have only to recall Iachimo's astonishment at the beauty of Imogen's chamber in *Cymbeline*. Apart from the ceiling and portions of the chimney-piece the room is largely Georgian. It was completed in 1785 and has hardly been touched since.

The commemorative purpose of the Saloon decoration is expressed in the restoration of the fine chimney-piece, where the arms of the newly confirmed peer and those of his two wives are found above the great central achievement of the first Earl of Suffolk's arms impaling those of Knyvett, with other quarterings. But it is most eloquently expressed in the series of elegant plasterwork panels, in which Biagio Rebecca painted full-length figures, most of them copied from original portraits, of successive owners of Audley End from Lord Chancellor Audley to the present lord, including the Countess of Portsmouth. The notable exception is the portrait of Lady Essex Howard (Lady Griffin), which is an original by Sir Peter Lely.

Outside the Saloon, the work by Adam at Audley End cannot be adequately appreciated to-day because the rooms he furnished and decorated have been turned to other uses. The principal suite was on the ground floor, where what was planned as a dining-room was later used as a billiard-room, while the drawing-rooms became dressing-room, bedroom, and boudoir. The dining-room has been altered so drastically that it is now difficult to recognize the remaining Adam work. The original library, which must have been a beautiful room when Adam completed it, was at the east end of the south wing. It is now broken up into sitting-room, bedroom, and dressing-room, and is referred to as the red suite.

The south wing has undergone more than one transformation. The ground floor was originally an open loggia overlooking the Mount Garden. Then in or about 1740 it was enclosed by the tenth Earl of Suffolk, who suffered from gout. When his effects were sold after his death they included 'a fine leather easy chair to turn into all manner of conveniences for the gout, on wheels, and a conveniency on wheels for the chair to be wheeled about in the fields and gardens.' After the Adam restoration it became the most lived-in part of the house, and continued in daily use until the third Lord Braybrooke, as we shall see presently, moved the suite upstairs. There is still much to admire, particularly in the ceilings and friezes, but the bedroom, for example, could be seen better if it were not over-furnished with the magnificent bedstead adorned with the Howard crest, a baron's coronet, and military trophies in the angles, which could never have been intended for a room of these proportions, and was evidently brought downstairs by the third Lord Braybrooke.

The dressing-room is interesting for the 'Etruscan' frieze by Rebecca, designed, no doubt, by Adam, with a representation of the Triumphs and Sacrifices from Montfaucon's *Antiquities*,[1] taking the female figures from Herculaneum—used frequently by Adam for the decoration of his apartments. Rebecca's cunningly deceptive craftsmanship is well exemplified here. This clever decorative artist was an inveterate private joker. One of his favourite tricks was to paint small paper disks to look like half-crowns, then leave them about the floor for the joy of seeing the annoyance of elderly gentlemen who stooped to pick them up. At Audley End he alarmed Lady Howard by painting a black kettle on a piece of card, which he placed on a white satin chair. And at a party he is said to have carried round a tray with bits of paper on it so effectively painted to look like cakes that many of the guests tried to take them. After looking at his 'Etruscan' frieze such anecdotes become perfectly credible.

Though Lord Howard was not a man of taste himself, he would derive great satisfaction from knowing that the Adams, by this time at the height of their fame, had served so many noble families, and that Audley End was thus being brought into line with such places as Kedleston, Syon, Luton Hoo, and Harewood.

Some details of the work done by the Adam brothers for Lord Howard, both before and after he succeeded to the peerage, are set out by Arthur T. Bolton in *The Architecture of Robert and James Adam, 1758–1794*. They include schemes for the decoration of these ground floor rooms, for which the estimate was

[1] Braybrooke, p. 109.

supplied by a Mr. Adair in 1763–5, and also for decorations and furniture at the Griffins' London home in Savile Row. Of the satisfaction of the family with what had been done we have delighted expression in a letter from Miss Emilia Clayton, Lady Howard's half-sister, to Miss Port, Mrs. Delany's niece, who was then at Windsor.[1] It describes a visit to Audley End in the October of 1786. 'The house,' she says,

is so much beautified and compleated since we were here last it is quite astonishing. I think the state apartment is as perfect as anything can be. It consists of a bedchamber, two dressing-rooms, two powdering closets, an antechamber and servants room. The bed-chamber, gentleman's dressing-room and antechamber are hung with grey water tabby, ornamented with crimson and gold. . . .

All the tables, chairs, &c. are suitably beautiful. The bed is grey, and embroidered most beautifully, and made up with the greatest taste I ever saw. The posts are white and gold. The lady's dressing-room is hung with some fine modern tapestry, the chairs, and tables inlaid, and Rebecca's paintings. I think this house is now the most comfortable, magnificent, and elegant one that it is possible to imagine. . . . The fine grounds, which really are delightful, are vastly improved since we were here.

In November of that same year, 1786, the elegant new chapel placed in the north-west corner of the house, which was fitted out under the direction of Hobcraft, with windows by Pecket of York to drawings by Rebecca, was used for the wedding of the Hon. Henry Fox with Lady Howard's half-sister Mari-anne Clayton, and again Emilia described the scene to her friend, Miss Port, in a letter written on the 14th of that month. 'The ceremony,' she says, 'was performed this morning at half-past eight. We were all in the *Galery* at that time. . . . Her [the bride's] dress was silver muslin night gown trimmed with white *sattin*, a very fine sprigged muslin apron, and hand-kerchief trimmed with beautiful lace, and white silver shoes. . . . Colonel Fox was in a dark green coat, with a very waistcoat she *net* him.' The costumes of the guests are then described, and Miss Clayton adds: 'After having signed our names as witnesses, we went to breakfast, which was vastly pretty.'

Thus throughout the thirty-five years of his residence at Audley End Lord Howard continued the work of converting the ruinous old palace he inherited into a seat befitting the rank and dignity of the Whig nobleman he became. As for the

---

[1] Mrs. Delany's *Memoirs*, vol. vi., p. 400.

estate, which will be considered later, when it was divided
between Lord Bristol and the Countess of Portsmouth and Mrs.
Whitwell, the river was made the dividing line, with small
adjustments.   Actually the boundary in front of the mansion
was the turnpike road; but even this meant that most of the
land seen from the windows of the principal rooms was Lord
Bristol's.   On the south the boundary was the Walden road,
along which the Countess of Portsmouth had owned two
cottages only.   This can never have been satisfactory to her
nephew as Sir John, let alone to him as Lord Howard.   So he
bought up the nearer land whenever opportunity offered and
steadily enlarged his park.   He also shifted his cottages, as
several other noblemen did theirs at this time, with the result
that practically everything we see as we look round us from the
front lawns to-day—including the trees—dates from these years.
And when his work was completed Lord Howard, who by this
time had a steady income of £5,000 a year, was able to walk
round his five manors without treading on any one else's land,
while at home he had seven miles of walks in his own pleasure
grounds, requiring twelve gardeners to keep them mown,
together with seven acres of kitchen gardens for the supply of
his household.   Altogether, fifty gardeners were employed at
Audley End by the seventeen-nineties.

XI

LIFE IN A GEORGIAN
MANSION

IF IN THE eighteenth century the village folk no longer
looked to the lord of the manor for protection as they
had done in feudal days, the majority might still look to
him for employment. At Audley End most of them had
looked in vain to the last three earls of Suffolk. With the
arrival of Sir John, therefore, a new era began for the villagers
of north-west Essex. If the completed gardens meant full and
regular employment for fifty gardeners, we can imagine what
the rebuilding must have meant; because if not the greater,
certainly a substantial part of the £100,000 spent by him was
circulated in the neighbourhood. And when in the summer of
1765 he and his second lady moved in, the kitchens and larders
of the house itself would become as important as the steward's
office or the builder's yard to tenants and tradesmen. But again
it was a rebuilding—in this case a rebuilding of the economic
life of house and estate—and again a rebuilding on a smaller
scale. Life in a Georgian household was still lavish enough for
the twentieth century to marvel at; but it was much reduced
from life in its Tudor and Stuart counterparts. If there was no
austerity, there was no longer the gluttony there had been, and
no longer the hordes of servants. When Sir John and Lady
Griffin set up house they paid, in fact, little more in servants'
wages at Audley End than the third Earl of Suffolk had been
paying at Chesterford Park a hundred years earlier, in spite of
the great difference in the value of money.

We have no household account books from the original
Audley End to compare with the *Derby Household Books*; but we
may assume from what we do know of his hospitality—at
Cambridge and elsewhere—that in the first years in his new

The Mansion from the South-west

house the Earl of Suffolk would kill his fifty or so oxen a year, and perhaps as many as five hundred sheep, to feed his household. Burghley's housekeeping at Theobalds during the first years of James's reign was at the rate of £80 a week, which may be multiplied by thirty, or perhaps forty, to arrive at its approximate value to-day. These great houses had taken the place in rural society of the old religious houses, and were still similar in their domestic economy. The flocks and herds, the warrens, the deer parks, and the fishponds that had supplied the abbot's table now supplied the earl's in similar style and measure, though the purveyor was called the achatour, not the cellarer. But greater changes had come by Sir John Griffin Griffin's time. The first three earls of Suffolk would employ such officers as chamberlains—or comptrollers—of the household, grooms of the buttery, purveyors of the spicery, yeomen of the chandlery, to say nothing of cup-bearers, carvers, gentlemen ushers, and pages. All these disappeared when liveries were abolished. Indeed most of the officers of Sir John's household had names familiar to ourselves, though some of them will sound strangely to our grandchildren. Perhaps the one eighteenth-century officer of the household whose title is already obsolete is the groom of the chamber, whose duty it was, apparently, to go the rounds after prayers in order to make sure that the servants were in their beds and had snuffed their candles. In 1768 Sir John paid only £370 to his indoor staff; but this increased steadily as he advanced in status. Five years later it was £509, and so on. The greatest increase came, as we should expect, with the peerage.

Cash payments were very small indeed in the early years. They amounted to no more than six or seven pounds a week. But buying was not done as we should do it. Those were days of extended credits. The grocer's bill, for example, came in at long intervals, though everything purchased from him was entered in what was called the *Contingent Book*,[1] which is in some ways the most interesting of the household account books. It contains such items as fishskin for cleaning locks, usually charged one shilling, a pair of scissors for trimming the lamps, a peck of scouring sand for the pewter, and ashes—one penny. Peppermint water is not infrequent. And each week the amount of soap and tallow candles used is carefully noted, usually between 16 lb. and 19 lb. of soap, and between 21 lb. and 26 lb.

[1] E.R.O. D/DBy. A.13.

K

of candles during the winter months, with suitable adjustments at festive seasons. Christmas 1765, for example, was celebrated at a cost of a little over £100. To be precise, the entry for the week ending 31st December 1765 reads:

Pounds Weight of all Sorts	Numbers of all Sorts	£	s.	d.	£	s.	d.
288	Beef, being 20 stone 81 lbs. @ 3½d.	4	4	0			
25½	Veal, @ 9½d.		9	6¾			
	Calves Head and four feet		3	0			
					4	16	6¾
224	4 Bushell Flour @ 5s. 4d.	1	1	4			
	Bran 1s. 2d.		1	2			
					1	2	6
	5 Chickens @ 6d.					2	6
	12 Larks						9
	5 Rabbits					3	4
	96 Eggs					4	0

Paid to Butcher for killing sheep and hogs:

		£	s.	d.	£	s.	d.
152	3 Sheep ⎱						
512	4 Hogs ⎰				1	11	0
1,483	27 Sheep @ 4d.				24	14	4
965	9 Hogs @ 4d.				16	1	8
	20 Quarters Barley to Poultry & Pidgeons				18	0	0
	Tares 10 Bushells to do.				1	17	6
684	Butter @ 6½d.	18	10	6			
361	Cheese @ 3½d.	5	5	4¾			
	101 Quarts Cream @ 6d.	2	10	6			
	117 do. Milk @ 1d.		9	9			
					26	16	1¾
289	68 Loaves eat						
	86 rolls						
	Butter used						
	Cheese						
	1 Turkey, 1 Duck, 1 Pea-fowl,						
	7 fowls, 3 Hares, 4 Partridges,						
	2 Woodcocks						

£95 10 3½

The total disbursements this week amounted to £101 0s. 8¼d.

The most detailed of the inventories made when the second Lady Griffin began her rule is that of Household and Family Linen.[1]   It is ruled to show: (1) the names of the various sorts of linen; (2) the number of linen articles of all sorts, 1st January 1765; (3) the number of linen articles of all sorts worn out or reduced in 1765; (4) the total remaining on 31st December 1765. This account was carefully kept each year and with good reason.   There were no fewer than 1,483 articles to account for: 324 sheets, 52 pillow cases, 132 tablecloths, 8 lay-overs for tablecloths, 49 breakfast cloths, 523 napkins, 218 towels, 8 toilet covers, 169 plate cloths, etc.   The various qualities were specified.   Of sheets, for example, there were long lawn, fine Holland, second Holland, Irish cloth, twelvepenny, eightpenny, and sixpenny flax, and finally 'common coarse sheets.'

The most important member of the indoor staff was the house-steward, who arranged and budgeted for everything, and was here, there, and everywhere about his master's business. Many of the duties that would now fall to a private secretary were his responsibility, as well as many that would later have fallen to the housekeeper.   Every one employed inside the house was answerable to him—the women no less than the men, though the maids were answerable through the housekeeper, whose importance increased as women gradually displaced boys in the kitchen.

To see what housekeeping meant at Audley End about this time, take the general account of things bought and used weekly, beginning Saturday, 8th October, and ending 31st December 1768, given on pages 130–1.

Probably the fact that Sir John and Lady Griffin were setting up an entirely new household at Audley End accounts for the extremely efficient housekeeper they had in the 1760s.   She was not, as it were, taken over with the fixtures.   Her name was Margaret Allen, and the account shown, giving particulars of all the food bought and used in the house during the three months ending 31st December 1768, will give an idea of what housekeeping entailed in such a house as Audley End at this time.

Most of this immense amount of food was produced on the estate.   The cash payments for the first week, for example, amounted to only £10 13s. 2d.   Two sheep were killed weekly, and of course game birds were important at this season.   The

[1] E.R.O. D/DBy. A.21.

	Pound Weight of the different sorts of Meat from the Butchers					Totall Pound Weight of Meat from Butchers	Number of Sheep Kill'd into yᵉ House	Pound Weight of each Sheep	Numbers of Hogs Kill'd into yᵉ House	Pound Weight of each Hog	Number of the different sorts of Game dress'd in yᵉ House						Number of [...]ferent sor[...] Poultry Bo[...] into Ho[...]		
	Beef	Mutton	Veal	Lamb	Pork						Hares	Pheasants	Parteridges	Quails	Woodcocks	Snipes	Geese	Turkeys	Ducks
1768 Octr 15th	338		35			373	2	122			2	1	4	5					4
22	290		38			328	2	121	1	89	2	2	4	2		1			
29	267		31½			298½	1	61			1	1	5		3	5			
Novr 5th	232		32			264	2	114	1	88	2	1	6						
12	232		27			259	2	122			2	1	4		1		1		
19	232		30			262	2	130	1	86	2	2	2		2				
26	232		26			258	2	116			2		5		2	30			
Decr 3	232		22			254	2	89	1	86			2		2				
10	256		32			288	2	98			3	1	4		1				6
17	296		27½			323½	2	103	1	104	1	2	4		2	3			
24	287		25			312	2	89			1	1	4						
31	288		25½			313½	3	152	4	512	3		4		2				
	3182		351½			3533½	24	1317	9	965	21	12	48	7	15	39	1		10

Ducks	Fowls or chickens	Pidgeons	Pea Fowl	Guinea Fowl	Rabits	Pounds of Candles us'd	Pounds of Soap us'd	Pecks of Flower bought into yᵉ House	Number of Quarter Peck Loaves made	Number of Rowls made	Total Pounds of Flower us'd in the House	Eggs Bought	Eggs Gather'd	Eggs used	Butter Bought	Butter Fresh made	Butter Potted	Butter used	Cheese Bought	Cheese made	Cheese Remains of Last Year	Cheese used
1	2	4			2	13	4	20	48	25	196	27	60	62		10	174	20	49	730	305	22
1	4	15				21	14	11	48	32	154	36		50		10		21½				23½
2	2		1			21	16	16	38	20	154	52		44		10		21½				24
1	4	12				21	16	20	48	44	252	44		36		6½		18				26
1	2	4	1		3	23	17	14	42	45	168	48		35		8½		26				25
1	4				2	23	16	16	42	48	210	48		36		7		26				27
2	7	3			4	24	18	16	51	64	252	72		80		6		28				29
2	3				3	24	18	16	51	70	224	70		66		3		28				29
1	5		1		2	25	19	18	60	70	280	70		70		3½		31½				33
2	6				2	25	19	22	76	78	280	52		52	8	3½		28				34
1	5				4	26	19	20	68	83	280	96		96	25	6		31				40
1	7		1		5	26	17	16	68	86	248	96		96	19	7		26				42
16	51	38	4		27	272	193	205	640	665	2698	711	60	723	52	81	174	305½	49	730	305	354½

gamekeeper indeed, although not a member of the household, was an extremely important person at Audley End, and it so happens that one of the great characters about the place in Sir John's time, John Chapman, was apparently engaged as game-keeper in this very year of 1768. He was evidently one of those gentlemen who like to have a clear understanding of their terms of service, and consequently we have one or two interesting documents relating to him. On entering Sir John's service he undertook to give up all his dogs to his master and never again to keep any of his own. He agreed to find his own guns, leather breeches, and boots; but to be found a suit of green cloth—coat, waistcoat, and breeches, yearly, with one hat, a shooting jacket, or fustian frock, and a common flannel waist-coat. Every two years he was to have a new greatcoat and his wages were to be £26 a year. Five years later he entered into a different agreement: [1]

John Chapman Gamekeeper's Proposals, to take place September ye 29th 1773 as undermentioned.

The said John Chapman is to find his own Cloaths of all Sorts entirely, and to appear in Green whenever out with the Honble Sir John Griffin or any of his Friends and to be in Green likewise on Sondays, and on other occasions when Required, he is to find his own Guns of all sorts, and to keep them in repair at his own expence, and to serve from year to year as long as his Master Sir John G. Griffin pleases, at the yearly wages of

	£	s.	d.
Forty Guineas per year	42	0	0
To 52 weeks Board wages at 6ˢ per week	15	12	0
To allowance yearly for the use of two horses	2	2	0
To Shoeing, Farriary, Sadles, Bridles, Brooms, Brushes, Oil, Curry Combs &c. &c. with the allowance for two loads of straw for Litter as made out in Paper of Particulars	8	16	0
To maintenance of ten dogs, viz. seven pointers and three grayhounds, Feeding with Barley meal, milk, bread, & horse flesh, pails, couples, collars, chains, whistles, straw, medicines, copper for boiling and fireing	31	10	0
	£100	0	0

Evidently the aim in estimating the cost of these multifarious items was to arrive at the round figure of a hundred pounds

[1] E.R.O. D/DBy. A.11.

for everything.   At this rate, with the inevitable unmentioned perquisites the gamekeeper's job must have appeared an enviable one to some of his neighbours.   For all that he could still submit his expenses sheet, which that year was for £13 9s. od., in which the principal item was £9 for powder, shot, and flints.

Gamekeepers have often been privileged persons about an estate.   The indoor staff were much more easily controlled as a rule.   Perhaps the ones with the least easily definable position were the footmen.   A trusted footman might be both an important and a highly respected person.   He was under the house-steward's orders only while indoors, and as much of his time was spent in carrying messages and doing special jobs it was easy for him to give his steward the slip.   Even indoors the footman was exceptionally privileged, because he waited on his master or his mistress, as the case might be, and if the house-steward had a job for him to do he could plead a call from them. At Audley End there were now two footmen, Sir John's and Lady Griffin's.   They were always in attendance on their master and mistress whenever they travelled by coach, and were thus always in the know about their movements.   As Sir John's footman ran the errands and delivered missives, he knew every one who mattered in north-west Essex, and either was, or pretended to be, a very knowing individual indeed about private matters. If a footman happened to be a trustworthy person his master might sound him about local affairs, and find him useful as a kind of social weather vane.   On the other hand, if he was an irresponsible fellow, he could be a nuisance to everybody.   No one did more than he to develop the art of tipping, or the taking of 'vails' as they were called.

How the staff at Audley End must have preened themselves when Sir John became 'his lordship'!   Let us look at his staff this year.   John Chapman is still there with his £59 14s. od. The house-steward has 60 guineas, but is described as butler as well as steward, with an under-butler receiving only £16.   A French cook, Jacques Tulen, is now employed, and receives £50 a year, which is a considerable salary for 1784.   The maids who assist him have the usual wages of the period, £8 or £9—the rate varies little from one year to another about this time, although twenty years earlier 20 guineas a year had been the rate for a cook, 6 guineas for maids, with the curious allowance of 1 guinea for tea.   The housekeeper in 1784 has £30 a year; the lady's maid, £12; the housemaids, £9 and £8 respectively; the stillroom maid, £8; the laundry maid, £9, and the dairymaid, £8. Perhaps the best guide to their prescribed duties will be Mrs. Hannah Glasse, whose book, *The Servant's Directory or House-keeper's Companion*, was a standard work at this time. It is not necessary, she says, to tell the laundry maid how to wash—'she knows better than I can teach her, as being always a person brought up to it from her childhood; for every poor woman teaches her children to wash, that's a thing they can't do without.' But she finds it necessary to tell them how to wash linens. According to her, the most important thing was to lay chalk at the bottom of the well, and chalk would be easily come by at Audley End. Mrs. Glasse is at her most charming in giving directions to the 'little young house-maid.' She says: 'First take care to be up very early in a morning, as indeed you are first wanted; lace on your Stays, and pin your things very tight about you, or you never can do work well. Have no long Gown or Coats about your Heels; and be sure always to have very clean Feet, that you may not dirty your Rooms as soon as clean'd, nor make any Noise, but learn to walk softly, and not disturb the Family.' And so we can imagine her tiptoeing through her flight of rooms at Audley End.

This little maid would have to light the fires and clean the hearths, sweep the carpets and do all the dusting before the family came down. Then she would go into the bedrooms to open the windows and uncover the beds so that the air could cool them. 'Besides,' as Mrs. Glasse says, 'it is good for the Health to air the Bedding, and sweet to sleep in when the fresh Air has had Access to them, and a great help against Bugs and Fleas.' With the lighter, loftier rooms had come a new desire for cleanliness. The white ceilings had put the floors and walls to shame. That was why so much of the panelling was painted and why every conceivable excuse for having bright porcelain, brass locks, and everything else that could be made to shine and reflect the glorious light was seized. The wainscoting now was mostly of deal, and floors and stairs were scrubbed daily. Never before had there been such cleanliness.

As for the male members of the staff, a name that was to figure in the accounts at Audley End until our own day, that of Nockold, appears about this time. Martin Nockold is nursery-man in 1784, with £50 a year. In 1785 he appears as bailiff, but at the same wages. The chief kitchen gardener also gets £50 a year. After these we have the valet and the groom of the chamber, with £30 apiece, but they lived in, and their wages were thus supplemented by their keep. The two footmen have £16 each, in their cases supplemented with both keep and 'vails.' The head coachman has £26 10s., the second coachman £15, which, as with the two butlers, shows the customary large difference between the two. The groom has £16; the postilion, 6 guineas; the house and foot boy, £4 8s.; the porter, £21.

These wages do not vary much for the remainder of Lord Howard's lifetime. He maintained a reasonable, but not excessive establishment for a man of his station, and consequently he had always money to spare for the improvements to house and estate on which his heart was immovably set.

The peak of excitement in the Audley End household was reached in the late summer of 1786, when a royal visit was expected daily. In the August of that year Their Majesties paid their second visit to Lord and Lady Harcourt at Nuneham Courtenay, near Oxford. They arrived on Saturday the 12th, and on the following day, after attending divine service, the king and queen, accompanied by the Princess Royal, the Princesses Augusta and Elizabeth, visited Oxford. After this it was naturally expected that Cambridge would be visited, and if such a visit were arranged Audley End appeared to be the likely place for Their Majesties to stay. Indeed, after the court's return to Windsor the London newspapers went so far as to say that such a visit had been proposed for October,[1] and that the king had expressed a wish to visit the university from Lord Howard de Walden's house, about which he had heard so much. Everything, therefore, was prepared for the royal visit, and we have in the Audley End archives three letters from Lord and Lady Harcourt [2] to Lord and Lady Howard, instructing them how to arrange for the proper entertainment of Their Majesties when the expected visit took place.[3] They show, incidentally, how much more difficult such occasions were for the host and hostess thus honoured than they would be to-day.

'Your lordship and Lady Howard,' writes Lord Harcourt,

are to receive their Majesties at the door; yourself either in a full dressed coat (with your sword) or your uniform; Lady Howard in a sack, without a hat. Your lordship will have a glove on, to hand the

[1] Cooper, *Annals of Cambridge*, vol. iv., p. 416.
[2] Elizabeth, daughter of George Venables Vernon, Lord Vernon. She was a lady of the bedchamber.
[3] E.R.O. D/DBy. C.10/1–3.

Queen into the Drawing room—the carpet to be laid for their Majesties to step out of their coach on.

Your lordship and Lady Howard know, that during the whole time of their Majesties' stay with you, you are their Lord and Lady of the Bedchamber, and supersede any Lord or Lady they may carry with them.

The King brought *no* riding horses.

The first time their Majesties came here they only walked through the house and gardens; the second time, they and the Princesses drove about the park in their carriages and in mine. Lady Harcourt attended the Queen and the Princesses in her Majesty's coach and myself attended the King and the eldest Prince in mine. The last time their Majesties were here, the weather did not permit them to drive out till they got into their coaches to go away, when I preceded in my own carriage to shew a part of the park they had not seen before, and then Lady Harcourt and myself got out at the park gate on the London road to make our obeisance to them as they passed by.

No Guards came either of the times their Majesties were here.

Two dressers, two hair-dressers, two pages, twenty livery servants, twenty-two horses, three coaches, lodged, fed, and put up here.

Your lordship and Lady Howard are supposed to wait on the King and Queen at table, therefore no servants can be in the room when they go to dinner &c.; but their Majesties will probably order you to call them in. No servants *in livery* can ever at any time or on any occasion appear before them, and the King's pages never wait.

Your lordship must stand on the King's right hand at table, and Lady Howard on the Queen's and you are to present them with what they call for, but not to go for anything yourselves to the sideboard. The first time, I did actually wait on the King at dinner, and still always do so at breakfast, on which occasion Lady Harcourt made the tea, and an out of livery servant brings everything to me, who present it to the King. The same is done at coffee, and afterwards at tea, except that at the former no servant is in the room.

Though no man whatever can properly sit in the Queen's presence, however elevated his rank may be, yet (for the first time) that etiquette was dispensed with on my account both last year and this, and I sat at the lower end of the table on the King's right hand. However, I thought it proper, notwithstanding, to rise and present him with everything he ate or drank.

Your lordship and Lady Howard will present whatever sort of liquor their Majesties ask for, in a covered glass, the cover of which you will take off, as you deliver the glass to them. The Princesses will be waited on by the servants, without any particular ceremonial. Your lordship and Lady Howard will carve for their Majesties, or the dish they choose will be sent off the table and carved by a servant, as it may happen. They are very indifferent as to what they eat. The dinner to be served in the usual style of great entertainments.   Two courses and a dessert are sufficient.

Supper was always prepared, one course, *en ambigu*, with ice, fruit, &c. set on the table together with hot and cold dishes.

The first night it was served, as it was last year; but the tour to Oxford and Blenheim ended so late, that their Majesties only dined and forbad (after they were returned) there being any supper.   The King and Queen give notice when they retire at night, the former almost immediately follows the latter.   Your lordship will light the King with one candle to his apartment, and Lady Howard will do the same by the Queen.   Your lordship and Lady Howard will have two water glasses on salvers and a napkin prepared for you on the side-board, which you will hold to the King and Queen for them to wash after dinner.   No other washing glasses can be used in their presence, even by the Princesses.   The King and Queen to be seated on *the side* of the table in arm chairs, the Princesses opposite to them on common ones, without arms.   The bread, knife, fork, spoon, and salt cellar for the King and Queen to be covered with a spread napkin for each. Those for the Princesses in the usual common manner.   No other napkins, knives, &c. to be placed on the table; but if your lordship and Lady Howard are ordered to sit at the table, you will then call for them.

Lady Harcourt wrote:

Madam,

Your ladyship's letter was forwarded to me while I was at Windsor, and the little time I can command there must plead my excuse for not acknowledging it sooner.   I will now answer your questions as they stand, that I may omit nothing, and first I received the Queen in a negligee, with a dressed cap, but neither lappets [1] nor diamonds.   I put on the latter when I attended her Majesty to Oxford, but we wore hats and night gowns that day, and did not new dress for dinner.   At breakfast I made the tea, and gave it to the Queen; my Lord gave the King his cup, and we did the same in the evening when it was made out of the room.   Miss Burney slept near the Queen, and Miss Planta near the Princesses.   My Lord and I lighted their Majesties to their apartments.   They proposed what they chose to do.   At dinner there should be only two covers on one side of the table, and two armed chairs for the King and Queen, and covers and common chairs on the other side for the Princesses, and no other chairs or covers are to be placed unless they are ordered.   The Queen drinks barley water if she happens to want anything more than usual in her room, Miss Burney will ask for it.   We received their Majesties at the bottom of the steps.

I hope I have given your ladyship such information as may be of

---

[1] One of the streamers attached to a lady's head-dress.

use to you in case their Majesties should go to Audley End, and beg you to believe that I have obeyed your commands with pleasure.

In reply to the Howards' acknowledgment of these letters Lord Harcourt wrote:

Nuneham
14th September 1786.

My Lord,

I am much obliged to your lordship and Lady Howard for the expressions of acknowledgement with which you honour me, and shall be very happy to think that in any way I may have contributed to the ease of your lordship or Lady Howard during their Majesties' visit at Audley End, where I have no doubt that everything will be conducted with equal splendour and propriety.

The Rector of this parish, who is one of my chaplains, was in this house during the time of their Majesties' stay here, but was *never* called on to say Grace.

The Church of this parish is an ornamental Temple in the Garden, and not, I fancy, more than an hundred yards from the house, so that it is more like a domestic chapel than a Parish Church, and neither the path leading to it, nor the door by which the parishioners enter, have any communication with the garden from which the door of the family closet opens, which is a very spacious one and raised above the floor exactly similar to that your lordship describes. When their Majesties attended divine service no alteration was made in the disposition of the seats in the Church, but every person was admitted and placed as on other Sundays, but two arm-chairs were placed in the front of the closet for the King and Queen, and three of those which always remain in it were placed on either hand of their Majesties, and in the same line, for the Princesses.

Never, my lord, having held any office at Court, I am quite at a loss to answer your lordship's query respecting the presentations at Cambridge, because I know not whether in the absence of the Lord or Groom in waiting, the Equerry has an *indisputable right* to supply their place. The Groom, *I know*, has such a right in absence of the Lord, nor would, or indeed could, my brother (on account of his brethren of the Bedchamber) have surrendered that right *even to me* during the hours the King passed both last year and this at Oxford, had I not at his request asked the king himself, who made choice of me to officiate as his Lord; which was without precedent, and which I do not believe his Majesty would have made, had not the Groom then with him been my brother, and had he not known the terms of affection and friendship we live on with each other—for in every other case it would have given offence to the Groom superceded, and to every other person holding the same office at Court.

These hints will, I hope, enable your lordship to satisfy yourself as to the point in question respecting your acting as Lord of the Bed-chamber when at Cambridge. I beg leave to offer my respects to Lady Howard, and to assure your lordship of the regard with which I have the honour to be, my lord,

Your faithful humble servant,

Harcourt.

Lady Harcourt is still at Windsor.

The visit to Nuneham is described by Fanny Burney in her *Diary and Letters*,[1] where the house is said to be one of those 'straggling, half-new, half-old, half-comfortable, and half-forlorn mansions.' As for the way things were managed there, she complains with some bitterness about being handed out of the royal carriage by a common postilion, about the 'difficulties and disgraces' of her wanderings through endless passages as she searched helplessly for her own apartment, and of the humilia-tion she was put to by the 'prodigious fine yellow-laced' menials, the 'yellow-laced saunterers,' and the 'superfine men in laced liveries,' who were much too high and mighty to assist a mere lady-in-waiting. Affairs would have been managed, perhaps, more efficiently at Audley End, with a general in command! But the visit never took place.

Evidently Lord and Lady Harcourt were kept busy at this time instructing the nobility on the way Their Majesties would expect to be entertained, because after the visit to Blenheim from Nuneham we find the Duchess of Marlborough writing to the Archbishop of Canterbury that Lord and Lady Harcourt had told them what to do, and adding amusingly: 'Poor Lord Harcourt seemed quite happy to be able to rest himself, and the Duke of Marlborough found him sitting down behind every door where he could be concealed from royal eyes.' In the royal presence, of course, no one was allowed to sit, so the exhausted peer was obliged to conceal himself like a guilty schoolboy.

[1] Edited by Austin Dobson, vol. ii, pp. 446–79.

XII

LORD HOWARD AND THE
PEOPLE OF WALDEN

ENVIABLE AS Lord Howard's life may appear to us, it was never easy. It is wrong—though natural, perhaps—to regard the aristocracy of this age of their affluence and luxury as unburdened with responsibilities and untroubled with anxiety. There were many, no doubt, who did shirk their duties; but most of them quickly fell into decay, as did so many of the earls of Suffolk we have mentioned, particularly in the eighteenth century. Lord Howard, in common with the majority of his class at the time, had an extremely high sense of duty, and was incapable of shirking responsibilities which he and his kind sincerely believed they were divinely ordained to assume. It is true that their first concern was property: that they thought of themselves as custodians rather than as reformers, and governed the nation as such. But the preservation of property was then, in fact, universally accepted as the chief function of government, and those who ruled could hardly be expected to be more altruistic in private than they were required to be in public. And as later generations have benefited from the refusal of these favoured few to fritter away the nation's gains in the eighteenth and nineteenth centuries, it is hardly for us to complain about their acquisitiveness.

But if we cannot blame the landowners for their attitude of mind we certainly cannot blame the labouring poor for theirs. Let us look, then, at the relationship between Lord Howard and his less fortunate neighbours. The crucial point for both, of course, was the issue of work and wages. While his lordship provided these his authority was undisputed. But inevitably the day came round when the building and furnishing were practically completed, and when the workmen had to look elsewhere for their livelihood. It was the old story of too many depending on too few—on a single person, in fact. The neglect of previous generations had, however, taught its own grim lesson. The people of Walden had learned to fend for themselves, and had developed an independence of mind that had expressed itself from an early date in vigorous nonconformity —political and economic as well as religious. There was, no doubt, a remnant of feudalism surviving in north-west Essex in Lord Howard de Walden's time; but no more than a remnant, and great as the benefits that came with his residence were, there was no inclination among his neighbours to surrender their wills unquestioningly to his. Consequently there was bound to be a trial of strength sooner or later, and this came in the 1780s with a plan to connect the town, along with the adjacent villages, with the eastern counties' canal system.[1] The story is worth telling at some length.

On 26th October 1781 a public meeting promoted by the Committee of the Thames and Canal Navigation of the City of London was convened at the Crown, Great Chesterford, to consider whether it would be practicable to extend to Cambridge, by way of Saffron Walden, the navigation then open only to Bishop's Stortford, in order to give the whole of the region northward to the Wash water communication with London. But the meeting came to nothing because someone present— probably Lord Howard—objected to a chairman being appointed until the name of the person or body convening the meeting was announced.[2]

Seven years later a similar meeting was convened in the same place, and such was the interest in the scheme that not only were all the most influential gentlemen of the eastern counties present, but they were supported by hundreds of villagers and townspeople, many of whom had come considerable distances to show their interest in a scheme which they believed would bring new prosperity to East Anglia. Alderman Clark of the City of London was elected to the chair, and there was no secret about the meeting being organized by London business men, whose appearance in Essex was clearly resented by Lord Howard and his neighbour, the Hon. Percy Wyndham. Lord Howard had already made known his opposition, and at the meeting itself he acknowledged bluntly that he objected because he believed that such a canal would practically destroy the value of his property at Audley End, on which, he said, he had laid out

[1] E.R.O. D/DBy. E.33.
[2] *Cambridge Chronicle*, 20th October, 3rd November, 10th November 1782.

nearly £100,000 in improvements during the twenty-six years he had lived there. He therefore appealed for special consideration. But he had few supporters. When the votes were taken it was found that not more than twenty of the five hundred present had voted with him, and that the strongest opposition to his lordship's appeal came from his neighbours in Saffron Walden, who were, it seemed, solidly against him. Indeed, it was said that many of the local roughs had been packed into a wagon and driven over to Great Chesterford expressly to vote against Lord Howard, who, not unnaturally, was more than a little incensed by this demonstration of disloyalty.

The local press made the most of the occasion, arguing that Lord Howard's opposition to the present scheme was on a par with Sir Richard Brooke's opposition to the Duke of Bridgewater's, which was referred to as 'by far the most magnificent work ever done by one man,' continuing:

Lord Howard and Mr. Wyndham may be, no doubt they are, amiable men; their grounds, their game, what they see, nay what they wish, cannot fail of full regard, from the equity of English law, and the generosity of English gentlemen. Yet public utility must be an object no less than private expedience . . . and in this case, thus are they balanced—the Game and Pleasure ground of these two gentlemen, against the obvious interest of every gentleman and peasant from Lynn to London, in agriculture, habitation, and trade.

In September of the following year another public meeting was called, and at this a plan was submitted for the desired extension that would not, it was claimed, in any way injure the estates of Lord Howard and his neighbour, the Hon. Percy Wyndham. But these two gentlemen and a handful of supporters again objected, though apparently they had not made much headway with their opposition during the previous twelve months, for they were outvoted by 'at least fifty to one.' A further motion, for the extension of the navigation by way of Bourn Bridge, Burwell, Fordham, and Freckenham into the Brandon river was then submitted and carried by the same majority. And the meeting was so enthusiastic about both resolutions that a petition to Parliament for the schemes to be put into effect was prepared and signed there and then.

After the meeting a rumour was circulated that Lord Howard had accepted the will of the majority and withdrawn his opposition. This his lordship denied in no uncertain terms, declaring that whatever might be done locally he was confident that he

The Saloon, looking North

would find protection for his property and interests in the justice of Parliament.

To this the people of Walden replied with a letter to the press, which stated:

> As neighbours, we are no way behindhand with the noble Lord in any one act of respect or civility; but we do not hold ourselves as any part of his property, nor are we dependants on his will.
>
> The truth is, his property here, taking its value from the Parish Rates, is very little more than £1200 out of more than £3500 at which all the landed Property of the Town and Parish is assessed.
>
> It is a fact, equally to be depended upon, that not a single Gentleman, Maltster, Tradesman, or Inhabitant in Trade in the whole Town, lives under his Lordship or in one of his houses.
>
> The inhabitants of this place are populous, and as Traders value ourselves upon means sufficient to act with spirit and credit, to promote our own welfare; is it therefore reasonable for any one single person (let his station be what it may) to act so absolutely, as to deprive us, if he can, from receiving a benefit in common with the Public? Especially as his property will not be touched or cut through, otherwise than in places hardly to be brought within view of his house, park or pleasure grounds; or take any water from him. As his lordship's property will not be injured, nor his comfort disturbed, but in his mind's eye, we shall persist in our endeavours to do good to ourselves, having in view a benefit to the Public, and make no doubt of that protection which is to be expected from the justice of Parliament.
>
> Inhabitants of Saffron Walden.

Nine thousand pounds were promptly subscribed by townspeople for the scheme, and judging by their conduct both sides were equally confident of victory. From a twentieth-century viewpoint the townspeople, supporting as they were strong commercial interests, might be thought to have the stronger case. But this was 1788, and Lord Howard's confidence was to prove well founded. By enlisting the support of the Chancellor of Cambridge University and the Conservators of the River Cam, he put up to Parliament so powerful an opposition that leave to bring in the required Bill was refused.

Nor was the navigation affair the only one calling for what his lordship would regard as firm handling in 1789. In the summer of that year Archdeacon Hamilton, who has an impressive memorial in the chancel of Little Hadham church, reported: (1) that the roof of Saffron Walden church, one of the finest in

L

the county, had shifted and was in danger of collapsing; (2) that the walls of the south aisle were out of repair; (3) that the pavement throughout the church was very irregular and required attention.   Lord Howard had already drawn attention to the condition of the church fabric, and had suggested to the parishioners that a subscription list should be started, which he had offered to head with a loan of £500 free of interest.   But suggestions that came from Lord Howard were not being favourably received at this time, so nothing was done.   When, however, in May 1790, the Bishop of London came down for a confirmation, and expressed astonishment at the courage of the people of Walden in assembling in so dilapidated a building for public worship, Lord Howard thought it time the parish-ioners made up their minds about his suggestion of the previous year, and wrote to the churchwardens asking for an answer to his letter setting out his original proposals.[1]   So on 20th July 1790 a meeting of parishioners was held, at which these were discussed at some length, but rejected.   Instead, it was resolved unanimously that Lord Howard should be asked to undertake the restoration himself, 'solely and singly,' and that if he would do this the parishioners would undertake to bear half the cost, raising the money by annual instalments out of the parish rates by the assistance of a brief, by subscription, or by the aid of Parliament, as they should be advised, in sums not exceeding £250 a year.

The proposition was accordingly sent to his lordship, who promptly returned it without reply because, he said, it bore no signature to authenticate it, and he must know with whom he was dealing.   This drew forth a most eloquent letter, of which the writer must have been extremely proud, submitting to his lordship's kind consideration that the inhabitants of Saffron Walden were quite incapable of bearing so great a burden as the restoration of their parish church.   Therefore, the writer proceeded:

In this their difficulty the parishioners take leave to look up to the noble patron of the church, with humble hope and confidence that his Lordship will be pleased to consider the fabric of this ancient church, justly deemed a magnificent relic of Gothic Architecture, and standing as an eloquent monument of antiquity in a style superior to anything of the kind in the country, as a most valuable part of his Lordship's property and inheritance, and well becoming the splendour

[1] E.R.O. D/DBy. Q.9.

of his station and situation: and tho' the space which this building occupies and its extent far exceeds any real use to the Parish, its superabundant magnitude however may justly be considered as an additional and heavy burden on the parishioners. . . . Yet the parishioners in general would feel great reluctance to have it reduced . . . they therefore wish to have it made known to his Lordship, that they will cheerfully join with him in keeping up the original grandeur of this building, in such a way, as his Lordship shall be pleased to have it executed, according to his own taste and judgment, provided his Lordship shall be pleased solely and singly to take upon himself the whole design and execution of it, and will be pleased to bear one half of the expence himself.

The letter was in the name of the churchwardens, who themselves waited on Lord Howard with it. He replied promptly, expressing appreciation of the compliments they paid him personally, and of their desire to preserve their noble church; but pointing out that he would be put to great independent expense in repairing the chancel, for which he alone was responsible, and submitting that it would be unwise for a man of his years to undertake a long-term arrangement such as they suggested. He then offered to subscribe £1,000 towards the cost incurred by the parishioners in restoring what was, in fact, their own parish church. The letter had achieved its purpose. The new offer was gratefully accepted—gratefully and more readily, perhaps, than it would have been if the parishioners had known that the work would cost £8,000 and take three years to complete.

His own house and estate put into order, it was characteristic of Lord Howard that he should wish to set the neighbourhood to rights. It is easy to criticize much that he did as autocratic. So it was from a nineteenth—or twentieth—century viewpoint. But to his contemporaries there would be nothing unusual about his high-handed ways, although some of his friends—Dick Neville, no doubt—might have thought that in his bluff, soldierly way he did not always express himself as tactfully as he might have done. All, however, would agree about the scrupulous fairness of his character. This is well exemplified in an exchange of letters about the rating of the parish,[1] which arose out of the letter from the 'Inhabitants of Walden' quoted a moment ago in connection with the navigation dispute. Lord Howard evidently saw that there might be grounds for criticizing the

[1] E.R.O. D/DBÿ. Q.14.

rate at which his property was assessed, and on 13th October 1789 he wrote:

> Lord Walden having been informed that some of the inhabitants of Walden are jealous that his estates in the parish do not bear an equal proportion with those of his neighbours in the same parish, he desires to have them assured, that if he knew it from conviction, he should be the first to discourage any such partiality, and as the strongest proof he can offer of his sincerity he requests the vestry to give their opinion at large, whether they wish a new assessment on an equal pound rate, and that if they should, he will give them every assistance in his power.

A meeting of parishioners was called to consider this letter, and it was resolved that a new assessment should be made in accordance with Lord Howard's suggestion. But life moved slowly in the late eighteenth century, so it was not until the following April that proposals for the revision were ready for submission to his lordship, who received them from his steward, Mr. Pennystone, and it is pleasant to note that in acknowledging them, Lord Howard signed himself: 'Your Friend and Humble Servant, Howard.'

In consequence of this reassessment Lord Howard's property, which at this time paid two-fifths of the total rates in Saffron Walden, was assessed at:

Audley End Mansion House, lodges, etc., £100; other rateable property in his hands, including £280 for the Great Tithes of the parish and rectory, upon an average of three years' rent to Michaelmas 1789, £661 7s. 6d., making a total of £761 7s. 6d. Of this two-thirds was rated, namely, £507 10s. 0d. A memorandum in his own handwriting, dated 2nd November 1781,[1] shows how much this adjustment was costing him. It runs:

> I pay a composition of £10 a year to the parish of Walden in lieu of all parish rates of every kind for the old park and gardens and house at Audley End, which has been the custom time immemorial.
>
> For all other lands I occupy in Walden parish, whether descended to me, by purchase, or otherwise, I am rated according to the custom of the parish; but instead of team duty to the highway, I take upon myself to keep in repair the London highway from the end of the stone bridge to the east end of the village of Audley End. N.B. The bridge I built and am engaged to keep up. In regard to lands I occupy in the parish of Littlebury I am rated to all parish rates according to the custom of the place, but instead of team duty to the highway I

[1] E.R.O. D/DBy. Q.15.

take upon myself to keep in repair the road from the west end of the stone bridge up to the high London Turnpike road. Moreover I have engaged myself to keep in repair the new road leading from the ring into the Turnpike road at the back of the late made plantation.

Meanwhile work continued on the restoration of the church, culminating in the pew for the Audley End family described by the Rev. G. Montagu Benton, F.S.A.[1] as

a loft-pew, supported by five arches, across the chancel arch . . . the entrance being from the chancel by a double flight of steps. It was popularly known as 'the opera-box.' This structure may be termed a degenerate development of the chancel-screen, as it undoubtedly owed its origin to the fact that after the Reformation, rood-lofts were sometimes used as a pew by the principal inhabitant of the parish.

There is a model of this pew in the Tapestry Room at Audley End, and a picture of it in the vestry at Saffron Walden church. It was heated by a stove, and, according to family tradition, in the third Lord Braybrooke's time there was an understanding with the vicar that when her ladyship poked the fire it was time for him to wind up his sermon.

By the end of 1792 Lord Howard had paid out for the repair of Walden church £1,324, which increased to £1,763 during 1793. In the following year he completed the building of a new vicarage house at a total cost of £1,028, including a fee of £20 to William Ivory, and closed the account for church restoration, which by that time had cost him £2,321. Of this sum a very considerable proportion had gone into the gallery pew. The result, as we gather from a letter written to Richard Neville Neville on 22nd May 1793,[2] was entirely satisfactory.

'Our respectable Friend the Bishop of London[3] and Mrs. Porteus,' he writes,

came to us on Fryday Eveng. The next Morning we conducted them to the Church with which he was high [sic] pleas'd indeed, much pleas'd with its elegant Simplicity & complimented Me particularly on those Parts that were incidently of my own Construction, in keeping them so well in Union, as He was pleas'd to say, & corresponding with the Stile of the old Gothic Fabrick & admir'd much the Altar. On Sunday our Friend Gretton had prepar'd everything that was right to recieve the Bishop of London with due Respect. He had selected Psalms for singing proper for the Day & the Occasion

---

[1] *Essex Review*, vol. xxxiv, p. 1.   [2] E.R.O. D/DBy. C.3/42.
[3] Beilby Porteus, 1731–1808; Bishop of London, 1784–1808.

well perform'd too by our Band & the Voices—the Church was amazingly fill'd (comparatively with any thing ever seen before) the whole Congregation perfectly attentive thro'out—& when the Bishop began his excellent Sermon to the time of its finishing every Body's Eyes were fix'd on his Manner, & their Ears on his Eloquence. He did Justice to the Parish for their Exertions in the Restoration of their Church (which he had seen near crumbling) & gave them full Credit for the Institution of the Sunday Schools: their Leader & Promoter of these Works did not escape his Observation. Judge, my dear Neville, of my Feelings on this whole day, conscious I say to you, not only of having brought all these Matters forward, as what I felt right, but thro' an inveterate Oposition from some People, & who had at the beginning got with them in the more publick Meetings by far a Majority—but Perseverance in a Matter, that was in itself fundamentally right, has carried Me through finally with Content.

I must once more return to the Bishop, who would have alleg'd all Animosities, had there been any existing, by his Candour & Judgment—for by what I have been able to learn there was not an Individual but was perfectly satisfied & pleas'd with the whole of his Discourse (ch. 8, v. 22, First of Kings). I hope I have not written Nonsence, for I have run on without any other Consideration than that of writing to a Friend that I love perhaps the most of any, & as such have open'd my Mind, & Feelings—but I know at the same time that the good Wife of a good Husband has a natural Right to participate in any thing that will afford him Pleasure on this whole Occasion. Judge of dear Lady Howard's Pleasure & Comfort, who has been my Partner thro'out the Whole of all these Transactions, & from whom I have experienc'd every kind Assistance. My Heart is full. Adieu—ever yrs. H. & B.

But the sunset glow of the last years was not to remain unclouded. The year after the one in which this letter was written, 1794, brought one of the worst harvests for many years, and this, together with the rising prices and shortage of supplies brought about by the war with France, reduced the poor everywhere to the brink of starvation. The Hammonds have dealt with the tragic conditions of 1795 in their *Village Labourer*. Essex, as we should expect, was as badly hit as its neighbours, and Lord Howard, who was lord lieutenant at the time, early consulted a Mr. Black, a land surveyor with a considerable reputation in the eastern counties, on plans for poor relief.[1] From correspondence that passed between them it is clear that they were both impressed by a scheme drawn up at a county meeting held in Huntingdonshire on 30th June 1795 with the

[1] E.R.O. D/DBy. O.12.

Earl of Sandwich in the chair, at which, among other things, it was resolved:

1. That bread should be sold to the poor at 13*d.* a half-peck loaf;
2. That the landowners of the county should be invited to subscribe to a relief fund;
3. That any illegal exportation of corn and flour, or any forestalling, engrossing, or regrating of provisions should be severely punished;
4. That all the county justices, and every subscriber of more than £5 should be entitled to serve on the Committee that should put the resolutions of the meeting into effect.

The inadequacy of the measures taken for the relief of the poor at this time has often been pointed out; but before sitting in judgment on these men and their schemes, we ought in fairness to consider whether or not they did their best according to the knowledge available to them in their own generation. The question is too big to be dealt with here; but we can at least look into the minds and hearts of a few of our more enlightened Essex landowners. The majority, no doubt, shared the viewpoint of Mr. Black, who wrote to one of his own Huntingdonshire tenants:

As I believe you to be an honest and industrious man, I hope you will set a good example to those poor labourers whom Providence has placed in a small degree below you . . . that you will in every way pay due respect and submission to the laws that protect you and me and everyone, in the full and true possession of everything that belongs to us, for without such attention we shall soon be in the same wretched state that the unfortunate people of France are brought to by a set of designing knaves who had nothing to lose themselves and are now living on the plunder of those who were the Protectors of their country, and upon what every honest man had got by his industry. Let me recommend to you to fear God, love and honour your king, and respect the magistrates.

That, we may take it, was how Lord Howard saw his own and his neighbours' duty in such an emergency.

The first meeting at Saffron Walden was actually held the day before the Huntingdonshire meeting. Like most public meetings of the time, it was held at the Rose and Crown, following announcements in the church and several nonconformist places of worship on the previous Sunday. At this meeting it was resolved that the churchwardens and overseers should forthwith levy a rate upon the inhabitants of the parish of not more than fourpence in the pound for the immediate relief of the poor, and the mayor, Mr. Henry Archer, was authorized to buy all the corn he could get, at the rate of £26 per load. When it was pointed out that there was still the scarcity to contend with, and that Mr. Archer might be unable to find enough, even at the price agreed, Lord Howard offered to pay a premium of 2 guineas per load, over and above the market price ruling on the day of purchase. But there were soon complications. On 17th July 1795 we find Mr. Black writing to Lord Howard from Dunmow, that the mayor was being accused of having taken advantage of a young man named John Andrews, by contracting with him for the purchase of a quantity of corn, belonging to Andrews's uncle, a Mr. Horner, at a price below that ruling on the date of purchase. Consequently, Mr. Horner had given orders that none of his corn should be sold to Mr. Archer in future. The price had evidently risen above the £26, plus 2 guineas premium, at which the mayor was authorized to buy. Mr. Black dealt with the matter in the only reasonable way, namely, by agreeing with Mr. Horner that the price in future should be that ruling on the day of delivery.

There was another serious food problem, that of potato supply. Let us hear about both from Lord Howard himself. To his friend Neville he wrote: [1]

Why your Friend Mr. James Grenville wishes to impose on you the Task (from his own Information too) of instructing Ministers in regard to the Potatoe Business I know not—his Observation however of the abominable Practice of bagging them up, & sending them out of the Country, has prevail'd to that Degree in this Neighbourhood, that they are already here at the Price of 1s. 9d. per Bushell. Foreseeing what was likely to happen & to save our Poor from paying an exorbitant Price, I have purchas'd 3000 Bushell at one Shilling a Bushell, that they may have them at this pretty reasonable Price, when they may be distress'd. I have made a large Pit in a drie Chalk, well cover'd & thatch'd over under a Barn of mine at Walden, from whence they will be deliver'd as the Occasions may occur; it seems upon Enquiry half a Peck of Potatoes will make a Meal for Eight Mouths including ye Children in a Family—so that I trust my Plan may have its Uses.

The Parish of Walden had a Meeting to-day to take into Consideration, what would be best to be done for the immediate Relief of our distress'd Poor. It has been thought proper in many Places in this

[1] E.R.O. D/DBy. C.4.B/2.

Neighbourhood, to relieve by Money Weekly at the Rate of Six Pence per Head where there is a Family of Children, & the Parish have adopted a Plan that I have recommended to them, that they may have a regular System to proceed upon—that the Poor may know what they have to expect, viz: that as the Price of Wheat drops, so will their Allowance be proportion'd, and when, if ever, it should drop to £12 a Load, the allowance to cease entirely, the Money to be rais'd by a Rate on the Parish. Subscriptions won't do, at least with our Corporate Body, for it was so manag'd this last Summer that it went to buy Corn & Flower for the *Parish*, of which the Rich as well as the Poor participated. When the Accounts were laid before me, which were very complicated, I did however make this Discovery. So I trust that Mode is put a Stop to—& so I will venture to say, if We take a reasonable Care of our Poor, & that the Magistrates, the Mayor in particular will properly discharge his Duty, & determine to be obey'd, The Police of the Place might be so regulated, that we might defie all Attempts to Tumults or Riots—or at least nip them in the Budd. But after all I find I am got into a long Tale of a Tub, that altho' it interests me very much, may tire you to Death. So down goes my Pen!

The following day, by the way, he added a postscript to this letter:

I forgot just to mention to you last Night that the Duke of Rutland had been here on Thursday to see the Place—lavish to a Degree in his Praises, & said he never saw such a House in his life for Magnificence & Convenience. In the Dairy, or rather in the Bake House, he desired to taste our brown Bread, which he lik'd so well that be beg'd a Loaf. The Morning before, the Duke of Somerset came to see the Place, & partook of our Family Breakfast. Very Chearful and easy. Both the Dukes went afterwards to see our Church.

This 1795 crisis is well known to students of economic history, if only for the Speenhamland System, the famous remedy devised by the Berkshire justices, and later adopted in most parts of the country, which provided for wages to be supplemented out of the parish rates. However well intentioned, this, it is now agreed, was unfortunate in its effect because it pauperized the poor, doubled the rates, and gave the farmers cheap labour at a time when they were getting high prices for their crops, though the crops, it must be admitted, were poor. The farmers' side of the argument has not always been stated fairly. It is worth noting that Mr. Black even went so far as to recommend relief funds for small farmers at this time, as well as for their labourers.

It was towards the end of this same year that Pitt came down into Essex to stay with friends, who, when the great man complacently dilated on the good fortune of industrious and virtuous labourers in this favoured island, was taken by his host to see for himself the conditions endured by the poor in Halstead. 'The Minister,' says Lord Rosebery, 'surveyed it in silent wonder, and declared he had no conception that any part of England could present a spectacle of such misery.'[1] It was probably this eye-opening experience that induced him to bring in his own poor-relief measure, laid before the House in November of the following year.

The nation would have been better advised if two of our Essex economists had been consulted at this time! There were at least two gentlemen in the north-west of the county who grasped the significance of what had led up to the crisis of 1795. These were the Rev. John Howlett, vicar of Great Dunmow, and Thomas Ruggles of Clare, Suffolk, and Spains Hall, Finch-ingfield, Essex, a justice of the peace for both counties. Howlett realized that during the past half-century wages had lagged behind prices, and he argued in favour of a minimum wage regulated by what we should to-day call a cost-of-living index. It was calculated that in the second half of the eighteenth century the price of food had risen by 60 per cent.[2] This was too great a gap to be bridged by poor relief. Ruggles, in a book entitled The History of the Poor, written in 1797, expresses the firm belief 'that, in no instance, through any breadth of country, did the additional increase the poor received to their income, from wages, gratuitous donations, and parochial relief, approach the increased price of bread' (p. 378). The justices might have pegged wages, but they had been unable to peg prices, which had continued to rise throughout 1795 and 1796, until it had become impossible for an average family of five—the number arrived at by Howlett as the average in his own parish—working as hard as they could from sunrise to sunset, to gain more than what they would need for bread alone. Wages were then 7s. a week in winter and 8s. in summer in north-west Essex. This, said Ruggles, might be supplemented by 1s. 6d. to 2s. a week earned by the rest of the family—rarely by more. With an allowance from the rates of 6d. per head, the breadwinner—and how well he was named!—would only have 11s. 6d. in winter

---

[1] Lord Rosebery, Pitt, 1891, p. 169.
[2] See also Nathaniel Kent, Notes on the Agriculture of Norfolk, p. 165.

and 12*s*. 6*d*. in summer. Allowing even an extra shilling on wages, he would only have 13*s*. 6*d*. at most. Yet the quartern loaf went up to 1*s*. 3*d*. when, in the spring of 1796, wheat was being sold at £30 a load. At this rate Ruggles—who was himself a man of substance—reckoned that bread alone was costing 10*s*. to 12*s*. 6*d*. per week for an average labourer's family. Tickets were issued to the poor of Saffron Walden which enabled them to buy bread at threepence below the market price; but even these did not meet the need, though at one time as many as 1,254 persons per week were assisted in this way.

In the letter from Mr. Black to Lord Howard informing his lordship of the agreement with Mr. Horner, it is mentioned that barley had been bought from Mr. Horner to be mixed with wheat for the bread being issued to the poor. In the letter from Lord Howard to Mr. Neville we learn that brown bread was being baked at Audley End, and that the Duke of Rutland liked it so well that he begged a loaf to carry away with him. These are two interesting scraps of information that have an important bearing on each other. From what Mr. Black says it is clear that the poor were not used to having barley mixed with their wheat. How they liked the new bread in Essex we are not told; but the Hammonds inform us that the labourers in some parts of the southern counties objected strongly, stating that the coarser flour upset their bowels. The gentry, on the other hand, baked the despised brown bread for themselves and liked it. When the poor objected, the rich replied that they had it on their own tables and suffered no ill effects. This fastidiousness of the poor seemed to the rich both wicked and foolish. They contended that what was good enough for his master ought to be good enough for Jack. What nobody realized at the time was that the labourers on arable farms had for a long time lived on a diet of white bread and tea, and as a result had become delicate and queasy. It was the riding, drinking, hard-living squire who was the sturdy creature.

In the north of England white bread never had been enjoyed by the poor; but there the coarser diet was balanced with milk. It is estimated that in pastoral regions of Cumberland, Westmorland, and Yorkshire the labourers were drinking six or seven times as much milk as the Essex labourer would get. Even in those parts of the county where there was pastoral farming, the milk was being made into butter for sale in London. There was little retained for the poor.

Lord Howard, as we see from his letter to Neville just quoted, hoped that there would be no riots or tumults in Walden. He was disappointed in this. On the morning of 27th July 1795 several of the Walden roughs burst into the yard of a local innkeeper named Thomas Gardiner, climbed a ladder leading to the room where he stored both his own corn and a quantity of wheat belonging to a Mr. Hall, and this they carried away in sacks to the Market Cross, where, alleged Gardiner, he heard them say they would sell the wheat at five shillings a bushel. This was followed by demonstrations in the Walden streets, during which a certain William Church was heard to say that as soon as the corn was ripe at Buckenhall Leys they would go and cut it, and their wives would carry it away. There were also threats to steal potatoes and cut down the trees on the common for winter fuel.

The mayor appealed to Lord Howard for protection, and a messenger was sent post haste to Lord Cornwallis at Warley Camp, who replied that he was at a loss to know how to afford relief, because he had only one weak troop of Pembrokeshire Fencibles, almost all of them untrained recruits, the First Dragoon Guards having been sent by government orders to Romford, and the Surrey Fencibles being then encamped at Colchester. Only from the last named, as Lord Cornwallis understood the position, could help be gained. So Lord Howard, with all the authority of his office as lord lieutenant, addressed a request for help to Lord Onslow at Colchester. Meanwhile the rioters, according to his lordship, continued to demonstrate—'a very disaffected class indeed, by whose workings threats of various kinds are much in circulation—firing and burning down houses &c. and among the rest the audacious one of forming bodies for harvesting crops of corn on the neighbouring farms.'

The appeal to Lord Onslow was successful. On 28th July he wrote:

In all places and in all capacities, civil and military, I am happy to render any services to Lord Howard, and am now particularly so to receive my good general's orders to furnish two troops of the Regiment I have the honour to command. . . . For myself, it will ever be my pleasure and my pride, that their first services have been to defend Audley End and its neighbourhood, and that my good Lady Howard and your Lordship have her old County Fencibles stand sentinels at your door.

Accordingly, one troop of Surrey Light Dragoons marched from Lexden Camp at five o'clock on the morning of 29th July, with orders to put themselves under Lord Howard's commands and to march into Saffron Walden on the following day at exactly half past twelve o'clock. Another troop was sent on the 30th with orders to march through Braintree to Dunmow and Thaxted. The latter, however, were returned, and General Whyte, who was in command, acknowledging their arrival at Colchester, wrote that he was particularly happy to have them back as there were constant demands for their services from the magistrates, adding significantly of the rioters: 'I cannot find out that these poor deluded people have ever assembled in this neighbourhood from any other motive than that of getting corn from farmers who would not bring it to market.'

Poverty and hardship long remained the lot of labouring families and when, on 27th May 1797, Lord Howard died, leaving his wife the sole executrix of his will, it was found that he had endowed a fund [1] for supplying clothing to twelve poor men and twelve poor women of Walden, and five poor men and five poor women of Littlebury, selected or nominated by the occupier of Audley End, advised by the vicars of the respective parishes, with certain reservations. The clothing thus provided, which became known in Walden as the Howard Livery, was to be distributed a few days before Christmas each year, and those who received it were to appear in their new garments in their own parish churches on the following Christmas Day, Easter Day, and Whitsunday, both morning and evening, for the inspection of their respective vicars. No person was to be clothed out of the trust more than once in three years, and no two persons from the same household were to be clothed in the same year. Furthermore, the garments provided were to be as nearly as possible the same, both as regards quality and colour, as those Lord Howard had himself been in the habit of distributing personally.

Lord Howard's income at the time of his death was approximately £7,000 a year. There was neither son nor nephew to succeed him. The Audley End estate—excluding the house—in accordance with the Countess of Portsmouth's will, devolved to his only surviving sister, Mary, wife of Dr. Parker, rector of St. James's, Westminster, for whom Lord Howard had long and unsuccessfully tried to obtain a bishopric. Of his eight brothers

[1] E.R.O. D/DBy. F.33.

and sisters not one left children. He and Mrs. Parker were the last of their race. Recording his passing in the Saffron Walden parish register on 2nd June 1797 his old friend and chaplain, 'our friend Gretton,' wrote:

John Griffin Griffin, Lord Howard de Walden and Lord Braybrooke of Braybrooke in the County of Northampton, was buried in the family vault with his ancestors. The procession from the house began at eleven o'clock and the concourse of people of all ranks who were assembled at this awful solemnity to offer the last mark of esteem for that truly respectable nobleman was very great. The funeral service was read by the Revd. Wm. Hamilton, Archdeacon of Colchester, and accompanied by the heartfelt sorrow of multitudes who have lost a most valuable protector and friend. To detail his several and numerous perfections would indeed by an arduous attempt. Suffice it to say of him that if unfeigned piety, if humanity, beneficence, charity, philanthropy, be virtues estimable in heaven, laudable on earth, all these he practised in a superior manner. For these he will be rewarded above and long, very long, be recorded in the memory of every grateful survivor. His Lordship died full of years and earthly honours on the 25th of May last in the 79th year of his age, lamented by no one more sincerely than by him who attempts this imperfect sketch of his character, his very humble and most obliged friend for thirty-two years during the twenty-six last of which he officiated daily as his domestic chaplain at the Chapel in Audley End House.

It was the passing of one who had reigned like a king in the land, whose wealth had transformed the landscape, and whose character had dominated the life of north-west Essex for thirty-five years.

XIII

FROM HOWARD TO BRAYBROOKE

TO A MAN who built and planned for the future as Lord Howard did, the succession to his property must have been a serious matter, particularly when it became plain that he would have neither sons nor nephews to inherit it. The Countess of Portsmouth's will provided that in that event Richard Neville Neville, or his heir, should inherit the estate on the death without issue of the last of Anne Whitwell's children. So as time went on the association between Audley End and Billingbear, always of the friendliest, became increasingly intimate.

The Nevilles of Billingbear trace their descent from Sir Edward Neville of Adlington Park in Kent, second son of the George, Lord Abergavenny, who died in 1492, and the most distinguished member of this particular branch of the family, the Elizabethan courtier and diplomat Sir Henry Neville, looks down at us from the walls of the Great Hall at Audley End, as also does his son, a second Sir Henry. Richard Neville Neville was a worthy successor. He was a delightful personality, charming and accomplished, and a well-spring of happiness to all who knew him. While in Geneva as a young man he was a member of that brilliant group of friends,[1] nine in number, who in the 1740s formed an English club called the Common Room, for the discussion of their various literary interests—botany, fencing, military history, philosophy, politics, music, moun-taineering, and apparently every other polite and gentlemanly accomplishment. One of the group, Benjamin Stillingfleet, botanist and *littérateur*, composed sonnets for each of them, and to Neville, who was then known as Aldworth, he wrote:

> Dear Dick of soul that answereth to thy birth,
> Generous and noble, and of open brow,
> Form'd to be chearful and make others so,
> Come let's enjoy the hours design'd for mirth.

[1] See R. W. Ketton-Cremer, *Norfolk Portraits*, pp. 96–109.

157

Let low ambition tempt the sons of earth
    To tread her gloomy paths, thou ne'er shalt bow
    To that false mistress. Nature's glass shall show
To thee whate'er in life has real worth.

Since she, kind mother and true Prophetess,
    Points out the blessings of a chearful mind
    To all her sons on easy terms and plain,
Let us not think that blessing therefore less,
    And like the leprous Namaan, proudly blind,
    To cleanse ourselves in her pure stream disdain.

Richard Neville Neville reached the peak of his career in 1762, when at the age of forty-five he was sent to the embassy at Paris as secretary and special plenipotentiary, with a commission to assist the Duke of Bedford, under whom he had served at the Admiralty, in negotiating the treaty of the following year. His official papers have been deposited at the Public Record Office; but his more personal letters have been retained, and one to his friend, Mademoiselle Goudet,[1] so well reflects his pleasure at the success of his mission that it is worth giving.[2] Writing from Fontainebleau on 26th October 1763 he says:

As I love to have my best friends partake of every agreeable circumstance that befalls me, I steal a moment to communicate them to you. The first, and greatest, is that my Royal Master has deigned to honour me with his most gracious acceptance of my services at this Court. This from himself, signed by himself. His brother king[3] has said and done everything that an honest Englishman could wish. I took leave of him yesterday, and have in my pocket his picture nobly set in diamonds. I have wound up all my bottoms, and I flatter myself in every point to the honour and advantage of my country. Don't from thence imagine I expect the approbation of it. In short, I am happy to have done my duty, have gained by so doing the approbation of my own court, and yet preserved the friendship of this. I hope to be in London about the 12th of next month. You shall know the time exactly as soon as I can tell you. God bless you all.

Whether he expected approbation or not, it is gratifying to find that his services did not go unrewarded. On 12th November 1763 he again wrote to Mademoiselle Goudet to inform her that he was to kiss the king's hand for the appointment of Paymaster

---

[1] Mademoiselle Goudet was a friend of Mrs. Neville Neville, who died in 1750, two years after marriage, leaving two babies. Mademoiselle Goudet devoted her life to the Billingbear family.

[2] E.R.O. D/DBy. C.2/73.   [3] Louis XV of France.

The Fire-place in the Saloon

of the Pensions, an office which he evidently expected to bring him in £1,000 a year. But much as his friends would appreciate such services as he was able to render to his country, their chief source of pleasure was himself. He was the most lively character, brimful of high spirits and almost bursting with amiability.

Sir John and Lady Griffin were frequently at Billingbear, Richard Neville Neville frequently at Audley End, particularly for birthdays and festivals. Thus we find the Griffins at Billingbear for Mr. Neville's sixty-second birthday, and how charmingly he notes the occasion:

'Sept. 3rd 1779: Sir John and Lady Griffin dined with us on their way to Harleyford, and hailed my entry into my *Grand Climacterick*. God make me thankful for all His blessings.'

Doubtless at these meetings Richard Neville Neville's son, Richard Aldworth Neville, in whom the hopes of both were centred, was the principal topic of conversation. In 1779 he was twenty-nine and still unmarried, though plans for the event, solemnized at Stowe in the following June, must already have been maturing. The bride was Catherine, youngest daughter of the Right Hon. George Grenville, and sister of George, first Marquess of Buckingham. After the wedding the two households were enlivened by regular and affectionate messages from the couple, and in course of time by visits with their children, who arrived rather quickly, bringing, as usual, both joy and sorrow to their parents. The first-born of the marriage, twin boys, died on the day of their birth, 2nd March 1781. The second daughter died in infancy, and the youngest son at the age of six in 1803. But six of them lived, and the third, a son, who eventually became third Lord Braybrooke, was always a favourite at Audley End, and loved the house from infancy. It was he, as we shall see presently, who was to bring it to completion. Meanwhile Richard Neville Neville and Lord Howard grew old together and completed their plans for Dick and his family after their death. Their estates, of course, would pass to him automatically; but Lord Howard was concerned that he should bear a title befitting the wealth and dignity he was destined to enjoy. Since obtaining for himself the Howard de Walden title in 1784, Lord Howard had always known that at his death it must either again fall into abeyance or be claimed by the earls of Bristol. So after he had formally adopted Richard Aldworth Neville as his heir he took steps to secure a title that could be inherited with the estate. And the title

M

chosen was not, as it might have been, one that would perpetuate a Neville connection, but the Griffin title of Braybrooke.

The first intimation we have of this new creation being sought comes in a letter from Lord Howard to his heir dated 5th June 1786, in which he says:

My dear Dick,

What must depend on greater folks than ourselves cannot be answered for; but after a long conversation with your brother the Marquis,[1] who seems to have a great affection for you, we have agreed that I shall lend my name to a fresh creation, to descend from me to yourself, and Lord Buckingham undertakes to move it on a proper opportunity.

But on 20th August of the same year the marquess wrote to Lord Howard from Stowe:

My dear Lord,

I have been extremely uneasy for some time past lest I should appear inattentive to your lordship.'

There had, however, been reasons for the delay until the previous Friday, 'when,' Lord Buckingham continued,

Mr. Pitt desired me to inform your lordship that his Majesty had received with 'the utmost graciousness your lordship's request, so full of kindness to Mr. Neville, to whom in default of your issue you wished the title should be limited; that it was impossible at the present moment to bestow that mark of his favour which he was fully inclined to give at the first opportunity, but that he could not (for obvious reasons) engage positively for the exact time in which it would be done.'

Having himself received many such letters Lord Howard cannot have felt at all reassured; but whether with Pitt's help or not, the barony of Braybrooke, with special remainder to Richard Aldworth Neville, was granted to Lord Howard in 1788, and the two who were to enjoy it in succession exchanged their felicitations and compliments. Dick came out to Audley End at once, and from there wrote to his friend, Viscount Bulkeley, on 10th August 1788:[2]

My dear Bulkeley,

Our Dignity in Perspective is to be settled on the king's return from Cheltenham, & I lose no time in giving you the earliest tidings of an event in which you will both so much and so kindly rejoice. It is yet a Secret, so you will be so good as to let it rest in your breast and in that of Lady Bulkeley until it comes out. The title will, I

---

[1] His brother-in-law.   [2] E.R.O. D/DBy. C.5/15.

believe, be Braybrooke, an old family business, formerly enjoyed by the ancestors of both Lord Howard and me.[1]

Richard Aldworth Neville was as popular as his father had been. Hundreds of his racy, informative, and entirely delightful letters have been preserved in manuscript. There are two bound volumes of them in the Berkshire Record Office, a large collection in the Essex Record Office, and another bound collection in Lord Braybrooke's possession at Mutlow Hall. Lord Howard's affection for him was unbounded. Writing to Richard Neville Neville in July 1778—ten years before the creation of the barony—he had said:

My dear Friend, whenever I speak of my friend Dick it is with much pleasure; and when it is to you it is with double the satisfaction, as it is impossible doing him justice, but it must be in his favour. We are just returned from spending three or four days with Lady Harriet Conyers in the neighbourhood of Cock's Heath. Lieutenant Neville [Dick] dined with us on Sunday; and I have besides had the pleasure of seeing a good deal of him every day—the ladies waited on him in his tent on Tuesday evening. I am sure it will give you some pleasure to hear (though you hear it every day) how much he is loved and esteemed by everybody in camp from highest to lowest. General Kepple, with whom I have had a little correspondence lately, spoke to me of him in the handsomest and kindest manner imaginable. These are his own words: 'A more pleasing young man in every situation of life that I have had the good fortune to see him in, I have never met with.'

The frank, manly face of the portraits supports all that is said of him by his friends, and indeed there is nothing surprising about his qualities, inherited as they were from a father who had been equally beloved. Let us look at one or two of his letters, for if the houses these noble families lived in reveal to us something of their lives, it is in their letters that they become most real to us as persons. Perhaps Dick was most completely at ease when writing to his friend Bulkeley, who was of his own generation and his most intimate friend. Here we have him on 9th November 1784:

My dearest Bulkeley,
    We have been six weeks at Brighthelmstone and are now on our way to Stanlake [2] for about a fortnight, when Catherine returns to

---

[1] An error. It had been enjoyed by Lord Howard's ancestors, but not by Neville's.
[2] The Aldworth family estate, now held with Billingbear by the Aldworth Nevilles.

attend Hester in her lying in. . . . We bathed our children, but the sea disagreed with the boy, and his health was not good afterwards, owing to a rash which is now nearly gone. The girl is livelier and more improved than ever, and has received uncommon benefit from bathing, which she thought good fun. Our life was very pleasant and the place very comfortable and much suited to my disposition, who like lounges, old magazines, and good riding and eating.

The Prince used to ride past and drive four post horses in hand backwards and forwards, and gave frequent dinners to George Hanger, Dick Beckford, Sir John and Lady O'Byrne. . . . Besides the usual entertainments, we had the pleasure of seeing two gentlemen dance a minuet for a wager.

Lord Howard had never written such letters as these. The man who was to succeed him lived in an easier, friendlier world. Consequently we feel in his letters a warmth of humanity that Lord Howard, fine old warrior that he was, neither possessed nor inspired. Neville was a family man. That, perhaps, was the essential difference. In his letters children and politics, balls and elections, follow each other as topics in a serene, confident flow of language, not unlike his father's, perhaps, but entirely different from anything in old Lord Howard's, which so often begin with an apology for having been so long in replying to his correspondent's last and end with an apology for having wasted so much of his time with the present. Here is a letter from Dick to Viscount Bulkeley on 19th May 1786, which, after referring to the death of his youngest child—'the sweetest child ever seen'—goes on to say that Pitt would do well to pay a little more attention to the refractory members of his party; 'but,' it continues,

his back is too long and straight, and his dinners are too few. But indeed it is hard to say how we are to be managed, and I believe any future minister, tho' he may invite every man of us, and bow and caress us with every appearance of sincerity, will want those essential qualifications which Pitt abounds in, and not keep up a majority for two sessions. The influence of the Crown ought now no longer to be diminished. We have taken up half this session in East India business, and I have already seen enough to pronounce Hastings the greatest man of almost any age. So far from deserving blame, he deserves a seat in your House.

Routs and Balls flourish more than usual this year, at most of which Mrs. Fitzherbert appears, and it is very ridiculous to see the awkward curtsies and humble gestures of the Great Ladies in the country, pressing her to enter rooms before them—however, this strange business is beginning to be stale in this strange country; neither at present are the print shops so full of pleasantry on the subject, as they used to be for two whole months. . . . Our dear Bess is still a spinster, and, I fear, likely to continue so. She has mounted a very neat little phaeton by Leader which she drives. Her health is better than usual. The Buckinghams are at Bath, where I hear the waters agree wonderfully with both. . . .

And so he runs through all the news about their mutual friends.

Always in reading letters from Richard Neville Neville and Richard Aldworth Neville we have the impression of charming unaffected people, without a shadow of pomposity about them. Indeed, it seems likely that the grandeur of Audley End in Lord Howard de Walden's time was too great for his heir. In a letter to Bulkeley from there on 13th August 1787 he says:

I have been living in all kinds of noisy feastings and in music since the commencement of this month. We are now here for a week, after which we shall go to Elton, and return home on the 25th. This place is most wonderfully improved indeed, but unfortunately there is too great observance of punctilio to be palatable to those of a less mincing and conformable turn.

Like his father and Lord Howard, Dick was a loyal subject of the third George, and he felt, no doubt, that the removal of George III was the end, politically, for himself and his friends. His father's association with the royal family having been so friendly, he would undoubtedly have been advanced at court if the king had remained in his senses. He had sat in Parliament as member for Grampound from 1774 to 1780, for Buckingham from 1780 to 1782, and was now member for Reading, which he continued to represent until he succeeded to the Braybrooke barony in 1797. When in 1791 the lord lieutenancy of Berkshire became vacant by the death of Lord Craven the claims of the Nevilles were laid before Pitt, to whom it was stated that they were as old a family as any in the county—they had claims, in fact, through two of its oldest families, the Aldworths of Stanlake and the Nevilles of Billingbear, and their property was inferior only to that of Lord Craven. Pitt, however, replied that Lord Radnor, who had applied for the office many years earlier, had been appointed.

In 1793 Richard Neville Neville died, and Lord Howard himself began preparing for the end. As we should expect, there were many letters to Richard Aldworth Neville at this time, carefully designed to secure the successful transfer and continued good management of the estate, although he was not to enjoy it in full until the death of Mrs. Parker—Lord Howard's last surviving sister—and her husband. He did, however, enjoy some benefit immediately, and the reservation of the remainder was no hardship to him. He was already a rich man, and four months before he died Lord Howard wrote to say that he had provided for him to have £1,600 a year immediately on his death, £1,200 of which would come from property in the parish and neighbourhood of Saffron Walden. The letter concluded: 'Be kind and friendly to my wife as long as you live, and inspire your children with love and respect for her. I'll say no more.' These last letters from Lord Howard have a tenderness that might seem out of keeping with the vigorous letters of his prime. Here is one written in the last November of his life, which appears to indicate that Neville, who as head of the family was no longer addressed as Dick, had suggested bringing his family to spend Christmas at Audley End:

My dearest Neville's very kind letter has given me great comfort indeed, and has afforded Lady Howard and myself a pleasure and happiness not to be expressed, by the kindest hopes you hold out to us both of bringing with you your two dear eldest girls: in short my dearest Neville, if you had asked us what was the greatest favour you could have done us, it would be just what you so affectionately propose to us.

Adieu my very very dear Neville,
Your most affectionate H. & B.

Two months before the end, on 26th March, came the last pathetic note:

My dearest Neville, I am sorry to inform you that I am too unwell to do more than [thank] you for your last two kind letters. My appetite you know has long failed me. Want of nourishment, attended with different complaints attendant naturally at my late age of life do not animate, and the effect of my blister left me very low and nervous, and so I continue; but must beg you won't think of making me a visit, which can do neither of us any good.

At Lord Howard's death the second Lord Braybrooke took possession of Audley End, and as early as 8th June—less than a fortnight after the old lord's passing—we find Lady Howard writing:

Dear Lord Braybrooke,
It is quite impossible for me to express what I feel from the repeated kindness, friendship, and delicacy of your conduct, but it only proves

you the more deserving of the distinction you have received from the best and most valued of men, who from his partial tenderness and affection for me, and seeing the interest and tender fondness I have ever felt for this place, would I know have been pleased to have left me in possession of it.   He always told me your friendly wishes expressed to himself, but it was in his judgment so impossible to be done, and the idea that you would come into immediate and undisturbed possession so smoothed his death bed that I cannot reconcile the thought of not facilitating his every wish.   I never could forgive myself if I was the means of delaying your being established here, as whenever that happens I am very certain affection for yourself and family will soon follow. . . .   Indeed I do fear I should be very unequal to it alone in any season, for tho' it has, I will allow, afforded me indescribable happiness for thirty-two years, its principal charm is gone, and tho' I trust I shall ever feel a composed resignation to the Will of God, who has so mercifully lengthened my prosperity, yet I daily feel the anguish in this place would be great.   I have been twice in the Elysian Garden, and my feelings out of doors tell me I should be sadly unequal to enjoy, or restore that cheerfulness to the place which you and yours will be so amiably capable of.

The transfer was completed in the following September, and at the conclusion Lord Braybrooke made this memorandum:

It has been a very satisfactory thing to me to have gone thro' such a variety of matters with so many persons interested without the least murmur or semblance of distrust amongst any of the parties. With Lady Howard there has been a constant and expressed wish to oblige and acquiesce, and I must do Dr. Parker and Mrs. Griffin the justice to say that I have met with great civilities from them in very intricate and difficult circumstances.

But not until the death of Dr. Parker at the age of eighty-eight in 1801 did Lord Braybrooke enjoy the revenues of that part of the estate which Lord Howard had inherited from the Countess of Portsmouth. By the doctor's death he benefited, according to his own statement, by £3,000 a year.

The expectations of Lord and Lady Howard were fully realized in him, both as man and landowner. If there was a fault in his character it has not come to light. His friends seem to have vied with each other in his praise, and his family of three sons and three daughters brought new life to the house. Unhappily his wife, who incidentally was herself descended from Theophilus, second Earl of Suffolk, and would therefore have given her husband a dual claim, died shortly before Lord Howard himself.

XIV

IN THE SECOND
LORD BRAYBROOKE'S TIME

THE SECOND Lord Braybrooke did little to the
house. It was already, perhaps, too fine for his
personal taste. At all events, he seems to have preferred Billingbear. If Lady Braybrooke had lived to
enjoy it perhaps she, accustomed as she was to the magnificence
of Stowe, would have induced him to continue the work of
aggrandizement. He could well have done so, living as he did
through a period of unimagined prosperity for the landed gentry.
After the first four years—that is to say, after Dr. Parker's death
—he was far richer than Lord Howard had been, and the
Napoleonic wars had the effect of enhancing land values as
never before. Indeed by the time of his own death in 1825 the
value of his estates must have increased to several times their
1797 value.

Much of the new wealth that came to landowners at this time
was the result of enclosures. Between the time of Lord
Howard's death and the end of the Napoleonic wars 1,800
enclosure bills passed through Parliament, and Lord Braybrooke
was as forward in the work as any. His activities belong,
therefore, to the progress of the estate rather than to the progress
of the house and will be dealt with in a later chapter; but the
social aspect ought to be considered at this point.

Many of the problems that had embarrassed Lord Howard
became still more serious in the second Lord Braybrooke's
time, aggravated as they were by the Napoleonic wars, and by
the problems of providing for a rapidly increasing population.
The Braybrookes may be said to have come in with the turn of
the tide in our economic history. The population of England,
which had taken 250 years to double itself before the middle
of the eighteenth century, was again doubled in a little more
than seventy years. In Audley End terminology, there was a
greater increase in the national population between the accession

166

of the first Lord Braybrooke as Sir John Griffin Griffin in 1762 and the death of the second in 1825 than there had been under Lord Chancellor Audley, the duke his son-in-law, and ten earls of Suffolk. And economic adjustment had been as haphazard here as elsewhere. As Saffron Walden had made its own life while the earls of Suffolk had been at Audley End, it had flourished on a variety of industries. It had been one of the wool towns of Essex and East Anglia. John Player [1] tells us that he remembers how on the festival of St. Blaize, the patron saint of the woolstaplers, the people of the town, accompanied by the town band, would be led in procession by the mayor and corporation along the bounds of the parish from Newport to Littlebury, passing in front of Audley End. One of the boys would be dressed as the bishop. There would be shepherds and shepherdesses, and one of the girls would carry a lamb in her lap. The day would reach its climax at sunset with a noisy jollification in the Rose and Crown. The last of these festivities was in 1778.

Then there had been the interesting saffron trade. But this also had died out. Other trades, such as malting, continued to do well enough; but for the majority agriculture was the only permanent employment, and the second Lord Braybrooke, like most of the landowners of his day, developed and extended it, enclosing, draining, bringing the waste into cultivation and improving the existing farmland. During his twenty-eight years at Audley End he recovered for the estate the whole of the manors granted at the partition to Lord Bristol, as well as other farms and woods that had formerly belonged to the earls of Suffolk. He was in all respects a progressive and enlightened landowner. Like his predecessor, Lord Howard, he did his best for both land and people. But it has to be admitted that neither had any grasp of economics. It was not, of course, to be expected of them. But here as elsewhere the consequences of this failure of those in power to understand what had happened was grave indeed. The effect of enclosure, essential as this was for agricultural development, aggravated by war-time and post-war shortages, is well known. It is estimated that by 1818 more than one-fifth of the rural population of England and Wales were receiving parish relief.

There is another side to the picture, it is true. The waging of war against Napoleon kept the nation at full stretch. That is

[1] *Sketches of Saffron Walden and its Vicinity*, 1845.

admitted. But to explain the shadows is not to dispel them. And to see them at close range is to see both light and shade intensified. On the other hand we have pride in property—in itself commendable—and an honourable and successful endeavour to transform the countryside and improve the cattle and sheep that grazed in the new pastures until they could hardly be recognized as the same creatures. These things weigh heavily in favour of such men as the Lords Braybrooke. The rebuilding of their houses and the cultivation of their estates by the great landowners of the day created enormous wealth. The tragedy is that this new wealth was not distributed. So while on the one hand the increase in population and the consequent increase in the demand for food was advancing both prices and profits, the labouring poor on the other hand were being steadily impoverished. Thus the gulf between rich and poor became wider each year, and the distress of 1795, which Lord Howard had dealt with in the manner of his time, continued throughout the war years, degrading and even brutalizing the poor. Then at the end of the war came a general depression attended by the usual wave of crime. In October 1816, for example, a gang of robbers who had terrorized the neighbourhood for weeks came before the Walden justices after an honest man had been shot while defending his home. When caught they were so defiant that they went off to jail laughing and whistling. These, it is true, were ruffians; but there were scores of honest men who were sorely tempted to take the law into their own hands after watching their children grow hollow-eyed and pot-bellied. It could not be otherwise when many able-bodied men were receiving only sixpence a day, and eightpence at most. Although much of this evil was certainly due to the war—to exhaustion at the end of the long struggle that had begun in 1793 and only ended in 1815—much also was attributable to failure to understand and cope with the nation's changed economy.

We have a reflection of the lawlessness of the Walden neighbourhood in Bishop Blomfield's *Letter on the Present Neglect of the Lord's Day*, published in 1830. Blomfield had held the livings of Great and Little Chesterford from Lord Bristol, a personal friend, after having already served them as assistant curate when he first took orders. Previously they had been served either by non-resident rectors, or by worldly minded gentlemen-in-holy-orders, who had been accustomed to ride past the cottages of their humble parishioners on their way to

Cambridge or London, and sometimes, no doubt, to Newmarket, with no more than a haughty nod in recognition of the bobs and curtsies of their flock. Blomfield was as sincere as Lord Braybrooke, and so energetic in those days that one of his farmers amused his neighbours by always referring to him as 'Mr. Snap-trace.'

At that time the Chesterfords lay on the Newmarket road, which now bypasses them, and it was the custom for horses to be changed at the Crown, the inn adjoining the church, already familiar to us as the place where the navigation scheme meetings were held in Lord Howard's time. In those days the New-market spring meeting began on Easter Monday, which meant that racegoers were riding and driving past Audley End and through the Chesterfords on Easter Sunday. With so much excitement on the road it is not surprising, perhaps, that the church should have been empty on the very day that it ought to have been full. In fact there was a country fair at Great Chesterford on Easter Sunday, with booths set up on the green in front of the inn. Blomfield's own account of what happened relates how:

More than forty pairs of horses have sometimes been changed there on Easter Day, a great porportion of them while I was celebrating Divine Service. Not only all the servants and dependents at the inn, but a great number of the young men of the parish were taken away from their own sabbath duties to assist in this flagrant violation of them by others; not to mention that hundreds were engaged in observing their betters thus ostentatiously setting at nought the ordinances of religion . . . while others were seen engaged in gambling, and scattering the implements of their unholy pastime about the road.

With Lord Braybrooke's help Blomfield got the first day of the races changed from Monday to Tuesday.

And while we have the Crown at Chesterford in mind, it might be mentioned that the canal scheme came up again in the second Lord Braybrooke's time. Indeed it reached the com-mittee stage in Parliament in 1811; but was thrown out there. Then, in the following year, an Act was actually passed; but for all that the canal was never made, although this time there was no obstruction from Audley End. Indeed the Hon. Richard Neville, who became third Lord Braybrooke, was to be a director.[1]

---

[1] See Cooper's *Annals of Cambridge*, and *Index to Local Acts, 1801–1899*, Stationery Office: 'London and Cambridge Junction Canal,' and 'Stort Navigation.'

But while the cleavage between rich and poor was as great at Audley End as elsewhere, the casual records of the period show that the second Lord Braybrooke and his family were much more approachable than most of their rank and wealth during the first quarter of the nineteenth century. A national school was started for boys in Walden in 1815, and shortly afterwards the Hon. Miss Neville opened her working school for girls, conducted on the mutual instruction system introduced by Dr. Bell. Seventy girls, we learn, were enrolled during the first week, and two years later a schoolroom was built by public subscription.[1]

Of life in Saffron Walden at the middle level during these years, our best record is the diary of Susanna Day,[2] a Quakeress, whose husband was the town's most prosperous shopkeeper. We may assume that Day was a man of considerable substance, because at the beginning of the eighteenth century there would be no wholesale merchants calling on the farmers, and no weekly trips by the farmers themselves to Cambridge or Bishop's Stortford. Mr. Day would supply scores of well-to-do families, hundreds of cottagers, as well as Audley End and one or two other houses of the landed gentry in the neighbourhood, with a range of supplies that in our day would do credit to a London store. Nevertheless, the social status and general intelligence of the Day household as reflected in Mrs. Day's diary might surprise us. Among apprentices and assistants who lived with the family were Robert Lloyd, the Quaker poet, who mentions Mrs. Day in his letters, and whose friend, Charles Lamb, visited him at Walden,[3] and Thomas Rickman, the architect, who gave names to our distinctive architectural styles. With men like these in the house, the conversation at that tradesman's table must often have been equal to that in Blomfield's parsonage at Chesterford or in the dining-room at Audley End. And one at least of these two assistants did not miss the attention of Lord Braybrooke. Rickman designed both the Ice-house Lodge and the lodge at what was then the principal entrance to Audley End—the one on the Newmarket road—and also the spire of Saffron Walden church.

On 3rd March 1802 Susanna Day recorded in her diary the passing of the man who had known Audley End better than

---

[1] Benton, *Essex Review*, vol. xxix, p. 13.
[2] *Essex Review*, vol. xviii, p. 151 et seq.
[3] E. V. Lucas, *Charles Lamb and the Lloyds*.

even its owners, the faithful steward, Thomas Pennystone, himself a Quaker:

The interment of Thomas Pennystone's remains was on this day previous to our usual meeting. A large appearance of our respectable neighbours were there, among them Lord Braybrooke, with his children and his chaplain. The meeting was crowded, and our dear friend E[lizabeth] G[ibson] had a very favoured open time, bearing lively testimony to the purity of true religion.

Pennystone must have been steward of the estate for about fifty years. It was he who had ridden to London to fetch a physician to attend the last of the earls of Suffolk at Audley End, and whose father, whom he succeeded as steward, had advised Colonel Vachell about the partition of the estate.

The Pennystones were a fine old Essex family. Their pedigree is recorded in the 1634 Visitation. Apparently they were early converts to the Quaker faith. One member was distrained upon in goods to the value of £8 12s. in 1670 for attending meetings at the house of John Churchman in Wenden, and again in 1675 for a similar offence in Saffron Walden.

During his fifty years as steward Thomas Pennystone had accumulated land and money by prudent and honourable means, and died a comparatively rich man. But in spite of his great care in administering the Audley End estate he died intestate, and his property went to his wife's nieces, who added his name to their own name of Day—no doubt they were related to Susannah Day's husband. These nieces lived at Wood House, Stansted. But the money did them no good. One died by her own hand; the other married a ne'er-do-well who quickly went through the estate so shrewdly built up by the old Quaker steward.

Nor is Mrs. Day's diary the only one that has come down to us from these years. Lord Braybrooke's second son, Henry Neville, who was a captain in the 14th Light Dragoons, and died of exhaustion in Spain after the battle of Talavera, kept a diary [1] which, although it has only indirect bearing on Audley End, is interesting both for its sidelights on the progress of the army during the Peninsular campaign, and for its descriptions of the country.

[1] E.R.O. D/DBy. F.16.

After Henry Neville's death on 21st August a friend wrote home:

My dear Neville, I have deferred till now acquainting you of the different arrangements that have been made of your poor brother's effects. I should indeed have wished to defer it to some later period, but I think it right to give you previous notice of the arrival of his favourite horse, Harlequin, which he had expressed a wish might be sent to England.

Then comes a particular commendation of the groom, 'for his constant and unremitting attention to his master during the whole of his illness; and I understand that poor Henry was so sensible of it that he had frequently expressed his gratitude.' After reading this we can imagine how anxiously the family would await the arrival of the groom, and how relieved they would be to hear from him, as they did, that apparently there had been no suffering at the end. The cause of death was evidently a fever brought on by exposure and fatigue. They had been without shelter for two nights and a day during which the rain fell incessantly, owing to the guide having mistaken the way.

This was the first of many sacrifices made by the Nevilles of Audley End in defence of their country. This also comes into the reckoning. But we have had enough of shadows. Let us look at the brighter side of life in the Braybrooke household during these years. There is nothing spectacular to produce; but there is a mass—in fact, a bewildering mass—of material to show what manner of life it was. The difficulty is to bring it into focus. Every bill and voucher was kept, and from these thousands of documents a most valuable picture of life at this time could be built up; but this would require a detailed treatment more suitable for an academic journal than for a book of this kind. There are, for example, no fewer than 26,000 documents in forty-one parcels, each containing twelve monthly bundles, forming what is apparently a complete series of household and estate bills for the years 1765 to 1805,[1] followed by many thousands for subsequent years. They are a fascinating collection. Even in their appearance tradesmen's bills over a longish period can tell us a great deal about the social conditions of an age. Let us glance at a few bundles for the post-war years—say 1815 to 1821.[2]

[1] E.R.O. D/DBy. A.23–63.   [2] E.R.O. D/DBy. A.315–36.

How proud these tradesmen were of their distinguished patrons at this time! Here is B. Odell, of Old Bond Street, 'Gold and Silver Lace Manufacturer, Embroiderer, &c., to Her Royal Highness the Princess of Wales,' who specialized in epaulets, sashes, swords, belts, plates, buttons, and every other military and naval appointment. His bills have a fine heraldic decoration with the Prince of Wales's feathers incorporated. Taylor and Doggell, late Martin, of Davies Street, Berkeley Square, announce that they are boot and shoe makers to His Royal Highness the Duke of Gloucester; Ralph Lonsdale that he is hosier to Her Royal Highness the Princess Charlotte of Wales; John Manton & Son that they are gunmakers to Their Royal Highnesses the Prince Regent and the Duke of York. There are still one or two tradesmen's pictorial signs surviving. At the Sea Otter, for example, all sorts of baizes, flannels, fleecy hosiery, and gloves could be purchased, and the accounts rendered on a bill with a delightful engraving of a sea otter as headpiece.

It is dangerous to jump to conclusions about the cost of living at different periods, because custom and fashion influence expenditure so irrationally. But considering the elaborate nature of costume at this time the tailor's bills do not seem as large as we might expect. They illustrate, on the whole, a downward trend if compared with those of the eighteenth century. A stout olive-green shooting jacket, lined with cotton and fitted with metal buttons 'as usual' costs only 3 guineas in 1817; black cashmere breeches appear regularly at £2 10s. a time; frock coats are £5 16s., with 9s. 6d. charged separately for the buttons, bringing the price up to £6 5s. 6d. Here is a bill for a 'Cocked Hat, cockade and sewing on trimmings, £2 8s.' The hosiers' bills, on the other hand, seem high. In the six months from January to June 1817 Ralph Lonsdale has sold to Lord Braybrooke:

4 pairs	embroidered black silk hose		@ 18s.;
2 —	fine china silk	—	@ 21s.;
12 —	china spun silk	—	@ 12s.;
2 —	embroidered black silk	—	@ 16s.

The complete account for hosiery in that one six months was £24 15s., and sometimes it was as much as £30.

Thomas Cartwright, his lordship's tailor, was evidently of the old school. Unlike most of his contemporaries he had not yet adopted a printed heading for his account sheets.   Here he is with:

	£	s.	d.
To a fine claret cloth great coat,	6	16	0
To silk serge sleeve linings and breast pocket,	1	1	0
To a fashionable velvet collar the colour		9	6
To two white Marcella waistcoats @ £1 14s. 0d. each	3	8	0

After the Napoleonic wars we find small sums added to bills for 'additional wages.'   Thus in 1820 Thomas Cartwright's bill has 16s. added to the usual charge of 5½ guineas for a frock coat, and 7s. to the usual 50s. for a pair of dress breeches. The most interesting item before 1820 is the purchase in April 1818 of:

A Lord Lieutenant of the County Dress Coat, of superfine scarlet cloth, richly embroidered in gold, superfine blue cloth cuffs and lapels &c., white cassamere turn-backs, body and skirts lined with fine white alapine, calico sleeve linings &c., &c.

	£	s.	d.
44/2 gilt 'Crown and Laurel' buttons,	25	0	0
A pair of rich gold epaulettes,	7	7	0
A pair of rich gold leaf ornaments for skirt,		9	0
A white cassamere waistcoat, sattinet back, cotton lining,	1	18	0
Ten gilt 'Crown and Laurel' buttons,		2	0
	£34	16	0

But by far the most expensive year was 1820, the year of the old king's death and of George IV's coronation.   For mourning we have quantities of black crape and a large number of 'fine mourning handkerchiefs.'   A round hat with a crape band for his lordship costs £1 17s., the trimming of a cocked hat with crape is charged 7s. 6d.   A crape bugue, apparently a form of cravat, is charged 12s.   Then come the ceremonial:

	£	s.	d.
A single-fronted black cloth Court Dress coat, lined throughout with black silk serge	8	18	6
India muslin weepers		3	6
A crape bag for the hair		13	6
Additional wages		16	0
A rich black sword belt and knitt	6	16	6
A sett of black buckles	1	11	6
A sword bag		2	6

Queen Charlotte's Sitting-room, looking North-east

These are followed by bills for the coronation robes, which illustrate the great difference in cost between ordinary and ceremonial dress:

The Right Honourable Lord Braybrooke,

To William Webb, Robe Maker to His Majesty, the Prince of Wales. and Royal Family, No. 37, Hollywell Street, near the New Church, Strand.

1820, July 19th.

To a silver gilt Baron's Coronet, trimmed with the richest crimson silk Genoa velvet, the choicest of spotted ermine, gold tassel, silk lining &c.

A Coronation Mantle & Surcoat of the richest crimson silk Genoa velvet, trimmed with the choicest spotted ermine, lined with rich white silk &c.

A Doublet & Trunks of very rich white satin trimmed with the richest gold brocade plate lace & vandyke fringe.

A pair of white China silk pantaloons with feet.

A pair of white cotton drawers with feet.

A Coronation Sword, scabbard & belt covered with rich crimson velvet, best gilt mountings &c.

A pair of the best white kid gloves trimmed with the richest deep gold fringe.

A pair of the best white kid shoes.

A pair of knee and shoes crimson ribbon rosettes.

A fine linen robe & coronet case.

A Cedar Chest for robes with patent lock, brass hinges, handles, inscription plate &c.

£250 0 0

Each season a return is made of the game killed, sometimes at one country house, sometimes at another—Escrick, Woburn, Holkham, Euston. Another account shows the wine drunk each year at Billingbear during the Ascot racing season. Evidently there was always a house party for this event. Thus in 1816, the first year of peace, we have:

Port, 6; Madeira, 14; Claret, 28; Sherry, 6; Champagne, 10; Hock, 4; Red Hermitage, 2; White Hermitage, 5; Barsac, 4; Burgundy, 1.

These were drunk during the four days, Tuesday, 11th June, to Friday, 14th June. And all the time improvements to the park and estate are being made. There are innumerable items relating to these, all of which eventually found their way into Jacob

N

Nockold's [1] beautifully kept *General Account*. In the last year of the second Lord Braybrooke's life, 1825, this showed:

	£	s.	d.
Housekeeping and Board Wages	472	8	2
Firing	131	18	10
Beer	0	0	0
Servants Wages	23	6	0
Stable Expences	174	9	6
Shooting Expences	732	14	9½
Menagerie Expences	96	3	8½
Travelling and Carriage	34	13	4
Audley House, Gardens, &c.	2,630	8	9½
Stationery	8	17	0
Contingencies	2	16	6
	£4,307	16	7½

At this time Jacob Nockold's inventory of Lord Braybrooke's personal effects reads:

	Audley End £	s.	d.	Billingbear £	s.	d.	London £	s.	d.	Total £	s.	d.
Household Goods	1,581	19	0	1,258	3	0	761	1	0	3,601	3	0
Plate Linen China	182	9	6	1,386	1	6	91	19	0	1,660	10	0
Books Prints and Pictures	1,432	0	0	306	0	0	30	0	0	1,768	0	0
Wearing Apparel				35	10	0				35	10	0
Wine & other Liquors	1,328	13	0	256	0	0	101	5	0	1,685	18	0
Horses and Carriages	46	14	6	236	19	6				283	14	0
Farming Stock &c.	4,351	10	0	2,293	15	6				6,645	5	6
Sundries	1,063	7	2	745	17	3				1,809	4	5
										17,489	4	11
Arrears of rent due										785	3	0
										£18,274	7	11

So while we cannot in the space available produce a complete and accurate picture of life at Audley End at this or any other time, from such items as these we can, given adequate knowledge of the social and political background of the age, get a clear—if general—impression of its character and quality. And always

[1] Jacob Nockold succeeded Thomas Pennystone as steward.

there is the continuing background of a healthy and vigorous life in the country, culminating in the shooting seasons and the great sporting events of the year. When the family were in town no letters were scanned more eagerly than those that told of sport. Here is a sample. It comes from Mollony on 23rd September 1822:

> The Rev. L. Barham had the luck to kill three woodcocks to-day in the Warren Copse, which will go tomorrow by the Venetian basket to Audley End. The deer continue to lie good, notwithstanding the sharp frost of last week. The weather being dry and without snow, the Park and other pastures are yet sound and healthy, and as yet we have wanted little fodder for store things. Burton has agreed to give eightpence per foot for the beech, and take a hundred load. We have forty-five down . . .

and so on.

It was a busy, energetic life. The second and third Lords Braybrooke lived in the heyday of the English aristocracy, at a time when town and country, work and pleasure, freedom and responsibility, were perfectly balanced for this small and favoured class. So although it was achieved at great cost to the rest of society, it was an achievement. In spite of all that can be said against it, the truth is that while other ages produce other ideals, and other modes of life produce other excellencies, this age produced the flower of our English nobility, among whom the Lords Braybroooke of the day were worthy representatives. When he died at Billingbear on 28th February 1825 the second lord was buried, not with the Howards at Saffron Walden, but with his own ancestors at Waltham St. Lawrence in Berkshire.

XV

VICTORIAN PRIME

IT IS WITH the third Lord Braybrooke, scholar and man
of letters rather than man of affairs, that Audley End, as we
see it now, was brought to completion.   He continued his
father's work on the estate, completing the park walling
under Joseph Ward's supervision, but with workmen employed
at piece rates instead of at fixed wages, an innovation by which
the cost per rod of brickwork was reduced by one-third.   He
fitted sash windows to the house, releaded the roofs, capped the
turrets with copper, and built new lodges: the two we have
mentioned to designs by Thomas Rickman (the Ice-house Lodge,
1827; the Main Gate Lodge, 1834) and also the Cambridge
Lodge, 1842, and the Audley End Lodge, 1846.   But his most
important work was indoors.   Between 1826 and 1831 he spent
over £15,000,[1] mainly in taking the living-rooms—the dining-
room, drawing-room, library, and so forth—upstairs, and turning
the ground floor into bedrooms.   In doing this he spoilt the
Adam suite on the ground floor, but made a new suite above
it, with a set of noble apartments to range with the Saloon—
obviously the determining factor in the plan.   From this we
now pass through the drawing-room and south library to the
beautiful library at the east end of the range, which balances
Lord Howard's Saloon at the west end.   When completed,
these new apartments were both larger and brighter than those
discarded, and undoubtedly improved the house, notwithstanding
the loss downstairs.   We cannot date them precisely.   They
may have been started towards the end of the second Lord
Braybrooke's time; but the scheme was the third lord's, and the
major part of the work belongs to the years 1826–31.
    In 1819 the third lord, then the Hon. Richard Neville, had
married Lady Jane Cornwallis, daughter of the second and last
Marquess Cornwallis of Culford Hall, Suffolk, by Lady Louisa
Gordon, daughter of the fourth Duke of Gordon; and by
this marriage the valuable collection of Cornwallis furniture,

[1] E.R.O.   D/DBy.   A.321–6.

portraits, and household treasures of various kinds came to Audley End on the death of the second marquess in 1823. Such an accession would itself suggest alterations. Moreover, the Neville-Cornwallis marriage introduced into the house a new and distinguished family with an ancestry equal in lustre to that of the Howards, Griffins, and Nevilles. And the Braybrooke finances were equal to the aggrandizement. At the time of this marriage the second Lord Braybrooke was able to provide [1] for his heir an income of £3,500 a year during his own lifetime, and for his wife a jointure of £1,500 a year if she should outlive her husband. The provision for the younger children of the marriage was on a proportionate scale. There was to be £10,000 if one only, £15,000 between them if two, £20,000 if three, and so on; but no child by survivorship was to inherit more than £10,000. There were, in fact, eight children of the marriage; but the estate was much less impoverished than it might have been because three of the sons succeeded as fourth, fifth, and sixth lords, returning their shares, as it were, to the common pool.

But while the importance of this marriage, and the background of Culford, would be enough in themselves to move the third lord to undertake yet another major restoration, his wealth and personality may already have disposed him towards it. His aunt, Lady Williams Wynn, writing to her daughter in January 1826, says:

Lord Braybrooke called upon me the day before yesterday, and sat with me nearly an hour talking all the time. He came on a flying visit to town for the purpose of letting his Burlington Street house for a twelvemonth. He intended to let it for eight hundred guineas, which he is told he may be sure of getting, and with which he means, for the next season entirely to new furnish and decorate it. In the meantime he says he shall have plenty of amusements and employment in watching the indoor improvements at Audley End, upon which he is going to begin immediately, and where he expects to make himself as magnificent in the interior as it is in the exterior. This can only be done by the entire abandonment of the ground-floor, which though I must consider as a great sacrifice in a country residence, was I believe in this instance an indispensible one.

The change meant more—much more—than carrying the downstairs furniture upstairs and bringing the upstairs furniture down. The first room to be completed, apparently, was the

[1] E.R.O. D/DBy. F.12.

dining-room, for which two rooms were thrown into one. Their plaster ceilings, Lord Braybrooke tells us,[1] were not disturbed, which explains their different designs. But he tells us less than we could wish about his work. We should like to know, for example, what exactly he did to the chimney-pieces, both of which have achievements of the royal arms and the initials of the kings and queens who owned the house during its thirty-two years as a royal palace—C. II and J. II on the one, to commemorate the association of Charles II and James II, and W.M. on the other, for that of William and Mary.   It is probable that these features were introduced by the third lord; but some of the work is earlier.   Indeed it may well be that one chimney-piece is largely original, the other a copy.

Of the pictures in the dining-room the most valuable is a full-length study of George II, painted towards the end of his life, which is claimed to be the only original portrait there is of him.   George II, as we know, hated 'boetry and bainting,' and would never consent to sit.   This one, we are told, was done by Robert Pine from sketches made while concealed in a closet overlooking the main staircase at Kensington Palace.   It did not, as we might suspect, come to Audley End through the association of George II with Henrietta, Countess of Suffolk, but was bought for the house by the fourth Lord Howard de Walden.   It has a curious history.   The original buyer was Lord Baltimore, who intended to present it to the colony of Maryland.   But the ship that carried it was attacked by a privateer, and the portrait, along with the rest of the cargo, captured. Later, however, it was recovered, and in accordance with the usual practice was condemned and ordered to be sold by auction. Lord Howard heard of the sale and bought it.

Among other portraits in the dining-room are those of Algernon Percy, tenth Earl of Northumberland, who married a daughter of Earl Theophilus, and Robert Carr, Earl of Somerset, who married the first earl's daughter, the notorious Countess of Essex.   We see him here, a slim girlish figure, resplendent in the robes of the Bath, wearing the collar and George, the Garter, and with the Garter motto worked in pearls round his left knee. Dobson's study of Sir Charles Lucas, hero of the siege of Colchester, is another fine study; but the room is dominated by Sir William Beechey's full-length portrait of the first Marquess Cornwallis in his Garter robes.   It is appropriate that it should

[1] Braybrooke, p. 111.

be so because Lord Cornwallis was now the most imposing figure in the family background. His part in the War of American Independence is well known,[1] and, incidentally, the sword he surrendered with at Yorktown in 1781 is said to be at Audley End, though which of the ceremonial swords in the Great Hall is the one in question seems doubtful. It was he who succeeded Warren Hastings as governor-general of India, and whatever views we may hold of his success or failure as an administrator, he is a genial figure in an English country house because he was himself so thoroughly English. Shocked by the conditions of the Bengali peasantry, he conceived a plan which he believed would 'make the country flourish, and secure happiness to the body of the inhabitants,' mainly by a revision of the land-revenue system. His idea was to get India settled with prosperous farmers like those of his native East Anglia, by establishing in the country a class comparable with the English squirearchy, who were, he believed, the backbone of the old country. Unfortunately he cannot have understood the people he was trying to govern. When disputes arose over these proposed reforms they were referred to the law courts, which were notoriously corrupt, and so horrified Cornwallis that he determined that, so far as his own authority went, in future no Indian should hold important administrative office. It was a serious error, involving a grave wrong to the people; but his intentions were sound, and he did in fact set standards of honour and integrity that were eventually to his credit, although at the time they were unattainable in practice.

We find Cornwallis portraits again in the Great Hall, and a bust of the first marquess in the drawing-room, another of the rooms altered by the third lord. The ceiling and frieze, although based on others in the house, are his work. There are other Cornwallis heirlooms in the room; but the most interesting piece is a curious little chair which belonged to Alexander Pope. It was given to the third lord by the Rev. T. Ashley, for some years curate of Binfield, the village in Windsor Forest where Mr. Pope senior had

> A little house with trees a-row
> And like its master very low,

and where the poet spent the happiest years of his life. Binfield

[1] See *Correspondence of Charles, First Marquis Cornwallis*, edited by Charles Ross, 3 vols., 1859.

is near Billingbear, which explains Lord Braybrooke's acquaintance with Mr. Ashley, who on 15th March 1844 wrote:[1]

My dear Lord Braybrooke, By Shawe and Co's Boats, Bull Wharf, Upper Thames St., I have sent, directed to Burlington Street, Alexander Pope's chair, with the hope that it may be deemed worthy of a place in the Hall or Gallery of Audley Hall. Its legitimacy is unquestionable. In the early part of my Binfield career, old Bobby Butler (who sat for the portrait of Crabbe's Old Dibble) frequently put to me this question: 'I suppose, sir, you have heard of one Mr. Pope, who lived near the Turnpike gate. My mother washed him.' But whether as nurse or laundry maid is still a doubtful point of history.

Some years afterwards I saw in the cottage of Bobby's brother a chair of singular formation and I enquired of the 'gude wife' from whence she obtained it.

'Ah, sir—the ould chair—the ould chair!! My husband's mother wou'd grow stark wild if she saw it in the condition it is now: she used to take as much care of it, as if it was made of gold; but the lads (meaning her sons) set no store by it and use it roughly.'

'Well, but where,' I asked again, 'did you get it?'

'Why,' she replied, 'my husband's mother lived many years with Mr. Pope, and this was Master's chair and given to her as a keepsake.'

The writer goes on to speculate on the apparently symbolic carving on the chair-back, which might conceivably be intended to represent a scene from the *Iliad*. There is Cupid, a flaming heart, and a town in the background, which Mr. Ashley suggests might stand for Helen of Troy, while the phoenix in the design, he thinks, is intended to suggest that Troy was again raised from the flames by the poet's translation.

It is particularly appropriate that we should recall these literary associations at Audley End while thinking of the third lord, who will always be remembered as the first editor of Pepys's *Diary*, which had been kept, as every Pepysian knows, in the Pepys Library at Magdalene College, Cambridge, to which the owners of Audley End have always been hereditary Visitors.[2] Diaries had recently come into fashion when the third Lord produced his edition of Pepys, the value of which was recognized at once, and we have in the Audley End archives[3] a copy of the original agreement between the publisher, Henry Colburn, and the Hon. and Rev. George Neville, the third lord's brother, who was then Master of Magdalene, and later became Dean of Windsor. It is dated 2nd October 1823, and shows

[1] E.R.O. D/DBy. Z.49.   [2] See p. 40.   [3] E.R.O. D/DBy. Z.15.

that the copyright of the diary and correspondence was sold for £2,200, of which £2,000 was paid at once, and the remaining £200 on the issue of the third edition. From this sum Lord Braybrooke allocated £1,000 to found an annual benefaction of £52 to deserving students in the college, now known as 'the Pepysian Benefaction,' and the second £1,000 went towards the building of the new Master's Lodge, completed in 1835.

George Neville, incidentally, was the only one of the second lord's six sons, apart from the third lord himself, to survive their father's death. Subsequently he assumed the name of Grenville on receiving an estate from his maternal uncle, Thomas Grenville,[1] and became known as George Neville-Grenville. It was he who engaged John Smith, an undergraduate of St. John's, to decipher the 3,012 quarto pages of shorthand of the original six-volume diary.

The third Lord Braybrooke wrote the history of Audley End published in 1836, which has frequently been quoted in these pages, and in 1842 edited and published at his own expense *The Private Correspondence of Jane Lady Cornwallis* (1581–1659). His name does not appear on the title-page of the latter, although the preface is addressed from Audley End.

The most valuable Cornwallis heirloom that came to Audley End by this marriage was the beautifully illuminated psalter of the time of Edward I, now in the Fitzwilliam Museum, presented to the third Lord Braybrooke by the second Marquess of Bristol, which is believed to be the work of a monk of the monastery of Austin Friars at Gorleston in Suffolk, and to have come into the family at the Dissolution. It had a worthy setting in the sumptuously appointed library, which is as much a memorial to the third Lord Braybrooke as the Saloon is to the fourth Lord Howard de Walden—the one to the man who completed the house in the nineteenth century, the other to the man who restored it in the eighteenth. We have thus three rooms at Audley End that enshrine the three branches of its family: the Great Hall, the Howards; the Saloon, the Griffins; the Library, the Nevilles.

In order to achieve this beautiful room at the east end of the south wing several small bedrooms had to be thrown together to gain length, the floor lowered about four feet to gain height, and the spacious bay window looking towards the east thrown out to gain breadth. The walls were completely

---

[1] The book collector, who left the Grenville Library to the British Museum.

encased in white painted bookshelves enriched with gilding to hold the 7,000 volumes of a typical gentleman's library of the period, most notable for its antiquarian and topographical works; but with many volumes from Lord Howard's library below, which are easily recognized by their uniform red and gold chequered binding, designed for the library in the Adam suite about 1765, and copied by the third lord for the successive volumes of the *Annual Register*.

The much-repaired chimney-piece, with musical instruments carved on its Corinthian pilasters, is one of Adam's, refixed here; but like the chimney-pieces in the adjoining dining-room it was enriched by the third lord, in this case with the arms of Audley and Neville. The ceiling, like that of the drawing-room, is nineteenth century, but with a graceful design based on others in the house. The ottoman is said to have belonged to Queen Charlotte, and to have been embroidered by the queen and her ladies.

In the next room, the south library, which was probably the room in which most of the writing was done, hung the curtains of crimson Florentine damask presented to a son of the third Sir Henry Neville of Billingbear by Cosmo, Grand Duke of Tuscany, who described so vividly the original Audley End. Over the low chimney-piece in this room is a portrait by Benjamin West of the fourth Lord Howard de Walden in his general's uniform, with a military cloak thrown over his shoulders and wearing the star of the Order of the Bath, while his two wives, Anne Schutz and Katherine Clayton, in the costumes of the Sibyls of Domenichino and Guercino, are represented in portraits, also by West, over the doorways.

The third Lord Braybrooke was clearly a man who lived in the tradition of his ancestors and took pride in perfecting their work. There are few great houses that have such unity of design in their decorations as this. Whatever the third lord did was in harmony with Lord Howard's work, which means that he accepted the discipline of both the house and its personalities. He accepted also the duties of his station, and discharged them faithfully. Like the first and second lords he represented Berkshire, sitting for the county from 1812 until his succession to the peerage in 1825, after previously representing in turn Thirsk, Saltash, and Buckingham. Like the Nevilles in general he took a moderate view in politics, voting with the Whigs for Catholic Emancipation and the Reform Bill, although later in life he joined the Conservatives, supporting Sir Robert Peel from 1834 to 1845. He broke from him, however, on the repeal of the Corn Laws, and afterwards followed Lord Derby.

Meanwhile the wealth of the family was steadily increasing. In a deed of settlement dated 1849 [1] it is stated that Lord Braybrooke had spent £65,000 in extending his estates, and had laid out £50,000 in improvements. He still held the extensive Berkshire properties of the family, which at this time were bringing in about £3,500 a year net.[2] By far the greater part of his land, however, was in Essex, and he seems to have preferred Audley End to Billingbear, his father's favourite seat. This pride in the Essex house is reflected in the accounts. During the 1830s expenditure at Audley End was at the rate of between £5,000 and £6,000 a year; during the 1840s it was at the rate of between £6,000 and £8,000. For example, in 1844 the *General Account* showed expenditure of £6,187 16s. 8d.; in 1847 it was £7,771 9s. 4d., much of which, though passing through the ordinary tradesmen's accounts, was obviously spent in improvements, because the third lord's housekeeping was never lavish. His household was usually made up at this time of housekeeper, governess, lady's maid, three nursery maids, three kitchen maids, three laundry maids, two still-room maids, four housemaids, and a dairymaid, which makes a total of nineteen women. There were now only half as many men: butler, under-butler, two footmen (later increased to three), house-boy, one or two coachmen, groom, and two stable-boys. This, it will be noted, is a reversal of the eighteenth-century ratios. In fact, the gradual displacement of men by women had been the trend all along—that is to say, throughout the reigns of the third and fourth Georges, and it was to continue throughout that of Victoria.

Although the third lord's interests were predominantly intellectual, the stables remain prominent in both accounts and correspondence. He played the part that an English nobleman was expected to play as a sportsman, just as he played it as a politician. Indeed, he and Lord George Cavendish owned and bred racehorses here, using part of the extensive kitchen gardens as paddocks. The most famous horse from the Audley End stables was Sir Joshua, a horse that won eight times at Newmarket, gaining its greatest renown by beating—in April 1816— the St. Leger winner, Filho de Puta, for the 'thousand-guineas,'

[1] E.R.O. D/DBy. A.375.   [2] E.R.O. D/DBy. A.351.

a triumph that was celebrated by giving the horse's name to the bridge being built at the time on the road from Saffron Walden to Wenden, which is still known as Joshua's Bridge. The third lord was offered 10,000 guineas for this famous horse —an unheard-of sum in those days.

What a rich and well-balanced life the third lord's was! He renewed the house; he extended the estate; he hunted, shot, sat in Parliament, bred racehorses, wrote, and had both luck and honour in every field. To have bred Sir Joshua, or to have restored and refurnished Audley End might have seemed enough for one man's lot; but what shall we say of the luck of giving Pepys to the world? As for honour, he enjoyed it fully, although probably the two distinctions that gave him the greatest pleasure were his election to the presidency of two important learned societies, the Camden and the Surtees.

Such are the pleasant reflections of life at Audley End and Saffron Walden in these leisurely times. The third lord had lived through an age of abundance for such as he, culminating in a period of security, if not of plenty, for his cottage neighbours. It came to its end, and not unnaturally the last four years of his lordship's life were shadowed by the loss of fourteen of his nearest relations, to all of whom he had been devotedly attached. They included Lady Braybrooke, his brother the Dean of Windsor, his sister Lady Glynne, three nephews, who fell in the service of their country, and finally the hardest blow of all —the loss of two sons who died within a week of each other from wounds received during the Crimean War in the winter of 1854. Henry, who was a captain in the Grenadier Guards, was mortally wounded at the siege of Sevastopol on the 5th November; Grey, an officer in the 5th Dragoon Guards, died in Scutari General Hospital from wounds received at Balaclava.

Three and a half years after losing his sons the third Lord Braybrooke died on 13th March 1858, and was succeeded by his eldest son, the Richard Cornwallis Neville already mentioned, who had married on 27th January 1852 Lady Charlotte Sarah Graham Toler, daughter of the Earl of Norbury, by whom he had three daughters but no sons. He had been brought up from childhood to take an interest in the antiquarian and topographical studies that were his father's lifelong delight, so, entering into these studies, as it were, at a second generation, he matured early, and although he died at the age of forty-one, after holding the estate for only three years, he was able to leave his enduring mark as a scholar. His chief works are: *Antiqua Explorata*, the outcome of excavations made by him during the winters of 1845 and 1846 and the spring of 1847, in and about the Roman station at Chesterford; *Sepulchra Exposita*, an account of the opening of some barrows in the neighbourhood of Saffron Walden; *Saxon Obsequies*, illustrated by ornaments and weapons discovered by Lord Braybrooke in a cemetery near Little Wilbraham, Cambridgeshire, which was printed in *Archaelogia*, vol. xxxii, p. 357; a memoir on Roman remains and villas discovered at Ickleton and Chesterford, contributed along with many other learned articles on similar subjects to the *Archaelogical Journal*. His collection of British and Roman antiquities, most of them brought to light in the course of his own excavations, and his collection of Dactyliotheca, which became one of the finest private collections in the country, are now in Cambridge. His collection of birds, however, another astonishing achievement for a man who died at the age of forty-one, is at Audley End.[1]

There is little to be said of the fourth lord as landowner; but he made a decisive contribution to the history of his family by abandoning the use of the name Griffin, which by the terms of the Countess of Portsmouth's will all who came into the estate were to assume, and reverting to that of Neville. At his death in 1861 he was succeeded by his brother, Charles Cornwallis Neville, who thus became fifth lord.

The fifth Lord Braybrooke, who married a daughter of the third Viscount Hawarden, held the estate for forty years, and throughout that time lived quietly at Audley End, serving his county in many public offices; but living the life of a wealthy country squire and never aspiring to be a national figure either in politics or scholarship. Such fame as he had was as an agriculturist. He was a regular winner of prizes at county shows for his Southdown sheep and Jersey cattle, of which he was justifiably proud. He was chairman of the Saffron Walden bench, and for some years vice-lieutenant of the county. Cricket was a passion with him. He had been a member of the Eton eleven, and never lost interest. It was he who in 1842 levelled the lawn in front of the house and laid the very fine pitch there.

As the house came to completion under the third lord's rule, the estate, as we shall see in the next chapter, reached its peak

---

[1] A list of the fourth Lord Braybrooke's works may be found in the *Annual Register*, 1861, p. 406.

under the fifth. In 1883 he owned 9,820 acres in Essex and 3,691 in Berkshire—a total of 13,511 acres valued at £18,173 a year.

Let us look at the fifth lord's establishment in the 1870s, the period in which agriculture was at its most prosperous in Essex. The tide may be said to have turned in the late 1870s, and the ebb was to continue until few, if any, large agricultural holdings could pay their way. A summary of the Audley End General Account for the years 1875, 1876, and 1877 is given opposite.

When the fifth Lord Braybrooke died suddenly at breakfast on 7th June 1902 there was again no son to succeed. The estate passed to his seventy-five-year-old brother, the Hon. and Rev. Latimer Neville, Master of Magdalene, who for more than fifty years had been rector of Heydon on the Essex-Cambridge border. Latimer Neville was the fourth son of the third Lord Braybrooke, and the third to inherit the title. He had succeeded his uncle, Dean Neville-Grenville, as Master of Magdalene in 1853, and celebrated his golden jubilee of office the year after succeeding to the Braybrooke title. His life, therefore, belongs to Cambridge University, which he served as vice-chancellor in 1859–61, rather than to Audley End. Indeed he held the estate for two years only, and although he had been a regular visitor at Audley End all his life and was intensely interested in the house, it was not to be expected that at his advanced age he would be able to disentangle himself from the university and begin a new life as a country gentleman. At his death in 1904 he was succeeded by his son, the seventh Lord Braybrooke, who held the title and estate from that time to his death at the age of eighty-six in 1941. With his passing in the middle of the Second World War, in which both his sons, Lieut. Richard Neville, eighth Lord Braybrooke, who had inherited the family love of cricket, and the Hon. Robert Neville, R.N., the long tradition broke. But more of that presently.

Summary	1875 Paym^ts			1875 Recp^ts			1876 Paym^ts			1876 Recp^ts			1877 Paym^ts			1877 Recp^ts		
	£	s.	d.	£	s.	d.	£	s.	d.	£	s.	d.	£	s.	d.	£	s.	d.
Housekeeping	953	17	½				1,080	5	3				908	14	2			
Firing	396	17	8½				343	6	11				264	15	10			
Salaries	640						398	2	4				613	15				
Stables	365	5	4				351	4	9				345		6			
Shooting	1,310	6	4	655	4	5	1,360	10	9	639	15	4	1,451	19		639	17	6
Menagerie	120	5	4	6	16		120	15	6	39	17	7	119	11	7	12	12	6
Gardens	865	13	11	13	18	10½	859	12	8	55	11	6	883	12	10	5	16	7
Carpenters	335	8	3				303	13	5				358	2	9½			
„ Materials (Timber, etc.)	89	6	9	121	12	[crossed through]	175	17	2				89		10	153	1	9 [crossed through]
Plumber	141	10	10				122	6	2½				112	7	6			
„ Materials	156	6	9	40	17	6	84	9	8	14	19	2	70	14	8			
Blacksmith	110	17	6				112	13	6				106	11	6			
„ Materials	157	9	3				135	7	1				142	11	5			
Bricklayer	261	16	10½				148	14	9				218	4				
„ Lime and Cement	53	3	4				22	5	10				32	19	11			
Brickmaking	515	15	6	105	19	1	501	4		422	13	6	534	18	7	147	19	10
Extra work	357		7				431	12	2				350	19	10½	27	10 (Stone)	
Woodwork	151	8	9½	121	12		174	4	5½	177	13		189	17	8	153	1	9
Rates & Taxes	32	15					1	14	2				65	17	4			
Lodgekeepers	46	19	10				47	9					47	5	4			
Deer	124	11	6	171	17		93	1	9	147	1	9	112	1		179	6	
Trade Horse	31	10	9				32	11	6				32	10	9			
Incidentals	236	6	½				278	15	5				277	4				
	7,454	13	2½	1,116	4	10½	7,179	18	3	1,497	11	10	7,328	16	1	1,166	4	2

XVI

ESTATE AND FARM

IN ONE OF his letters home Richard Neville Neville, while fulfilling an engagement of historic importance at the British Embassy in Paris, wrote: 'I am not so much a statesman as to have forgotten that I am full as much a farmer, or country squire. I therefore expect you should give me an account of my hay harvest, and of Forrester, and Jock, their friends and acquaintances.' So it was with his descendants at Audley End, and so it was with Lord Howard. Each had his own personal ambitions and pleasures, which might even raise him to fame, as with the third and fourth Lords Braybrooke; but always there was the estate, the farm, the property, to guard and enjoy. And as the family must be seen in its social setting to be understood, the house must be seen in relation to the estate that sustained it, and indeed to the home farm that met its day-to-day needs.

The Audley End estate was run as a commercial undertaking, with carefully kept accounts, from Sir John Griffin Griffin's time, and the papers connected with it that have been preserved, although too detailed to be studied in full here, present an admirable example of able management by wealthy landowners, particularly in the nineteenth century.

The estate as a whole is first set out for us in the middle of the eighteenth century, for the purposes of the partition then made between the Countess of Portsmouth and Mrs. Whitwell on the one hand and Lord Hervey on the other. The surveyor was Colonel Vachell, who had been appointed receiver on behalf of the successful claimants. His notes on the various farms and their tenants are most enlightening.[1] Of John Foord and Thomas Pennystone, junior (who succeeded his father as steward), he notes that they rented a hop-ground at North-end, near the Park, which had been in hand when the late earl died, and that

[1] E.R.O. D/DBy. E.9.

The State Bedroom

they had made a compliment of that year's crop to the dowager. They had articled for a twelve years' lease and had bought the hop poles. The reference is interesting because although hop growing has now disappeared from Essex, in the seventeenth and eighteenth centuries the county had some of the best hop gardens in England.

At Almshouse Farm, which in 1951 became St. Mark's College, a place of retirement for elderly clergy of the Chelmsford diocese,[1] 'there are,' he reports, 'apartments for ten poor persons to live in, which have time out of mind been allowed one shilling per week to each person.' This farm was let to a John Headland. Vachell goes on: 'This is certainly the worst conditioned farm belonging to the Walden estate. The present tenant is not in arrears, but it is evident he loses rather than is paid for his labour and industry. The man is an honest, good character, and a good tenant.' Colonel Vachell recommended a reduction of rent here.

Of Little Walden Park, with a mid-seventeenth-century house that still retains some original panelling—though much of this was removed at some time to Chesterford Park—he writes: 'This farm was in hand when the late earl died. The crop and stock was sold by the owners of the Personal Estate, and house, barns, stables, &c., &c., &c., paling, hedges, ditches, gates, bridges, stiles, in the worst condition I ever saw.' It was essential, therefore, that it should be put into tolerable order that some profit might arise, and that whoever came to look on it might not be frightened, or give it a bad name. Several reports of this kind give a general impression of neglect and decay, and no one after reading the whole could have a doubt in his mind about the state of dilapidation into which the last four earls of Suffolk had allowed the estate to fall. About a mile out of Walden were the flaxfields, which Colonel Vachell reported had not been cultivated for seven years, and were now 'overrun with thistles and beggary, the fences all out of repair.' They paid a land tax of four guineas a year and did not bring in one penny. The only man who had offered to take them was Mr. Pennystone, the steward, who proposed to add them to the land he already farmed, and said he would be willing to accept these lands in lieu of salary. 'If I had power sufficient,' says the colonel, 'I would have immediately tied him down.'

---

[1] See *The Times*, 28th September 1951.

Up to Henry VIII's reign England imported practically the whole of the linen used; but about 1533 it was enacted that every person who occupied sixty acres of arable land should grow a quarter of an acre of flax or hemp annually.[1] The best flax land in Essex was about Stratford, but it is interesting to find the fields so neglected at Walden, because saffron and flax were so often grown together, the saffron roots being said to afford the best sward on which to bleach the linen.

Hospital Farm, Newport, is referred to as the manor house of Newport. The building, we learn, was large and old, and there was a toll for cattle brought to Newport Fair connected with it, the income from which is set down as 'uncertain,' because 'Since the infection has been amongst the black cattle, the tenant is a considerable loser for few cattle have come up since, and last year the fair was cried down. I cannot look on this farm as a ready pennyworth,' says the colonel, 'if it should be untenanted. Joseph Todd rents the toll bridge and has likewise suffered by the crying down of the fair.'

Littlebury comes out badly on the whole. Of Catmer Hall he writes: 'This is an ill conditioned farm.' The rent had been raised a few years earlier by nine pounds annually, but had been reduced to the old rent for a new tenant, and 'his bargain,' says Vachell, was 'dear enough.' George Buck of Great Bradleys, a man of morose temper, was always in arrears with his rent, though well able to pay and in the main a good tenant. His only trouble as a tenant was that he disliked parting with his money. The tenant of the water mill, which was then in a miserable condition, was an honest hard-working man, but refused to article for a lease because in a dry summer there was insufficient water to turn the wheel. Littlebury Mill, Vachell says, was 'the worst conditioned of any on the river.' Bowsers Lands, Littlebury, rented by Thomas Mool, was a sheep walk for a hundred and twenty sheep that had been without a tenant for some years. If Thomas left it another tenant would be hard to find, in Vachell's opinion. But there were brighter spots on the manors, and one of the brightest was Wenden Hall, rented along with Westbury Farm by Lancaster Rickard. Wenden Hall was the manor house, and a dinner was provided there when the manor court was held. Rickards put in a bill for this. In addition the lord of the manor gave five shillings to the servants for their trouble and paid a shilling for the church

[1] 24 Henry VIII, c.4.

bell to be tolled. Colonel Vachell says of Lancaster Rickard and Wenden Hall:

The present tenant is an old man, honest and substantial. His son receives and pays all, and is, in fact, the tenant. Should the old man die the son must not be parted with. He is a prating, whimsical fellow, but will prove a good tenant. These farms will hold their rent. Its a pretty estate, and well tenanted.

Little Chesterford was less satisfactory. Place Farm, about two and a half miles from Walden and formerly a seat of the Walsingham family, was rented by a Francis Killingbeck. At some time the rent had been raised £40 a year, since which every tenant had broken. Little Chesterford Park, on the other hand, was set down as a good farm with a bad tenant. 'He is indeed the oldest tenant to the estate,' says Vachell, 'but he is now a sott or crack'd-brain'd, so that a landlord can expect no alteration for the better.' Several of the farms were thought by Colonel Vachell to be too large for their tenants to run properly and pay the required rent.

Thomas Pennystone, the steward, who was a prominent member of the Saffron Walden meeting of the Society of Friends, seems to have been a good hand at getting in the money. The one part of his duty that may have disturbed his Quaker conscience somewhat was the collecting of tithes, due on 2nd February. Each year on that date, or on the nearest convenient, he invited the tenants to a dinner and ale at the Rose and Crown. That was the steward's invariable custom when dues were to be collected, and it answered well, as the accounts passed before the Master in Chancery showed.

There was a fair amount of underwood, normally felled between November and February, which sold readily to the maltsters of Saffron Walden, who used it for drying. It was bought also in great quantities by the poor. By long-established custom this underwood was sold in May of each year to chapmen, who hawked it round the villages during the summer months. Payment was never demanded until November, when the chapmen came in to a gathering called the wood-feast, at which each settled his account and received a shilling for his meat and drink. There was other wood in the accounts, referred to as hoblins. These were stunted trees, and a number of them were allotted to every acre of underwood sold. They were valued chiefly for their bark.

In the management of large estates the sale of timber was always watched carefully. Not only was it an important source of revenue, it was also one that was extremely difficult to check. Woodwards often lined their pockets by irregular sales, and the land steward had to be constantly on his guard. At Audley End the woodward at the time of the partition was John Foord, who sold the wood and collected the money, and who also collected the quit rents. His wages were £20 yearly. Colonel Vachell was by no means satisfied with the way he kept his accounts.

In valuing the timber on an estate it was necessary to take the cost of transport into consideration. This applied to under-wood as well as to large timber. The Walden woods, for example, had a great advantage over those on the other manors, because they were more conveniently placed for sale. The maltsters were at hand, and even the chapmen tended to be more reliable than those who worked the other woods, largely because they could sell to Walden householders, whereas the others had to tramp round the villages, which were inhabited by poorer people.

Here is the colonel's valuation of the estate at the time of the partition:

| | Rent | | | Land Tax at 4s. | | |
	£	s.	d.	£	s.	d.
Saffron Walden	1,743	6	0	227	10	8
Newport	179	10	0	25	16	0
Littlebury	392	2	5	61	6	0
Wendens	273	5	0	36	16	0
Little Chesterford	227	4	0	38	13	8
Great Chesterford	718	4	10	108	6	6
Mr. Reynolds of Bumpstead	6	5	0	1	4	0
Cambridgeshire	16	0	0		16	0
	£3,555	17	3	500	8	10

	Arable	Pasture	Meadow	Ley	Woodland
Saffron Walden	2366·3	427·3	140·2	48·3	79·2
Newport	187·3	32·2	33		
Littlebury	788·1	8	39		
Wendens	414	43	2	22	
Little Chesterford	350·3	73	3	42	30
Great Chesterford	686·2	145	64	25	
Cambridgeshire			14		
	4792	729	295	137	109

The timber on the estate was valued at:

	Walden			Other Estates		
	£	s.	d.	£	s.	d.
Oak @ 11d. per foot	2,748	6	6	1,585	13	5
Ash @ 9d. per foot	207	3	9	88	6	3
Elm @ 9d. per foot	74	15	6	80	7	8
10,067 Standils @ 6d. per stand	251	13	6	234	4	0
	£3,281	19	3	£1,988	11	4

To equalize, £646 13s. 11d. worth of timber was transferred from one side to the other, bringing the value on both sides to £2,635 5s. 3¾d.

At the partition in 1653 the net value of the Walden estate was £1,876 11s. 9d.; the net value of the others together, £1,872 15s. 0½d. It was a low valuation, though on the whole we may feel, as the colonel did, that the Walden estate was the better half. Rentals might be more or less equal on the two parts; but the farms in Walden would be more likely to hold their own, and proximity to the town was an advantage. Another disadvantage to the farms in the other parishes was that they were exceptionally large. This was particularly true of those in the Chesterfords. We have not yet reached the time when smaller farms were being thrown together to make larger units. In the middle of the eighteenth century tenants for farms as large as that of Chesterford Park—the third earl's place—were hard to come by. On the other hand, it had to be borne in mind that in Wenden Hall the Bristol half had the best farm on the whole of the Suffolk estates.

The manor courts—at which, incidentally, the lord of the manor appointed a constable for each parish—were now held a little before Easter each year, and it was the custom in all manors except those of Newport and Great Chesterford for the lord to take rather more than one year's purchase in cases of copyhold transfer, and rather more than a year and a half purchase on a descent; while in Newport there was a fine at the fixed rate of sixpence per acre; in Great Chesterford at a shilling per acre.

These charges were low in comparison with most. Agricultural writers of the day were very critical of rapacious landowners, who by the severity of their exactions at the determination of leases discouraged tenants from spending much on improving their holdings. But insecurity of tenure had been the main cause of dilapidation on the Suffolk estates, and the low charges were doubtless intended to encourage prospective tenants to take over what were not at the time very attractive farms.

Such then was the general condition of the estate at the time of the partition. As Lord Hervey was never resident in Essex we may assume that his half was not improved as quickly as Sir John Griffin Griffin's. Indeed we have evidence of neglect in the improvements made after its purchase by the second Lord Braybrooke. The Walden estate on the other hand was steadily improved throughout Sir John Griffin Griffin's time, though not for profit. His first concern, as we have seen, was to lay out his parkland in the manner of the age, and from this he would naturally go on to replenish the timber on the estate as a whole. The landed gentry of the day had suddenly become timber conscious. At last they had realized the necessity of making good the inroads that had been made for a century or more on behalf of the navy. When in 1771 a committee of the House of Commons was set up to inquire into this particular problem its findings were deemed so alarming that they were hushed up. Numerous articles in the *Annals of Agriculture*, the *Gentleman's Magazine*, and kindred publications show how alarmed the nation was. Then, twenty years later, came the eleventh report of the commissioners, with statistics to show that unless there was immediate and widespread replanting a famine in timber was inevitable. It is estimated that in six of the royal forests four-fifths of all the timber suitable for naval purposes had been cut down, and the impoverished earls of Suffolk, in common with all too many of the landowners of their day, had taken advantage of the continued demand to sell as much as they could. Nor did the demand end at the time of the transfer of the estate. If we glance at the figures for the steadily rising tonnage of the Royal Navy in George III's reign we see what a ready market there must have been for English oak. Sir John, as a wealthy and public-spirited man, like most of the great Whig landowners who became so proud of their estates at this time, replanted vigorously.

The principal crop at Audley End was barley, which rose to 35s. a quarter in 1783, after being as low as 14s. a quarter the previous year. Normally it was about the middle twenties. Oats, which fluctuated between 8s. and 20s. a quarter—usually between 12s. and 16s. 6d.—seems to have been a very speculative crop. Wheat was never important. It was grown for the first time on Windmill Hill in 1784. More of it was sown in 1785 and 1786, when the price was 44*s.* a quarter; but the soil was too light and the crops were poor. Hay made as little as 30*s.* a ton in the earlier years of this 1770–90 period, and as much as 70*s.* in the later. Wool, of course, varied considerably. One year it might be 14*s.*, another 26*s.* Among occasional items in the accounts we have such entries as:

'To Shepherd and Archer, for watching the sheep three nights to detect a dog killing a lamb, 5*s.*'

'Paid for a pint of ginn for the fowls by order of Lady Griffin.'

Once Sir John had organized the estate the general picture is much the same here as elsewhere in the eastern counties. Progress was steady and continuous, and farm profits, though modest, rose accordingly. They were prosperous decades. Most men of landed property would have agreed with Lord Auckland, who on 3rd July 1792 wrote to Lord Grenville: 'Our good old island now possesses an accumulation of prosperity beyond any example in the history of the world.' But that same year came war, with its consequent high prices and artificial economy, although these have surprisingly little effect on the farm accounts for several years. Let us look at the full accounts for 1775 and 1809, with the profits for the thirty-three intervening years, given on pages 198–9.[1]

As the second Lord Braybrooke was a farmer in a way Lord Howard never had been there was rapid advance in his time over the estate as a whole, although there was no immediate difference to be noted in the running of the home farm. With the purchase of the Bristol estate at Great and Little Chesterford, however, widespread changes were made everywhere, resulting in the main from the enclosure of about three thousand acres of land by Act of Parliament in 1803. In doing this, of course, the second lord was in line with most of the great landowners of his day.

For any special features of the second lord's farming we may rely on Arthur Young's *Agriculture of Essex*. There we read that the prevalence of mildew was the chief reason for avoiding wheat on the four hundred acres of arable land farmed by Lord Braybrooke himself. Young goes into considerable detail about

[1] E.R.O. D/DBy. A.291.

1775

Payments	£	s.	d.	Receipts	£	s.	d.
Wheelwright	19	7	6	Barley	188	4	3
Blacksmith	21	0	0	Tares	9	18	9
Collarmaker	7	19	0	Grass	126	17	$9\frac{1}{2}$
Horse Corn	87	6	0	Hay	73	11	6
Straw	5	18	0	Four Horses, from			
Pease	5	14	6	Gardens to Farm	107	18	0
Seed Corn	17	3	6	Bullocks	47	17	0
Harvesting	28	9	4	Calves	6	19	6
Threshing	15	0	0	Sheep	12	12	0
Manure	8	16	3	Lambs	89	2	0
Journeys	3	3	$5\frac{1}{2}$	Horses	12	1	0
Horses	58	14	0	Swine	3	16	0
Bullocks	53	8	0	Mutton	80	5	6
Sheep	63	10	0	Pork	46	9	9
Tithes	8	4	9	Butter	31	10	$3\frac{1}{2}$
Church	1	5	0	Cheese	7	12	6
Poor	32	16	$11\frac{1}{2}$	Cream	19	1	0
Highway	11	10	3	Milk	2	0	9
Labour	128	6	$0\frac{1}{2}$	Wool	40	4	0
Other Items	11	18	10	Hides	4	1	0
	£589	11	$4\frac{1}{2}$	Sheep skin	6	10	0
				Tallow	4	9	0
Balance	£331	10	$2\frac{1}{2}$		£921	1	7

The profits for the years 1776 to 1808 were:

	£	s.	d.		£	s.	d.		£	s.	d.
1776	109	2	1	1787	354	17	$6\frac{3}{4}$	1798	527	7	11
1777	232	3	$6\frac{1}{2}$	1788	444	8	$7\frac{1}{4}$	1799	564	1	$9\frac{1}{4}$
1778	347	10	8	1789	385	9	$8\frac{1}{4}$	1800	591	19	$2\frac{1}{4}$
1779	326	1	$10\frac{1}{2}$	1790	401	0	$1\frac{3}{4}$	1801	645	0	1
1780	318	3	$10\frac{1}{2}$	1791	480	16	$0\frac{1}{2}$	1802	784	6	4
1781	316	7	$0\frac{1}{2}$	1792	518	13	9	1803[1]	146	1	$10\frac{1}{2}$
1782	333	0	$4\frac{3}{4}$	1793	543	12	$9\frac{3}{4}$	1804[1]	51	11	$6\frac{1}{2}$
1783	510	14	$0\frac{1}{4}$	1794	490	19	$1\frac{1}{2}$	1805	463	16	11
1784	327	11	$2\frac{1}{2}$	1795	460	14	$4\frac{3}{4}$	1806	698	19	$2\frac{1}{2}$
1785	357	5	$10\frac{1}{2}$	1796	523	12	$2\frac{1}{4}$	1807	957	0	10
1786	438	18	$2\frac{3}{4}$	1797	438	15	1	1808	800	10	9

[1] The smallness of these two balances arises from taking in the new enclosed land in Littlebury parish.

1809

Payments	£	s.	d.	Receipts	£	s.	d.
Wheelwright	45	4	10	Wheat	22	14	6
Blacksmith	54	8	10	Barley	766	18	0
Collarmaker	22	14	9	Tares	—		
Farriery	34	9	3	Peas &c.	82	10	0
Straw	33	0	0	Oats	32	0	0
Wheat	6	17	0	Buckwheat	16	5	0
Tares	7	8	0	Small Seeds	42	10	0
Small Seed	63	6	11	Grass	83	15	9
Barley	27	10	0	Hay	99	15	9
Oats	21	12	0	Horses from Farm			
Harvesting	151	14	3	to Garden	100	19	9½
Hoeing Turnips	37	7	0	Horses	21	0	0
Hoeing Peas	3	12	6	Cows	6	0	0
Threshing	65	6	5	Bullocks	475	0	0
Journeys	8	7	5	Sheep	164	16	6
Bullocks	281	5	0	Lambs	314	12	0
Sheep	256	3	0	Swine	45	15	6
Swine	3	3	0	Beef	69	2	2
Tithes	8	7	2	Mutton	71	7	4
Church	15	19	4½	Pork	92	6	11
Poor	176	15	9	Butter	69	18	4
Highway	45	12	11	Cream	27	12	0
Labour	344	10	4½	Cheese	7	17	3
Woodwork	117	1	2	Milk		16	2
Incidentals	164	14	4	Calves	32	5	0
	1,996	11	3	Hides	1	0	6
				Skins	6	7	6
				Wood	201	14	9
				Tallow	8	16	7
				Wood for fires	87	10	0
				Wood sold	80	0	0
				Incidentals	108	17	0
					£3,140	4	3½

	£	s.	d.
Balance	1,143	13	0½

the cultivation of potatoes at Audley End under 'his Lordship's very intelligent bailiff, Mr. Nockold,' [1] and gives us the rotation of crops on the various manors.[2] At Great Chesterford this was: 1, turnips; 2, barley; 3, clover; 4, wheat. At Audley End,

---

[1] Young, *Agriculture of Essex*, vol. i, p. 390.   [2] Ibid., vol. i, p. 239.

where the wheat was cut out, it was: 1, turnips; 2, barley; 3, clover and trefoil; 4, barley again. This was on newly enclosed land which had previously been under the husbandry of two crops of wheat, if the land would bear it, and one fallow, with barley substituted for wheat if the land was too poor. On the old enclosed lands which were in good heart the rotation was: 1, turnips; 2, barley; 3, clover; 4, wheat (if the land was equal to it); 5, peas, beans, or oats.

The rapid progress of agriculture in the second lord's time enabled him to double his rents when opportunities arose, and still leave his tenant farmers better off than ever before. These were great days for farming, largely inspired by the king him-self, who acknowledged himself more indebted to Arthur Young than to any other man in his dominions, and was in the habit of carrying the latest volume of the *Annals of Agriculture* about with him when he travelled. At his model farm at Windsor His Majesty experimented in stock breeding. So also did the Duke of Bedford at Woburn, Lord Rockingham at Went-worth, Lord Egremont at Petworth, and, of course, Coke of Holkham. Lord Braybrooke could afford to compete with them, and in course of time Audley End was to become as famous for its flocks and herds as it was for the magnificence of its mansion.

In Arthur Young's time polled Yorkshires were in favour at Audley End. He says: [1]

Lord Braybrooke, at Audley End, has a very fine dairy of polled Yorkshire cows and two bulls; and gives much attention to continue the breed pure, and improving by a due selection of calves for stock, and feeding them for the first two years on the best of everything: his yearlings and two and three years old are of such a size, and in such *case*, as mark the care which has been taken of them. Mr. Nockold assured me that they are excellent milkers, some of them giving in the height of the season three gallons at a meal. He has a three year old spayed heifer that promises to be an exceedingly fat beast: his Lordship's other cattle stock consist chiefly of spayed Welsh heifers, bought in at Harlow-bush Fair. These are first turned into sainfoin rouen; then are taken into the yards to coarse hay; after that to sainfoin hay for two months before turning to grass, and sells or kills before harvest.

In the summer of 1811, however, this herd was sold. The sale bills advertised:

[1] Young, *Agriculture of Essex*, vol. ii, p. 275.

To be sold by Auction on the Premises on Wednesday, July 24th, 1811, at eleven o'clock, the whole of the truly valuable

DAIRY OF COWS

AND YOUNG STOCK

The property of Lord Braybrooke at
Audley End, near Saffron Walden, Essex.

Consisting of 14 extremely large poll'd Yorkshire Cows, 6 Heifers, 2 Weaning Calves, and 2 Bulls, of the same breeds.

The above are parted with on account of the proprietor's wish to change his stock, are well worth the attention of gentlemen farmers or graziers, being beautifully marked in colour, excellent milchers, and have the greatest tendency to fatten; they have been reared on the premises, and at very great expence.

The Yorkshires were sold to make way for twenty-three Alderney cows and heifers, with one bull, bought for £429 14s. 0d. from a Mr. Shurmer, who was then importing cattle into England from the island; a fact of importance because this was the foundation of what came to be recognized as the oldest Jersey herd in the country.[1] These Audley End Jerseys were first shown in 1833 by the third lord. They were again shown at the Royal Society's Show at Cambridge in 1840. In 1844 the herd was improved by the purchase of an Alderney prize bull from Mr. Massey Stanley at the Royal Show at Southampton for either £30 or 30 guineas. The cost is recorded in the accounts as £33 18s. 9d., which evidently includes conveyance home.

The Audley End herd book, in which the birth of calves, their colour and distinctive marks are noted, dated from 1839; but unfortunately in the earlier years the names of the sires are not recorded.[2] When these are entered it becomes clear that great care was taken before introducing new blood, which came from such famous herds as those of Lord Chesham, Mr. Gilbey, Mr. Simpson, Mr. Cardus, and others well known in Jersey circles.

The calves were allowed to suck their dams up to eight or ten days old, and were then fed with new milk, later changed

[1] Thornton, *The English Herd Book of Jersey Cattle.*
[2] E.R.O. D/DBy. A.312-15.

for skimmed milk with a little boiled linseed or Thorley's Food
mixed with it.   They were not, however, fed on Jersey, but on
Shorthorn, milk, and in cases of scour a little linseed oil, followed
by a small dose of bicarbonate of potash, was given, unless the
case was severe, when oatmeal flour or ricemeal gruel was given
with an egg and a dash of brandy in it.   The calf was encouraged
to nibble a little hay, and was given rock salt and a piece of
chalk to lick.   When the calf was about three months old the
milk was gradually discontinued and replaced by bean meal, hay,
straw chaff, and linseed cake.   During the winter months the
cows were kept in an open yard with sheds to take shelter in,
and allowed to run on the grass for three or four hours daily if
the weather was not too inclement.   Their food was mixed
corn, linseed cake, bean meal, straw chaff, with sliced roots in
winter and a little clover or other green food in summer.
Heifers were bulled at from twelve to fourteen months old, and
were rested for a short time after the birth of their first calf.
After calving sliced roots were given in season, with salted straw
and hay chaff, crushed oats, bean meal, and malt culms.   The
older cows had the same food with the addition of brewers'
grains.   The diet varied little from one season to another, and
at all times there was free access to water.

   Milking times were 5 a.m. and 4 p.m., and by an interesting contrivance the pail itself formed a seat for the man who
was milking.   When drawn from the cow the milk ran into
a dish, from which it passed through a fine strainer and down a
telescopic spout, or hopper, into the pail.   The registration and
testing of the milk was not introduced until 1881, when the
method adopted provided for:

   1. The milk from each cow to be measured in a gauzed pail at every
milking.

   2. A portion of each cow's milk to be weighed on the first Monday
of each month, and the ascertained weight per gallon to be adopted
for the ensuing month.

   3. A portion of each cow's milk from both morning and evening
milking every Monday—dipped fairly from the pail—to be set in
testing tubes to ascertain the percentage of cream it contained, and the
mean of the two milkings to be taken as the cream percentage for
the current week.

   4. The quantity of milk from each cow having been ascertained,
her yield of butter to be determined by comparing the total quantity

of cream churned during the week with the quantity of butter made from it, the proportion of butter to cream from the entire herd to be thus ascertained and applied to each cow individually.

In 1882 the fifth Lord Braybrooke's agent, Mr. W. S. Hosley, won a £50 challenge cup offered by Mr. Thomas Higgins of Liverpool for the most complete and practically useful record of a dairy of not less than ten cows of any breed for a period of nine months between Michaelmas 1881 and Michaelmas 1882. Mr. Hosley's system was stated by *The Times* of 5th October 1882 to be a little less elaborate than one originated by a Mr. G. M. Allender of the Aylesbury Dairy Company some years earlier, and to be particularly valuable in enabling the owner of the herd to gauge the day-to-day condition and behaviour of each individual cow. It thus served both as a record and a guide to diet and general treatment.

Mr. Hosley's accounts showed that twenty cows during the nine months from December 1881 to August 1882 yielded £381 19s. 8d. worth of produce at a cost of £294 19s. 5d., showing a profit of £87 0s. 3d. In these accounts the price of butter varied between 1s. 5d. and 1s. 7d. a pound, averaging 1s. 6¼d. Skimmed milk was valued at 3d. a gallon. Calves were credited at £3 for heifers, £1 for bulls. Manure was valued at 2s. a week from each cow for the eighteen winter weeks, 1s. a week for the twenty-one summer weeks. Food grazing was charged at 1s. 6d. a week from 26th November to 1st May; 2s. 6d. a week from 1st May to 1st June; 3s. a week from 1st June to 12th August; 2s. 6d. a week from 12th August to 26th August. On this reckoning the twenty cows cost £202 11s. 9d. for feeding— £57 5s. 6d. for grazing, £145 6s. 3d. for other foods. Labour costs worked out at a weekly average of 1s. 5d. per cow, veterinary attendance at 1½d. per cow, wear and tear of utensils at 1d. per cow. The average value of each cow's produce per week, including manure, worked out at 12s. 5d., the cost 8s. 1d., leaving 4s. 4d. profit.

During the seventeen weeks of May, June, July, and August 1882, these twenty cows gave 9,288 quarts of milk, weighing 24,182½ lb. The weekly average per cow is given as 54½ quarts, or 142 lb., containing 14·2 per cent of cream. Each gallon of milk produced on an average 8 oz. of butter.

This fine herd of Jerseys was the pride of Audley End for a great number of years. But it brought glory rather than profit most of the time. There was no complaint about this. In Lord Howard's time, and for much of the second Lord Braybrooke's, the farm—as we have seen—showed a profit. Towards the end of the Napoleonic wars that profit became considerable, and remained high for several years after the war. But when conditions became normal again the profits were turned to losses and these were allowed for in the annual budgets. There was now an entirely new attitude towards farming among the aristocracy. Consequently, to the third, fourth, and fifth lords the farm and its pedigree herd was as much a matter of pride and absorbing interest as the gardens had been to Lord Howard. It was, if you like, an expensive hobby, and accepted as such.

The shifting of interest from the gardens to the stock-yard came later at Audley End than at many great houses. If Lord Howard had been a keen agriculturist, or a west country landowner, it might have come earlier. Agricultural societies, supported by the county gentry, sprang up in most parts of the country when the success of the Bath and West of England Society, founded in 1777, became known, although it was not until well into the second Lord Braybrooke's time that it became the generally expected thing for rich landowners to indulge in costly experimental farming and aspire to excel in the show ring. Obviously the elaborate system we have just described could not have been undertaken by the farmer who had his living to earn. Such systems were, in fact, evolved by groups of learned agriculturists that in character were more like our present-day literary and archaeological societies than farmers' clubs. These gentlemen met—not in the inn nearest the local auction mart, as the farmers of to-day would—but at their clubs in London or the provincial capitals. And their discussions were introduced by a carefully prepared paper read by one of the members. The inevitable result of this was that the early agricultural shows, which sprang up all over the country in the first half of the nineteenth century, particularly after the first national agricultural show held by the Board of Agriculture in 1821, were social events for the 'county.' They were certainly not intended for the ordinary run of farmers.

Under these conditions profits would have been almost unseemly. But what did these losses amount to at Audley End? Here is the account for the year ending Michaelmas 1858—the last year of the third lord's life:

	£	s.	d.		£	s.	d.
Valuation at Mich^s				Valuation at Mich^s			
1857	2,749	15	0	1858	2,772	18	3
Cash Paid	2,271	2	3¾	Supplies to house	17	7	4½
				Cash Rec^d· to			
				Mich^s 1858	1,470	3	2¾
				Balance	760	8	5½
	£5,020	17	3¾		£5,020	17	3¾

For the following seven years the losses were: 1859, £427; 1860, £438; 1861, £514; 1862, £606; 1863, £437; 1864, £532; 1865, £126. Then in 1866 came a profit of £560, due to a sale of stock, and from this time onwards the losses can no longer be taken at their face value. The figure at which the stock was valued did not vary much in the 1850s and 1860s. It fluctuated between £2,500 and £2,800. Nor was there much change in the following decade. Losses also continue to run at approximately the same figure. But on the other side of the reckoning we have a number of large sales of pedigree stock at very substantial prices, which, taken over a number of years, actually cancel out the losses. Thus in 1871 there is the usual loss— this year £575—and the following year a sale of shorthorns producing a profit of £2,476, which if it had been spread over the five years since the last sale would have wiped out the losses entirely. From 1872 to 1877 inclusive there was a run of profits, followed, however, with a loss of £1,368 in 1878. Then in 1879 comes another sale of shorthorns, bringing the year's profits up to £3,970. The next two years show losses; but again we have a substantial profit in 1882, when £2,900 was received for shorthorns exported to America. In 1883 there was a sale of Jerseys, followed by a £670 loss in 1884 and a £3,700 profit in 1885. The fifth lord's accounts are therefore not typical. He had become a renowned breeder of cattle and was able to command extremely high prices for the animals he sold. Nor was the success entirely his own. It has to be remembered that the foundations of the herd were laid in the third lord's time when profits were not expected, and when the only thing that mattered was the improvement of the herd.

While it is difficult, therefore, to take any years as representative at this time, in order to give some idea of expenses it might be useful to give figures for the three years for which we have already had a summary of the *General Account*, that is to say, the years 1875, 1876, and 1877:

E.R.O. D/DBy. A240

	1875 Paym^ts £	s.	d.	1875 Receipts £	s.	d.	1876 Paym^ts £	s.	d.	1876 Receipts £	s.	d.	1877 Paym^ts £	s.	d.	1877 Receipts £	s.	d.
Live Stock	884	7	3	3,447	18	4	1,305	8	8	3,265	15	8	1,068	19	3	3,723	10	10
Corn &c.	1,213		11	1,248	3	4	1,063	4	9	1,300	16	4	1,214	3	7	1,405	19	11
Cake	472	18	10				441	12	3				477	8	7			
Straw & Hay	124	15		322	19	9	133	17	6	243	4	2	213	8		245	17	6
Seeds	77	2	1				88	18	10				129	1	2			
Manure	52						76	16					99	14	2			
Rates &c.	240	15					153	10	7				184	11	9			
Labour	1,204	12	5½	180	7		1,199	9	6	230	13	3	1,152	3	9½	208	7	7
Incidentals	605	4	8½	63	11	1½	706	19	5	135	3	10½	699	6	11½	126	1	6
	4,874	16	3	5,262	19	6½	5,169	17	6	5,175	13	3½	5,238	17	3	5,709	17	4
				4,874	16	3				5,169	17	6				5,238	17	3
				388	3	3½				5	15	9½				471		1
	Inc: in St: *			180		6	Inc: in St:			467	5	6	Dec: in St:			129	8	
	Rental			568	3	9½	Rental			473	1	3½	Rental			341	12	1

* In pencil underneath: 'In in Stock.'

At all events, those were peak years. Elsewhere in the county they were followed by the long and tragic decline in Essex agriculture which continued into the present century. At Audley End the fifth lord's success as a breeder prolonged the family prosperity beyond that of most landowners in the county. But commercial success was never the object. The pride of the third, fourth, and fifth Lords Braybrooke, like that of so many other gentlemen and noblemen farmers of Victorian England, was in the astonishing improvement achieved by their enterprise in both animal stocks and agricultural methods. In these their success was incalculable.

The Library

XVII

PUBLIC OFFICE

I. CIVIL

IF IT IS important to remember that the noblemen of the eighteenth and nineteenth centuries had their feet on the earth—had soil on their boots—it is equally important to remember that their heads were high: that they held from generation to generation, in one form or another, their sovereign's commissions. The Griffins and Nevilles of Audley End were farmers and countrymen; but equally they were soldiers and diplomats, officers of the royal household, high stewards, and lords lieutenant. These commissions, bearing, as so many of them do, the sign manual of one king or another, and the signatures of a long succession of prime ministers, would make an interesting study in themselves. They are impressive enough when restricted to owners only; but if the study were based on the archives of Audley End, enriched by the papers of so many associated families, the contrast between the splendour of these and the prosaic routine of crops and rentals discussed in the last chapter would emphasize again the range of aristo-cratic authority and influence in Georgian and Victorian England.

But there is no need to go through these documents here. They were calendared and described in the eighth Report of the Historical Manuscripts Commission. That their relevance was national rather than local was recognized in their transfer to the Public Record Office, and to discuss them in these pages would unduly complicate the present study. It is, however, essential that we should see the family life of our great houses throughout the period covered by this book against a background of national politics, with letters from ministers of the Crown arriving in the country, and being as personal to their recipients as letters from land stewards and bailiffs were when delivered in town. As the one interest kept the aristocracy of these times—or the best part of them—physically fit, the other kept their minds alert. Authority was great; but it was balanced by responsibility. We have heard a great deal about what the wealthy landowners could get away with on their own estates, where their authority was unquestioned; but it has to be remembered that these mighty ones had themselves to step warily in dealing with those above them.

Many papers of national importance were transferred to the Public Record Office from Audley End by the fifth Lord Braybrooke in 1880. The remainder were sent in 1948. Few of them were connected with actual owners of the house. That is to say, the really historic documents that accumulated at Audley End did not relate to the activities of the earls of Suffolk or the Lords Braybrooke, but to those of their relatives or ancestors. There is little of importance from Lord Chancellor Audley; but there are letters relating to Sir Henry Neville's term of office as ambassador to France in Elizabeth's reign. There is nothing of national consequence from Richard Aldworth Neville, second Lord Braybrooke; but a large collection of the official correspondence of his father, Richard Neville Neville, covering both his term of office as under-secretary of state at the Admiralty at the time of the Treaty of Aix-la-Chappelle and his term as special plenipotentiary in the Duke of Bedford's embassy to Paris for the peace negotiations of 1762–3. Richard Neville Neville's papers as paymaster in the Pensions Office have also been transferred to the Public Record Office.

The most important section of the 1880 deposit was undoubtedly the fifty-nine bundles of the official papers of the first Marquess Cornwallis, which was enlarged in 1948 by a further deposit of two hundred bundles. Among other associated collections transferred to the Public Record Office were: documents relating to the office of Auditor of the Exchequor, held by members of the Aldworth family; papers relating to the payment of Mary of Modena's dowry, 1682–3; papers of Lord Grey of Werke,[1] who was governor of the Barbados at the close of the seventeenth century, which include three letters from William Penn, congratulating him on his return home and the success of his term of office.

Important as these collections are, however, they do not compare with such great national collections as those of the Cecils, for example. The original Audley End was quite as important as Hatfield at the beginning of its history; but it did

[1] See Genealogical Table, back end-papers.

not remain a political centre. The house as we see it to-day has never been the scene of meetings or conferences that can be said to have shaped our history. The family commissions and grants are interesting mainly for the purposes of social history —the long series of Lord Howard's commissions, for example, or the letters patent granted to Richard Aldworth Neville, afterwards second Lord Braybrooke, for the office of provost marshal of Jamaica, with correspondence about the fees and emoluments of the office. But all these documents may be described as incidental. They have no direct bearing on even the history of Audley End. Nor are they of vital importance in themselves. It is probable that Lord Howard could have had high and influential office in the Government of his day for the asking. But he never liked politics, as he confesses frankly enough in a letter to Richard Neville Neville on 7th June 1772.

'I shall be very short on Political matters,' he says,

of which I begin to be pretty heartily tired. That confounded Royal Marriage Act I never liked or relished, and tho' I hate all appearance of shuffling or not acting up to the Principles a man avows and professes, yet as that matter was supposed really to be a measure of the Crown, so far it became personal. . . . As to East India matters—the Committee goes on, and as Lord Clive told me t'other day at Court, may continue the whole of this Parliament, in the way it goes—I was put into the committee list (very unfit, God knows, both from want of Inclination and East India knowledge). Some of my friends to whom I intimated the difficulty I should be under to attend, & others who had better men to supply my place, kindly set me at Liberty: which I have taken, & enjoyed myself at Audley End.

It was, in fact, only about this time that the owners of such houses as Audley End had become sufficiently independent to be able to snap their fingers at state affairs in this way. We have seen how dependent the earls of Suffolk were on princes' favours. But gradually the power had passed from the sovereign to his ministers, to whom the aristocracy were much less inclined to toady. Gradually also the aristocracy had become economically independent. Lord Howard, therefore, could afford to take his choice.

As for the office of provost marshal of Jamaica, enjoyed by the second Lord Braybrooke, this was an instance of such offices being used as political rewards. It had first been obtained in 1762 for Richard Neville Neville, his father.

It is thus on the local plane, rather than on the national, that

we see the Braybrookes most effectively in office, and Audley
End as a social and political centre. Lord Howard, like several
of his ancestors, was both lord lieutenant and vice-admiral
of Essex for several years, and the latter office, in which, as in
the lieutenancy, he succeeded the fourth Earl of Rochford, seems
to have been somewhat ambiguous to him. On 4th September
1795 we find him writing to the Lords Commissioners of the
Admiralty about directions he had received from them, and in
the course of his letter confessing that he was not even aware
that he held the office! He says: 'It is true that Lord Spencer
obligingly in the Spring propos'd to me the acceptance of this
office; but never having heard any more about it, or of any
appointment to it, I am at a loss to know if there should be any,
or if it is a matter of course that follows the Lord Lieutenancy
of any maritime county.'[1] He was no less at a loss to know
whether he was expected to do anything about the orders he
had received, which had to do with ships trading between the
United Kingdom and Ireland. In reply to his inquiries he was
informed by the Admiralty that he had been appointed vice-
admiral of Essex as long ago as the 1st of May, but that
apparently the commission had never been collected, as it should
have been, by his lordship's agent. The letter proceeded: 'The
commission ought regularly to be registered in the Admiralty
Court at Doctors Commons, and deputies should be appointed
by your Lordship in different parts of the County to carry the
orders of the Council &c. into execution. The duty, if anything,
is trifling.'

Apparently the duties were so trifling that, although the
writer confessed that he had inquired of a dozen persons who
might have been expected to know what they were, he was still
unable to enlighten his lordship about what would be required
in general, although he could assure him that the Customs had
attended to the matter that started the correspondence.[2] This,
as we can imagine, was by no means satisfactory to so con-
scientious and punctilious a man as Lord Howard, particularly
when he began to receive such letters as one from John King
of Brightlingsea, who on 8th October 1795 wrote to say that
for five years he had managed the wreckage brought into the
port of Colchester on behalf of the Commissioners of Customs,

[1] E.R.O. D/DBy. O.14/3.
[2] For an account of this office see Sir George Sherston Baker, *The Office of
Vice-Admiral of the Coast.*

whom he served also as tide-surveyor, and that he would be grateful if the new vice-admiral would confirm these appointments. At last, however, enlightenment came from a Mr. Bullock of Little Burstead, who informed Lord Howard that although many duties were required of the vice-admiral by the terms of the commission, there were now in fact, so far as he could discover, neither duties nor emoluments in the office, but merely the honour of the title, the duties and emoluments having been diverted to the Customs.

At the death of Lord Howard in 1797 his heir, the second Lord Braybrooke, succeeded as lord lieutenant, *Custos Rotulorum*, and vice-admiral of Essex, and as England was then at war with France, the responsibilities of the offices were great indeed, particularly when invasion seemed imminent. The county had already been roused to action. The Essex Light Dragoons, a crack corps by volunteer standards, had been raised at his own expense by Montagu Burgoyne in 1796. Lord Petre had marshalled strong forces of his tenantry in Brentwood and Ingatestone for the defence of the highway to the east, Sir William Hillary of Danbury Park had a thousand men in arms, and almost every parish in the county had raised its quota of volunteers, large or small according to the number of men available and the vigour of their leader, when, in April 1798, Lord Braybrooke summoned his deputy lieutenants and communicated to them a plan he had received from the secretary of state, which was to be put into operation immediately the enemy landed. The plan provided that:

If an enemy should land upon our shores every possible exertion should be made immediately to deprive him of the means of subsistence. The navy will soon cut off his communication with the sea, the Army will confine him on shore in such a way as to make it impossible for him to draw any supplies from the adjacent country. In this situation he will be forced to lay down his arms or to give battle on such disadvantageous terms as can leave no doubt of his being defeated. . . .

In clearing the country the first principle is an indemnification from the Community at large to the individuals for the value of all stock which may be removed in consequence of an invasion, if not restored to the respective owners, as also for whatever moveable property may be destroyed by our own arms to prevent its falling into the hands of the Enemy, provided the proprietor comes forward and enters into such arrangements as may be proposed to preserve it rather by personal attendance at the time or otherwise by some mode of service at the moment of invasion.[1]

The militia were disbanded in 1802, but with the resumption of hostilities in 1803 the defences of the county had again to be organized, and the second Lord Braybrooke proved a popular and efficient leader.

The third Lord Braybrooke did not succeed his father as lord lieutenant. This office, along with those of vice-admiral and *Custos Rotulorum*, went at the second lord's death in 1825 to the third and last Viscount Maynard, who held them for forty years. During the last four years of his life, however, Lord Maynard was unequal to the duties, and the fifth Lord Braybrooke, as vice-lieutenant, acted in his stead.

Either because he was acting on another's behalf, or because such care was natural to him, the fifth Lord Braybrooke kept a record of all he did as vice-lieutenant in the form of a journal, which is particularly interesting for the light it throws on the county magistracy during those four years. Then as now, the recommendation to the lord chancellor of suitable persons for appointment as justices of the peace was an important part of a lord lieutenant's duties, and it was probably the one in which he was most open to criticism—at least in his own county, where in those days every country gentleman, and most clergymen of substance, expected to be appointed as a matter of course. If they were not they did not hesitate to ask why, and in view of the established custom of making such appointments almost automatically on the inheritance or purchase of an estate the question would not seem improper. Nathaniel Kent of Fulham, in his *Hints to Gentlemen of Landed Property* (new edition, 1793), seems to assume that every country gentleman will be a magistrate. He has a chapter on the duty of such a person in which he says: 'His public duty consists principally in his office as magistrate; in which station he has it in his power to render real service to his country, in just administration of the power the law has entrusted him with.'

Most magistrates, undoubtedly, had a high conception of their office, and exercised their authority with honour and discretion; but not every landed gentleman was suitable, and Lord Braybrooke was scrupulously careful about his recommendations. He had, in fact, good reason to be, because one

[1] R. B. Colvin, *The Lieutenants and Keepers of the Rolls of the County of Essex*, 1934.

of the justices appointed on Lord Maynard's recommendation was constantly bringing the Colchester bench into public ridicule during the fifth Lord Braybrooke's first few months of office. This obstreperous justice was a Mr. William Rawdon Havens, who between 15th December 1860 and April 1861 repeatedly interrupted the court proceedings until a rule of criminal information was obtained against him in the court of Queen's Bench for imputing corrupt conduct to his brother magistrates. On his making a full apology to them and their clerk, and paying the costs of the case, he was discharged; but in December 1861 he again caused a commotion in court by usurping the chair and refusing to vacate it for the duly appointed chairman, an undignified episode that was only settled by the adjournment of the court. Representations were at once made to Lord Braybrooke, and on his advice the lord chancellor ordered the name of this gentleman to be struck off the commission.

Much of the correspondence about the appointment of justices arose from the frequent and repeated nomination of clergymen. In the eighteenth century many of the beneficed clergy, when resident—which many of them were not—had served as magistrates; but by the middle of the nineteenth century this practice had come to be severely criticized, and lord chancellors were refusing to appoint any clergyman who had a cure of souls unless no suitable layman was available. In reply to letters asking for clergymen to be appointed Lord Braybrooke was in the habit of quoting the lord chancellor, who in November 1862 had written to him:

I have the honour to inform your Lordship, in reply to your letter of the 5th inst., that the Rule I have found laid down by my predecessors regarding the appointment of clergymen as magistrates is this: Never to divert the attention of any beneficed clergyman from his spiritual duties by inserting his name in the Commission of the Peace unless the Lord Chancellor is impressed by the Lord Lieutenant who recommends the appointment that there is such an absolute dearth of properly qualified laymen to undertake the office as to render the services of the clergyman really necessary for the administration of justice. This rule, however, would not apply in the case of a clergyman residing on his own property and who has no cure of souls.

The principle, no doubt, was sound enough; but there were at least two strong arguments in favour of appointing clergymen. In putting forward a name it was frequently pointed out that in the case in question the rector or vicar was the only educated man residing in the parish. For the other argument it was submitted that if the nineteenth-century parson was not allowed to sit on the bench he would lose the most powerful instrument for reformation that his eighteenth-century forerunner had possessed. Experience was proving, said the parsons, that pleas for honest and decent living from the pulpit were much less effective than orders—and not uncommonly threats—from the bench had been. This may well have been true in remote marshland parishes, where moral standards could not be described as high at this time, where smuggling was prevalent, and where lords of the manors were commonly non-resident. As an illustration, there is a letter bearing a date in March 1863 from C. Du Cane, Esq., with an enclosure signed by the church-wardens, overseers, and surveyors of Tollesbury, Tolleshunt D'Arcy, and the adjoining parishes, earnestly requesting Lord Braybrooke to use his influence with the lord chancellor on behalf of the Rev. Charles Leigh, rector of Goldhanger, whose appointment was sought on the ground that there were no suitable laymen in the vicinity. A similar request came from J. Gurdon Rebow, Esq., asking for the Rev. Dr. Hayne to be recommended for appointment as there was not a single resident magistrate within eight miles of the Mistley justice room, close to which the clerk resided.

These two clergymen were, in fact, appointed. So was the Rev. Edward James Hill of Panfield, of whom it was stated that he was a good business man and had, besides his living, 'a landed estate in the immediate neighbourhood, which was of itself more than a qualification.' His parish was said to be a very small one, and the duties of the two offices, it was argued, were in his case 'perfectly compatible.'

It must be admitted that there was another reason for so many names of clergymen being sent in. They were of the same class as the gentry! If they were rejected the only alterna-tives over a great part of the county would be tenant farmers. Indeed, this comes out in correspondence between Lord Bray-brooke and the magistrates of the Tendring Hundred, where the name of a substantial farmer had been put forward. On the rumour of this proposed appointment reaching the ears of the Tendring bench, the chairman wrote to inform Lord Braybrooke that, during his twenty-seven years as a magistrate, it had always been the custom for the lord lieutenant, before making any recommendation to the lord chancellor, to consult with the chairman of the bench on which the proposed magistrate would serve, and for the chairman then to consult with his brother magistrates as to the suitability of the person proposed. In these circumstances he thought he ought to inform Lord Bray-brooke—who undoubtedly would have consulted him—that although the gentleman whose name was being mentioned was

a most respectable man, he was merely a leading farmer and yeoman in the Tendring Hundred, without the position in society, or the education, to qualify him for the office of a magistrate, and that his appointment would probably cause the retirement of many of the present Bench. Furthermore, there was no present want of magistrates at the Tendring Bench, which now consisted of ten magistrates—six laymen and four clergymen, all more or less attentive to their magis-terial duties, and the introduction of Mr. B. would destroy the harmony now existing.

Possibly there had been a public petition for Mr. B.'s appoint-ment. Such petitions were not infrequent at the time. There was one from Loughton in December 1862, signed by fifty-one parishioners, asking for Mr. Williams of Debden Hall to be appointed to serve on the Epping bench. In the south-west of the county, however, where the population was already increas-ing rapidly, the boot was on the other foot in that there were too many new residents seeking appointment. Consequently from this part of the county Lord Braybrooke received warnings about the aspirations of such persons as the secretary of a large industrial concern recently established in the neighbourhood, or a builder interested in the development of the Metropolitan area. If more magistrates were needed, he was reminded, there were members of such established and respected families as the Buxtons, the Pellys, and the Howards available.

In short, there were thirty-eight appointments in all during those four to five years, of which only six were of clergymen. Three of these were gentlemen in holy orders living on their own estates, without cure of souls; the others were the three already mentioned. Of the fifteen persons whom the lord chancellor refused to appoint eight were clergymen and one a member of Parliament.

So much for the civil aspect of the public offices held by the Lords Braybrooke. They were such as the owners of the county's most historic seat would be expected to hold; but not

more.   Neither the Griffins nor the Nevilles can ever be said to
have dominated the county.   And for two reasons.   The first
is the remoteness of Audley End from Chelmsford and Colchester; the other is personal.   The Griffins and Nevilles never
thought of themselves as belonging pre-eminently to Essex.
The Griffins had their Northamptonshire allegiances, the Nevilles
had their roots in Berkshire.   Consequently neither was ever to
represent in the life of Essex what the Cavendishes have represented in Derbyshire, the Stanleys in Lancashire, or the Russells
in Bedfordshire.   Their town was not, in fact, the Essex county
town of Chelmsford, but Cambridge, which brings us to the
most important tradition of public service in the family, that as
Visitors and Masters of Magdalene College.

II. ACADEMIC

When Thomas Lord Audley refounded Magdalene College,
Cambridge, formerly Buckingham College, it was enjoined in
the Henry VIII charter that the owners of the former monastery
at Walden (*Domini nuper Monasterii de Walden*) should be hereditary Visitors, with the privilege of presenting to the mastership,
a condition that remained unvaried until 1925, when the commissioners, in revising the statutes, confirmed an arrangement
that had been agreed between the seventh Lord Braybrooke
and the Master and Fellows of the college, whereby the visitorship was alienated from the estate and attached to the Braybrooke title.[1]   It was a condition of exceptional importance to
the college because in the same deed of endowment Audley
conferred on the Master two votes, in addition to his normal
casting vote as chairman, a great if not excessive privilege for
the master of so small a college.   It was, perhaps, a tribute to
the way in which the family had discharged their duty that the
commissioners allowed this unique patronage to continue.   The
owners of Audley End, therefore, enjoyed a right similar to
that of the patronage of an influential benefice, which might, if
desirable, be kept in the family.   But so admirable were most
of the appointments that it was not until 1882 that even the
double vote, always open to criticism, was abolished—and again
the amendment was by mutual agreement between the college
and the Visitor.

[1] Universities of Oxford and Cambridge Act, 1923.

Audley's son-in-law, the fourth Duke of Norfolk, who was in fact the great-grandson of the earlier founder, the Duke of Buckingham, continued the lord chancellor's work, both by contributing generously towards the completion of the college and by giving it the benefit of his patronage, which, in view of his unique position as holder of the only surviving dukedom, was a considerable privilege. In the summer of 1564, when the queen rode through Cambridge in her 'black velvet pinked gown,' as Nichols has it, 'a call upon her head set with pearles and pretious stones, a hat that was spangled with gold, and a bush of feathers,' she had the duke in attendance, and as she passed the college gates on her way out—Magdalene being the last of the colleges—the Master stepped forward with a Latin oration composed in her honour. He was disappointed, however, because by this time the queen was suffering from the heat and the press of the townspeople, and rode on towards Huntingdon, bidding the duke present her compliments to the Master and explain the reason for the seeming discourtesy. But the duke himself, after conducting Her Majesty out of the town, returned and improved the occasion by promising £40 a year to the Master and Fellows 'until they had builded the quadrant,' as well as an endowment of land 'for the encrease of their number and studies.' With such munificent founders as these the college would have become extremely wealthy if certain of its city endowments had not been lost to it.

We saw in an earlier chapter how the link between Audley End and Cambridge was strengthened when, in another of Elizabeth's progresses through the eastern counties, Dr. Howland, the vice-chancellor, asked Burghley's permission for the heads of the colleges to wait upon her at Audley End and received the reply that Burghley 'liked well of their purpose.' And in the third generation the college's association with the house was continued by the first Earl of Suffolk, grandson of the founder and eldest son of the Duke of Norfolk by his second wife, Margaret Audley, who became high steward of the university in 1601 and chancellor in 1614. When the latter honour was conferred on him twenty doctors of the university, 'in their formalities and upon their footcloths,' along with fourscore of inferior rank, rode out to Audley End to present him with his patent of office. A banquet had been prepared for them, for which the vice-chancellor and the university orator expressed their appreciation in Latin. The earl himself replied in English,

promising to do all in his power to maintain the privileges and
dignity of the university, assuring his guests of his affection and
goodwill, as an earnest of which, he said, he was able to announce
that he had already persuaded the king to honour Cambridge
with a visit.   When James fulfilled this promise the occasion,
apparently, was one of glory for the earl no less than for the
king.   At all events John Chamberlain, writing in March 1615,
mentioning the predominance of the earl's family in the cele-
brations, remarks that there were few ladies present 'but of the
Howards, or that Alliance; as the Countess of Arundel, with
her sister, the Lady Elizabeth Grey; the Countess of Suffolk,
with her daughters of Salisbury and Somerset; the Lady Walden
and Henry Howard's wife; which were all that I remember.'   The
lord treasurer, he adds, 'kept a very great port and magnificent
table, with the expence of a thousand pounds a day, as is said.'

The fifth, sixth, and seventh earls were all members of
Magdalene.   Indeed the royal arms were painted over the
high table at the charge of the sixth earl in 1714, and it is
possible that Vanbrugh did work at the college, probably at
the earl's expense, at the time he was engaged at Audley End.

At the partition of the estate in the middle of the eighteenth
century, Colonel Vachell was invited to examine the terms of
the visitorship on behalf of the Countess of Portsmouth, and
on 16th September 1746 he wrote to her:

Madame, I beg leave to trouble your Ladyship with this to let you
know that I have made further enquiry concerning the Statutes of
Magdalene College and am inform'd that the mannor of Brooke
Walden is the Springhead, for Audley End house and Park are only
part of that Mannor: my information came from the Gentleman thats
Court-keeper for the Suffolk Estate.   I shall know more particularly
tomorrow, having wrote to an intimate friend, who is just return'd to
yᵉ University, to go to the President of that College, who will not deny
him any assistance he wants.[1]

At the time of this letter a new Master was required, and
one was in fact presented [2] by the Lord Effingham from whom
Lady Portsmouth and Lord Hervey were claiming the estate.
It was therefore important that the title to the visitorship should
be clarified, otherwise it might lapse and fall to either the
chancellor or the Crown.   The inquiries were evidently fruitful
but not decisive, because in his next letter Colonel Vachell

[1] From a bound collection of manuscript letters in Lord Braybrooke's possession.
[2] Thomas Chapman of Christ's.

reported that his view that the right to the visitorship went with the manor and not with the house and park had been confirmed by the fact that at vacancies of the mastership while the house and park were Crown property the third earl of Suffolk had presented. He conceded, however, that it might be argued that the earl had presented by the king's consent and not in his own right.

Lord Effingham's nomination, apparently, was accepted, though by all accounts Chapman, the Master in question, was not a success—Cole says he was most forward, arrogant, overbearing, and haughty. With the countess's purchase of the house and park from Lord Effingham the question that had exercised Vachell's mind became irrelevant, because she thus became possessed of all the properties to which the title might be held to be attached. It is interesting, however, to note that in the correspondence leading up to the purchase of the house and park it appears to be assumed by both parties that the visitorship was attached to these, in which case the third earl would not have been acting in his own right when he presented in 1668 and 1679, nor for that matter would the fourth earl when he presented in 1690. Anyhow, the visitorship did come to the Countess of Portsmouth, who gave it under 'bond to resign' to George Sandby, a Suffolk parson and fellow of Merton, who was put in as a seat-warmer so that the office could be reserved for her husband's grandson, Barton Wallop.

Wallop was duly presented by Sir John Griffin Griffin in 1774, but he also was one of the less successful appointments. He was, says Cole, of 'good breeding and behaviour, but totally illiterate. His whole amusement was horses, dogs, and sporting.' There was in fact an unsuccessful attempt to prevent Wallop's appointment, but appointed he was, although fortunately he agreed to be non-resident and spent most of his life as a sporting parson in a quiet Hampshire rectory. For a year, however, he took his turn as vice-chancellor, and we are told that he had the reputation of being a good magistrate. E. K. Purnell, the historian of Magdalene College, in recording this genial sporting parson's death at the beginning of the shooting season in 1781, is reminded of that capital story related by Cole of how Dr. Walker, vice-master of Trinity, an enthusiastic horticulturist, on hearing of the death of a fellow enthusiast who had shot himself in spring, exclaimed: 'Good God, is it possible? At the beginning of tulip time, too!'

Lord Howard was yet another benefactor of the college. His portrait hangs in the hall.   At his death Lady Howard, in a postscript to one of her letters to the second Lord Braybrooke, says: 'One buck used to be given in former days to Magdalene College from the Park, and as there is one to spare I ventured to ask Dr. Peckard if you and I should jointly give it this year.   He seems to like the idea, and I suppose the President will accept.'[1]

With the temporary separation of the house from the estate between Lord Howard's death and the death of his one surviving sister, Mrs. Parker, and her husband, who was rector of St. James's, Westminster, the question of which carried with it the visitorship might again have arisen.   Whether it did or not we do not know.   What we do know is that when a vacancy occurred during these years the presentation was by Dr. and Mrs. Parker, who jointly signed a patent admitting to the office the William Gretton, Lord Howard's chaplain, whose tribute to his patron has been quoted.   As at least three eminent scholars who were also members of the college were then available the appointment was not a popular one.

The coming to Audley End of the Nevilles, with their more scholarly traditions, brought a new intimacy to the association of the mansion with the college until finally, with the sixth Lord Braybrooke, the mastership of the college and the ownership of the estate were held by the same person, Lord Braybrooke himself.   This closer association began with the second Lord Braybrooke's presentation of his second son, George Neville, afterwards Neville-Grenville, to the mastership in 1813.   Subsequently, George Neville-Grenville became Dean of Windsor, but he continued to hold the mastership until his death in 1853, that is to say, for a period of forty years.   And as he was succeeded by his nephew, Latimer Neville, who held it for fifty years, uncle and nephew between them were masters of Magdalene for over ninety-one years.   Then as Henry, seventh Lord Braybrooke, was brought up in the Master's Lodge, which was his father's home before succeeding to the Braybrooke title late in life, the association remained of the closest, right up to the seventh lord's death at the age of eighty-six in March 1941. Although a man of retiring disposition, largely because of his deafness, he took a paternal interest in his tenants and the welfare of the estate, and was held in the highest esteem.   As for his academic privilege, Magdalene has always felt that the

[1] 11th August 1797.

seventh lord fulfilled in a most admirable manner his historic function of appointing a master to Magdalene, a duty that fell to him on three occasions, and each time his sound judgment directed him to a man who was able to preside over the destinies of the college with distinction.

Latimer Neville, sixth Lord Braybrooke, like the third and fourth lords, exemplified an order of men now, alas, almost extinct, that of squire and scholar.   Indeed if there has been one characteristic that has distinguished the Lords Braybrooke it has, in fact, been that so many of them have belonged to that order.   Equally it has been characteristic of them to carry their distinction lightly.   And of none was this truer than of the sixth lord, whose term as vice-chancellor, 1859–60, was one of revolutionary reforms in the university.   Although he himself was leader of the Conservative party in Cambridge, and by no means the man to inaugurate such reforms, his dignity, courtesy, and coolness of mind were of the highest value during the heated and sometimes acrimonious discussions of that eventful year, and when, in December 1903, he completed his fifty years as Master, the senate enacted a special grace for the purpose of conferring on him the unique compliment of an address of congratulation.   This was read by the vice-chancellor, in the presence of the member of Parliament for the university, the public orator, the masters of seven colleges, and many friends, and Lord Braybrooke impressed this learned assembly by replying at length in Latin, without the aid of any notes and without once faltering or hesitating.   It was, however, his last public appearance.   On the 31st of the same month he wrote from what proved to be his deathbed:

AD UNUMQUEMQUE AMICORUM

Jam mihi lustra decem datur explevisse; cubile
Stat comes, et medici lex, tenuesque cibi.
Advenit interea, longas ceu stella per horas,
Nuntia vox curae testis, amice, tuae.

Coll. S. M. Magd., Prid. Kal. Jan. MDCMIV.

My jubilee leaves me in bed on a diet
 Low, meagre, imposed by a ruthless decree;
But a light cheers the wearisome hours of quiet—
 The voice of your friendship and kindness to me.

With all good wishes for the New Year—B.[1]

[1] E. K. Purnell, *Magdalene College*, p. 198.

He died on 12th January 1904, and an obituary in the
Cambridge Review, 21st January 1904, paid tribute to his scholarship, his simplicity and goodness. Perhaps the character of the
man comes out best in the passage:

Of late years, there being no Fellow of the College in Orders, he
undertook the honorary office of Dean. In this connection may be
mentioned his sermons—remarkable for their brevity, their earnest-
ness, and their point. Avoiding all conventionalities of the ordinary
preacher, he never used a word too much, and the right word was
always in its place. The same qualities characterized his speeches.
There was no attempt at oratory, but the delivery was natural, and, be
the occasion what it might, almost every sentence had a happy turn
in it. . . . While all who came in contact with him will ever cherish
his memory, it is reserved for those who were his intimates to know
and feel that he was one of the men who may be truly numbered among
'the pure in heart,' for such his life had been from the beginning.

Thus in the academic realm, no less than in the civil, the
Braybrookes had a record of quiet distinction. In the eighteenth
and nineteenth centuries they had brought Audley End to a
degree of perfection that made it a place suitable for preservation
as a national monument. As we have seen, the spectacular part
of the achievement came to completion with the third lord's
work. But those who succeeded him are equally to be admired
for the way they maintained the best traditions of their kind
through later generations, in which such glory as they had
became increasingly reflected glory. They were living, as the
greater part of the English aristocracy have been living in recent
generations, through a long twilight; but they were good land-
lords, fair-minded magistrates, men of culture, whose intellectual
life was kept sane and healthy because they were a family rooted
in the land, whose privileges were balanced by responsibilities.

The Mansion and Bridge from the South-west

XVIII

'IN COMMENDAM'

HEN THE EIGHTH Lord Braybrooke, while
serving as lieutenant in the 3rd Battalion of the
Grenadier Guards, was killed in Tunisia in January
1943, the line of the Nevilles at Audley End
snapped. He was twenty-four. His father, the seventh lord,
had died two years earlier in his eighty-sixth year. His only
brother, George Robert Latimer Neville, had been killed in
action on 12th August 1941 at the age of twenty-one. Thus
between the beginning of March 1941 and the end of January
1943 the aged father and the sons who had brought joy and
confidence to his later years—the children of his second marriage
—had gone. That the father was the first to die was perhaps
the one comfort that his wife, Dorothy Lady Braybrooke, and
her daughter, the Hon. Catherine Dorothy Neville, were able to
find in those cruel years. When the seventh lord had succeeded
his father in 1904 there had been no children, and the house had
been let for some years to the eighth Lord Howard de Walden,
the holder of the title traditionally associated with the estate, but
which had been alienated from it since the death of the fourth
Lord Howard in 1797. Again considerable sums had been
spent by the family in redecoration, but as the house remained
Lord Braybrooke's property there had been no structural alterations, and when, in 1914, the seventh lord had himself taken up
residence it had been much as it was in his uncle's and grandfather's time. It had remained so throughout the rest of his
long life, and with two sons to succeed him he had naturally
believed that in spite of heavy taxation Audley End would be
the home of his family for at least one more generation. When,
however, his nephew, Henry Seymour Neville, the son of his
brother Grey, inherited the estate and title under such tragic
circumstances, continued residence—except, perhaps, in a few
rooms—was out of the question. Maintenance costs for such
a house were then running at a level that only the wealthiest
could sustain. And to have occupied a few rooms only would

inevitably have meant allowing the rest to fall into decay. Moreover, the revenues from the estate had been drastically reduced by the incurring of death duties twice in so short a time. The ninth lord was therefore forced to the painful decision that the family home must go, and by an arrangement with the Treasury it passed, not, as in the seventeenth century, to the Crown for the king's pleasure, but to the nation as a national monument. As with the passing of the centuries such houses inevitably become fewer, the appreciation of those who visit them is likely to increase, and it is to these future generations of visitors that Audley End is now entrusted. The Ministry of Works is their custodian.

There is nothing new, of course, about opening our great houses and displaying their treasures to admiring visitors. Wilton had its guide-book in the eighteenth century, and indeed Rowlandson sketched a party inspecting the 'Double Cube Room.' Knole, Penshurst, and the rest of them had their streams of visitors, and these same curious travellers rode or were driven into north-west Essex from East Anglia, London, or Cambridge to be conducted through the state rooms at Audley End. Evelyn, Pepys, Celia Fiennes, Cosmo of Tuscany, Daniel Defoe, and a host of others both visited the house and recorded their impressions either publicly or privately. Others left no record. A mere postscript to a letter from Lord Howard[1] mentioned visits of the Duke of Portland and the Duke of Somerset within a few days of each other. Both had come purely as sightseers. Thus the house has always been something of a showpiece. But what is not so well known is that there is nothing new about charging for viewing. Dr. J. H. Plumb, of Christ's College, Cambridge, has reminded us[2] that a satirical account of the Duke of Chandos's house at Canons by Alexander Pope created such interest that charges for viewing enabled the duke to employ three extra maids. And as often as not these charges went in the eighteenth century as they do in the twentieth towards maintaining the fabric.

There are, however, noteworthy differences between these earlier visitors and those of to-day—apart from the obvious one that then they came singly or in families, now they come in hundreds. The most important is that Evelyn and Pepys in the seventeenth century, and the Dukes of Portland and Somerset in the eighteenth, came to see the house—new in the seventeenth

[1] See p. 151.   [2] *The Listener*, 16th November 1950.

century, restored in the eighteenth—as the latest achievement of English craftsmanship and culture, as—to quote Dr. Plumb—'an obvious expression of the growing wealth and prosperity of their country,' while to-day it is viewed as a memorial to an elegance and magnificence in private life which the nation has decided, for better or worse, that it can no longer afford.

But while the nation has decided that it will not allow such houses to be lived in as they were in the past, it has also decided that it will not allow every trace and record of this vanished mode of life to disappear. Audley End was one of the first of our English mansions to be acquired by the nation for preservation as a place of exceptional architectural and historical interest. It was conveyed in 1948, that is to say, in the year in which a committee was set up under the chairmanship of Sir Ernest Gowers to advise the Government on ways and means of saving such houses, and before the committee had published its report it had already taken its place in the changed society as an example of wise and careful restoration.

Preservation of the fabric, however, is one thing; preservation of the life and culture of which it is so noble a symbol is another. Such houses can only have meaning so long as their visitors can appreciate the quality and substance of the life that was lived in them. This resolve to preserve our great houses must have a higher motive than that of providing the public with a new pastime. Happily more is desired. The new and wide-spread interest in social history so obvious to-day is encouraging evidence of a quickening of what may be termed social memory. Apparently we are realizing—and not a moment too soon—that loss of memory may be as tragic and bewildering to society as it is to the individual—that past experience is not something to be discarded, but something that has to be continually gathered up into the present if we are to keep our bearings and have wisdom for the future. Achievement begets achievement. Our great houses, therefore, must be preserved for a creative as well as for a commemorative purpose. They must be preserved not merely as an act of piety to our ancestors but because they are vital to ourselves.

There is, of course, one place in which they can never be lost: they are enshrined in our literature. More than once while turning over the politely worded letters and faded old diaries that are the foundation of this book, I have had to shake myself to make sure that I had not by some magic been transported into an earlier century, and become a member of Jane Austen's own circle. The Countess of Portsmouth might so plausibly have come out of her novels. So also might Sir John Griffin Griffin. Do you remember how in *Mansfield Park* a certain Miss Maria Ward of Huntingdon captivated a Northamptonshire baronet, Sir Thomas Bertram, with only £7,000, which her lawyer uncle allowed to be at least £3,000 short of what might have been expected of her? The date of the match would be somewhere in the 1780s, which was the very period of Sir John Griffin Griffin, himself a Northamptonshire knight.

So much of the family life at Audley End in its most vital phase turns within the orbit of Jane Austen's world that perhaps the best way to people its rooms again is to read *Mansfield Park*. There could be no better way of seeing it through contemporary eyes. Think, for example, of Mr. Rushworth in Chapter VI, who 'had been visiting a friend in a neighbouring county, and that friend having recently had his grounds laid out by an improver, Mr. Rushworth was returned with his head full of the subject, and very eager to be improving his own place in the same way.' Such a chapter could easily have been based on Sir John and his designs for Audley End. And Sir John, though not of a literary turn, might as easily have described to his friend, Richard Neville Neville, a visit to a mutual acquaintance in the words of this passage from Chapter VIII:

Here begins the village. Those cottages are really a disgrace. The church spire is reckoned remarkably handsome. I am glad the church is not so close to the Great House as often happens in old places. The annoyance of the bells must be terrible. There is the parsonage; a tidy looking house, and I understand the clergyman and his wife are very decent people. Those are almshouses, built by some of the family. To the right is the steward's house; he is a very respectable man.

And so the account goes on, all in the spirit and language of Sir John, of Mr. Rushworth, and of nine out of ten of the rest of the nobility and landed gentry of that self-congratulatory age. Then a page or two further on comes the tour of the house under Mrs. Rushworth's guidance, with the rooms described as:

. . . all lofty, and many large, and amply furnished in the taste of fifty years back with shining floors, solid mahogany, rich damask, marble, gilding, and carving, each handsome in its way. Of pictures there were abundance, and some few good, but the larger part were family portraits, no longer anything to anybody but Mrs. Rushworth, who had been at great pains to learn all that the housekeeper could teach, and was now almost equally well qualified to shew the house.

Jane Austen, of course, again satirizes this pride in the Georgian great house in *Northanger Abbey*.

But *Mansfield Park* represents only one phase of life at Audley End, and although it is the one to which most of the present house belongs, others must not be forgotten. The unity of design observed by its restorers has given it a peculiar value of its own. but has involved a loss. It means that the visitor cannot go through the various rooms of Audley End as he can through those of so many old houses, to find this architectural feature or piece of furniture evocative of Elizabethan, that of Caroline, and yet another of Georgian England, each with its own characteristic of the gay, the flamboyant, the restrained, or the austere. Apart from the Great Hall and the screens passage, there is little to remind him of the Jacobean mansion. Yet without this the composite picture of life at Audley End would lose its most brilliant if not its most characteristic colours. Sir Joshua Reynolds once remarked that architecture had many principles in common with poetry and painting, in particular 'that of affecting the imagination by means of association of ideas.' As the Thames is 'liquid history,' our buildings are solid history. It is in our great houses that we get the actual feel of this life that controlled the very pulse of the nation through so many generations.

To understand such life we must have access to the records. It is from these that we are able to trace the rise and fall, see the lights and shadows, and interpret intelligently the pageantry of such a house as Audley End century by century. It is in these that we meet the owners of such houses, not as portraits in oils or vague legendary figures whose names survive through two or three remembered incidents in their lives that may have little bearing on their true characters, but as men who bred their stock and farmed their land, and who in their public lives were able to act from a position of such strength as seems almost incredible to us now. Undoubtedly they were all too often corrupted by their immense power; but on the other hand they were much more inclined to take the long view than we are, confident, as they were, that as they ruled in one generation, their sons would rule in the next, and their grandsons after that.

Edmund Burke, writing to the Duke of Richmond in 1772, contrasted the passing of such 'annual plants' as himself with the continuing virtues of such noblemen as the duke. 'You on the contrary,' he said, 'if you are what you ought to be, are in my eye the great oaks that shade a country, and perpetuate your benefits from generation to generation.' The oaks are being felled to-day; but the seed may still be potent. After all, the present has no more finality than the past. The future is still, as always, unpredictable.

Reflecting on the best of our landed families we may feel that it was the balance of their lives that was most admirable. Not all achieved it, but a surprising number did. They were politicians, men of affairs, farmers, sportsmen, magistrates, churchwardens, and all the rest of it, and in the long winter evenings they sat by their library fires studying the ponderous folios ranged in elegant calf round the walls, then laying them down to write notes of their own, or to draft wills and settlements, always with an eye to posterity and to the good repute of their family. They were not remarkable for efficiency; they bungled a good deal; but what characters they were! Each age has both its characteristic virtues and its characteristic vices. It is futile to try to strike the balance between one generation and another. The nineteenth century was inclined to curse its landed gentry for impeding progress. Now that they are no longer in the saddle we are inclined to be sentimental and romantic about them when—heaven knows!—most of them were hard-headed realists and Spartans. Yet when the time comes for their golden age to be seen in perspective Edward Fitzgerald may prove to have been right when he said: 'Never were there such gentry as the English. They will be the distinguishing mark and glory of England in history as the arts were of Greece and war of Rome.'

APPENDIX

Ref.: E.R.O. D/DBy. F3

Presentment to Queen Anne concerning the office of Earl Marshal, 1705

The Presentm[t]

To the Queen's Most Excellent Majesty.

Whereas your Ma[ties] late Royall Uncle King Charles the Second Did by Letters Patents under the Great Seal of England bearing date at Westminster the 19th day of October in the 24th year of his Reign, Give and Grant to Henry then Lord Howard, Baron Howard of Castle-rising, the Office of Marshall of England together with the Name and Honour of Earl Marshall of England with all and singular the Dignities Precedencies Preeminences Jurisdictions Profits Commodities Emoluments Advantages Offices and Nomination of Offices with other Rights therein mentioned.   To have hold exercise and enjoy the aforesaid Office and p[r]misses to him the said Henry Lord Howard and the Heirs Males of his Body, (lawfully begotten or to be begotten,) by himself or his sufficient Deputy or Deputy's, And for want of such Heirs Males of his Body, Then to the Heirs Males of the Body of Thomas late Earl of Arundell Surrey and Norfolk, Grandfather of the said Henry Lord Howard.   And for default of Heirs Males of the body of the said Thomas Earl of Arundell, Then to the Heirs Males of the Body of Thomas late Earl of Suffolk with remainders over.   And Whereas the said late King did therein further Grant that the aforesaid Henry Lord Howard and the Heirs Males of his Body and every Deputy of them by reason of the said Office should have and bear as-well in the presence of his said late Majesty his Heirs and Successors as elsewhere a Gold Staff enameled at each end with Black with the Arms therein described As in and by the said Letters Patents (relac*i*on being thereunto had) it doth any may more fully appear.   And whereas the said Henry Lord Howard (afterwards Duke of Norfolk) dying so seized of the said Office, and other the p[r]misses before menc*i*oned, the same descended to Henry late Duke of Norfolk as his Son and Heir, By whose death without Issue, the said Office and p[r]misses are descended to Thomas now Duke of Norfolk as Son and Heir of the Body of the late Right Hono[ble] the Lord Thomas Howard of Worksop the second son of the said Henry Lord Howard Baron Howard of Castlerising (afterwards Duke of Norfolk aforemenc*i*oned).   And whereas in and by an Act of Parliam[t] made in the 25th year of the said late King Charles the Second, entituled, An Act for preventing dangers which may happen from Popish Recusants, It is among other things provided That neither the said Act nor any thing therein contained shall extend be judged or interpreted any wayes to take away or make void the Grant of any Office or Offices of Inheritance or any Fee Sallary or Reward for executing such Office or Offices or thereto any way belonging granted by his said late Majesty or any his Predecessors, to, or enjoyed, or which hereafter shall be enjoyed, by, any person or persons who shall refuse or neglect to take the Oaths enjoyned by the said Act or either of them, Or to receive the Sacrament or to subscribe the Declaracion menconed in the said Act in the manner therein expressed Nevertheless so as such person or persons having or enjoying any any such Office or Offices of Inheritance Do or shall substitute and appoint his or their sufficient Deputie or Deputies (which such Officer or Officers respectively are thereby impowered from time to time to make or change, Any former Law or Usage to the contrary notwithstanding) to exercise the said Office or Offices untill such time as the person or persons having such Office or Offices shall voluntarily in the Court of Chancery before the Lord Chancellor or Lord Keeper for the time being or in the Court of Kings Bench take the said Oaths and receive the Sacrament according to Law and subscribe the said declaracion And so all and every the Deputy & Deputies so as aforesaid to be appointed take the said Oaths receive the Sacram^t and subscribe the said Declaracion from time to time as they shall happen to be so appointed, in manner as by the said Act such Offices whose Deputies they be are appointed to do. And so as such Deputies be from time to time approved of by the Kings Matie under his Privy Signet. And whereas there is a Proviso to the same intent purpose nature and effect in another Act of Parliam^t made in the 7th and 8th years of the Reign of his late Matie of Glorious Memory King William the third, entituled, An Act for ye better security of his Maties Royall person and Governm^t. As in and by the said two recited Acts or other Act or Acts it doth more fully appear. Now your Maties Most Dutifull Subject and Suppliant Thomas Duke of Norfolk Earl Marshall and Hereditary Marshall of England &c having neglected to take the Oaths enjoyned by the said Acts or some of them and to receive the Sacram^t and Subscribe the Declarations mencioned in the same in the manner therein expressed Doth (at the desire of the right Honourable Henry now Earle of Suffolk being aged and infirm) in all humility beseech your Matie to approve, under your Privy Signet, of the Right Hono^{ble} Henry Lord Walden (Eldest son and heir apparent of the said Henry Earl of Suffolk Grandson and Heir Male of Thomas late Earl of Suffolk on whose heirs Males the remainder of the said Office and p^{r}misses is settled in the manner above mencioned) to be his sufficient Deputy to exercise the said Office of Marshall of England with all the Rights thereto belonging; And your said most dutifull subject and suppliant Thomas Duke of Norfolk doth in most humble manner crave leave to signify to your Majesty that he the said Thomas

Duke of Norfolk in pursuance of the said letters Patents and Proviso
or Provisoes Act or Acts above menc*i*oned hath ordained constituted
appointed and deputed and doth hereby ordaine constitute appointe
and depute the said Henry Lord Walden to be his true lawfull and
sufficient Deputy to exercise the said Office of Marshall of England
with all and singular the dignityes Precedencies Preeminences Jurisdic-
c*i*ons Profits Com*m*odities Emoluments Advantages Offices and nomin-
ac*i*on of Offices and all other rights thereunto belonging in as full large
ample and beneficiall a Manner as He the said Thomas Duke of Norfolk
can or may might or could substitute or depute by vertue of the said
Letters Patents and of the said Acts of Parliament or any or either of
them, To execute the same according to the Laws and Customs of this
your Ma^tles Realm and your Court Military for such time as by the
said Letters Patents Act or Acts is directed limitted and appointed.

All which your said most dutifull subject and suppliant prayes your
Majesty would graciously please in your great Wisdom and out of
your great Clemency to approve under yor Privy Signet as aforesaid
In Witness &r [1] whereof the s^d Tho. D. of Norf. has to these Presents
set his Hand and Seal this 27th Day of Febr. A°. Do*m*ini. 1705.

NORFOLK & MARSHAL

In another hand: 26 Feb^ry 1705 having perused this I thinke that
yor Grace may be pleased to signe the same
Wm Longueville

In another hand: Signd and seald in
the Presence of
Rob. Dale Blanch Lion
Tho. Waters.

[1] This was originally written: 'In Witness &c' and then the part from 'whereof'
to 'Febr.' was interlined.

INDEX

A

ADAM, ROBERT, 3, 115, 118, 123–4, 184
Aldworth family, 87, 163, 208
Aldworth, Richard, 87, 208
Aldworth, R. Neville. *See* Neville
Andover, 104, 107
Archer, Henry, 150
Arundel, Philip, Earl of. *See* Howard
Astry, Arabella, 6, 57
Astry, Sir Samuel, 6, 57
Aubigny, George, Lord, 69
Audley, Margaret, Duchess of Norfolk, 12, 13
Audley, Thomas, Lord, 9, 10–13, 216
Audley End:
  almshouses at, 33, 191
  architecture of, 26–8, 56–7
  building of, 2, 4, 24–32
  description of, 1–9, 26–8, 40–1, 42–3, 52, 124
  Elizabeth I at, 16, 20
  estate and farm, 190–206
  great hall at, 5–6, 117, 120
  grounds of, 2–4, 27, 114–15, 125
  housekeeping at, 126–35
  James I at, 2
  library at, 184
  rebuilding of, 112–25
  saloon at, 121–2
  site of, 2, 8–9
  sold to Charles II, 38, 41
Aylott's (St.), 19

B

Banbury, Elizabeth, Countess of, 66
Barbados, 87, 208
Beechey, Sir William, 180
Benton, Rev. G. Montagu, 147
Berkeley, George, 77
Berkshire, earls of, 65
Billingbear, Berks, 82, 94, 159, 163, 176, 184, 185

Blickling Hall, Norfolk, 72
Blomfield, Charles James, Bishop of London, 168–9
Bolton, Arthur J., 123
Braybrooke, Barons, 159–228
Braybrooke, first Baron. *See* Griffin
Braybrooke, second–ninth Barons. *See* Neville
Braybrooke Castle, Northants, 99, 107
Brighton, 161–2
Bristol, Earl of. *See* Hervey
Brown, 'Capability,' 3, 114, 115, 116
Buckenhall Leys, 154
Bulkeley, Viscount, 89, 160, 161, 162, 163
Burney, Fanny, 137–9
Buxton family, 215

C

Cambridge, 29, 135, 141
  chancellor of, 29
  Magdalene College, 12, 29, 40, 85, 86, 97, 182–3, 188, 216–22
  University of, 20–1, 29, 142, 216–22
Caroline, Queen, 71, 73–7
Carr, Ann, Countess of Bedford, 69
Carr, Robert, Earl of Somerset, 65, 67, 180
Cary, Lucius Charles, seventh Viscount Falkland, 65
Catherine of Braganza, Queen, 42
Catmer Hall, 192
Cavendish, Lord George, 185
Cecil, William, Lord Burghley, 15, 16, 20
Cecil, William, second Earl of Salisbury, 69
Chamberlain, John, 218
Chandos, Duke of, 224
Charles II, 1, 38, 41, 43
Charlotte, Queen, 184
Charlton, Wilts, 32, 50